//Rig//

Teacher's Book

Amanda Collins

Assessment sections: Julie Green

Nelson Thornes

Text © Amanda Collins 2008
Original illustrations © Nelson Thornes Ltd 2008

The right of Amanda Collins to be identified as author of this work has been asserted by her in accordance with the Copyright, Designs and Patents Act 1988.

All rights reserved. No part of this publication may be reproduced or transmitted in any form or by any means, electronic or mechanical, including photocopy, recording or any information storage and retrieval system, without permission in writing from the publisher or under licence from the Copyright Licensing Agency Limited, of Saffron House, 6–10 Kirby Street, London, EC1N 8TS.

Any person who commits any unauthorised act in relation to this publication may be liable to criminal prosecution and civil claims for damages.

Published in 2008 by:
Nelson Thornes Ltd
Delta Place
27 Bath Road
CHELTENHAM
GL53 7TH
United Kingdom

09 10 11 12 / 10 9 8 7 6 5 4 3

A catalogue record for this book is available from the British Library

978-1-4085-0229-7

Illustrations by: Mark Draisey
Page make-up by Pantek Arts Ltd
Printed in Great Britain by CPI Antony Rowe

Acknowledgements

The authors and publisher would like to thank the following people and companies, without whose support this book would not have been possible:

Julie Green – series editor and assessment author
Jim McElwee – manuscript consultant
Joyce Morrison – consultant for Scottish curriculum
Sara McKenna – teaching notes editor

Recordings produced by Footstep Productions Ltd.
Music composed and produced by Steven Faux.
Video stories by Nordpro Sweden KB.

Rigolo 2

Contents

Foreword	iv
Using *Rigolo* with the Scottish curriculum	v

How to use Rigolo

What is *Rigolo*?	v
How to use the *Rigolo* features and activities	
(a) Standard features	vii
(b) Whiteboard activities	vii
(c) Worksheets	x
How to use the *Rigolo* teacher tools	xi
Using *Rigolo* to measure pupils' progress	xii

Teaching notes

Unit 1: Salut Gustave!	1
Unit 2: À l'école	11
Unit 3: La nourriture	23
Unit 4: En ville	33
Unit 5: En vacances	45
Unit 6: Chez moi	55
Unit 7: Le week-end	67
Unit 8: Les vêtements	77
Unit 9: Ma journée	89
Unit 10: Les transports	99
Unit 11: Le sport	111
Unit 12: On va faire la fête!	121

Appendices

Appendix 1: *Rigolo* 2 Scheme of Work	133
Appendix 2: *Rigolo* 2 KS2 Framework mapping grid	146
Appendix 3: *Rigolo* 2 5–14 guidelines mapping grid	147
Appendix 4: Flashcards	148

Foreword

Rigolo is an exciting new course for Key Stage 2. It is not a traditional language course as it combines a variety of new and traditional media. Its structure serves the dual purpose of making French accessible and exciting to pupils, and of providing the classroom teacher with a flexible route through the range of resources.

Rigolo is also a new venture into Blended Learning; that is, a combination of traditional and new media, allowing the planning of taught lessons and flexible learning with the suite of multimedia materials. It is also particularly suitable for use with an interactive whiteboard, so that the whole class can work on the activities, particularly useful where time is precious. The course is closely matched to the Key Stage 2 Framework, both in its selection of teaching and learning activities, and in its promotion of language-learning strategies and development of knowledge about how the language works.

Background to the Virtual Teacher

A unique feature of *Rigolo* is the Virtual Teacher. She is there not as a surrogate teacher, but as a support assistant to the classroom teacher. The Virtual Teacher was developed as part of a three-year project, funded by the European Commission, called *Primary Letter Box*, which looked at ways of integrating reading into the primary foreign language programme. The project considered, among other things, the importance of showing children the link between sound and spelling, so that they could acquire fluent reading skills.

Recent research has shown that one of the factors influencing the sense of failure in the early years of secondary school is pupils' inability to decipher the correct pronunciation of French. This impinges on their ability to understand texts, since they are too concerned with its actual appearance. Experiments with primary school children showed that they were capable of responding to the Virtual Teacher and acquire good levels of pronunciation and intonation. Where the classroom teacher did not have high quality pronunciation, the children took the Virtual Teacher as their role model, but this did not detract from their professional relationship with their classroom teacher. Indeed, teachers often felt relieved that they could confidently point to their virtual colleague! It was found that children learnt and retained vocabulary more effectively with this method than those who were taught the same language in a more traditional way.

Presenting new language in Rigolo

Rigolo presents new language against an interactive backcloth, rather like an animated flashcard. Children tap on any part of the screen and the Virtual Teacher says the word. In a departure from common practice over the last 20 years, the text also appears as it is spoken, although it may be turned off if desired. It was found in *Primary Letter Box* that children who interacted with the Virtual Teacher in order to learn new language retained it much more easily than those who were taught in a more linear way with flashcards and OHP.

Moreover, children remembered the spelling of words even though these had not been pointed out to them. As one Year 4 pupil explained, 'I watched the lady's mouth and I noticed the word underneath her face, and then when I thought of the picture, I could remember the spelling and how to say it.' This is a naïve, but very succinct definition of the holistic nature of multimedia learning. Trials of *Rigolo* found the same phenomenon, with children noticing the spellings of words and also making observations such as *souris* being the only animal that was *une*.

We need to pursue the logic of this new approach and ensure that children are seeing the relationship between the sound and spelling of words, as the Key Stage 2 Framework demands: 'Recognise how sounds are represented in written form' (Year 3). *Rigolo* has the added function of presenting selected phonemes and graphemes in each unit.

Introducing literacy skills

Primary Letter Box also experimented with exploring words at text level. Research showed that children could cope with texts, particularly when they were presented on an interactive whiteboard. They were able to apply very sophisticated logic to texts and deduce the meanings of prepositions (*dans, sur*) and conjunctions (*et, mais*) from the context and illustrations. This meant that they also began to make inferences about sentence structure, an important skill that leads to writing.

Again, *Rigolo* includes a range of interactive exercises that help children to move into reading and writing. Regular animated stories use graphics and audio alongside the text to develop the engaging storyline. Exploring the written form of the language at word, sentence and text level contributes to the acquisition of Knowledge about Language (KAL) and Language Learning Strategies (LLS), both of which underpin the teaching activities set out in the Key Stage 2 Framework. Classroom teachers will be pleased to find that many of the activities reflect their experiences with the National Literacy Strategy, and *Rigolo* complements work in literacy, as indeed it does in other areas of the curriculum.

Learning away from the whiteboard

Let's not forget that ICT isn't everything! The Teacher's notes suggest classroom activities using flashcards and other props. Each lesson, guidance for starters, plenaries and extra oracy and literacy activities are suggested in the notes to help practise and consolidate the language presented in the whiteboard activities. Two worksheets are also provided for each lesson to help further practise the language. The songs are also a very powerful way of developing children's affective learning: they quickly learn and remember not just the whole song but also its elements. Singing is a very effective way of learning longer pieces of text by heart, and it helps to encourage recycling of language in new contexts.

Rigolo has the twofold aim of providing a route to excellence and of promoting enjoyment. We hope that those teachers who find the idea of teaching French somewhat daunting will find that the *Rigolo* Virtual Teacher and plethora of resources will help them to do the job with confidence.

Jim McElwee
Series Consultant to Rigolo
Modern Language Consultant for Redcar & Cleveland
Redcar & Cleveland Primary MFL Regional Support Group Co-ordinator

Using Rigolo with the Scottish curriculum

Rigolo is an exciting interactive course which appeals to all types of learner. The Curriculum for Excellence Review Group recommends that young people should be "successful learners, confident individuals, responsible citizens and effective contributors" and *Rigolo* encourages young learners to achieve success and be confident in their learning of the French language. The variety of activities and the visual impact of the DVD-ROM are relevant and stimulating and make learning enjoyable. This has a positive effect on children's self-esteem and promotes positive attitudes to language learning at present and in the future.

The course progression provides worksheets, games and follow-up activities for reinforcement and extension work. The fact that it can be used for all stages of ability adds to its value. Assessment is built into the programme and allows children to know what the Learning Intentions are (unit objectives) and thus know when and precisely what they have achieved. They can then go on to set their own goals, which is an aim of the Assessment is for Learning Programme – itself a major focus in Scottish schools.

The Scottish 5–14 Guidelines recommend that the teaching and learning programme for Modern Languages should provide "broad and balanced learning, coherent links and connections, continuous pathways for learning and a progressive development for learning". *Rigolo 2* is a course that meets these aims in a fun, comprehensive way. It links to the Listening, Speaking, Reading and Writing attainment outcomes and provides a framework for the development of the knowledge, understanding and skills identified within the strands A–D.

The included Appendix 3: *Rigolo 2* 5–14 Guidelines mapping grid matches the 5–14 strands to the different units in *Rigolo 2* at the relevant levels, allowing teachers to identify activities easily for their planning and, at a glance, enables them to focus on certain strands across some or all of the units.

Joyce Morrison
Class teacher
Ancrum Road Primary School
Dundee

How to use Rigolo

What is Rigolo?

Overview

Rigolo is a ground-breaking new Key Stage 2 French course from Nelson Thornes. It provides a wealth of exciting activities for pupils, and as much or as little support for teachers as they need. It fully meets the requirements of the Key Stage 2 Framework for Languages.

The course is chiefly aimed at pupils in Years 3–6, with *Rigolo 1* covering Years 3 and 4, and *Rigolo 2* Years 5 and 6. However, if schools are starting French earlier or later (for example, in Year 1 or Year 5) they can still use *Rigolo 1* as it is designed to cover the first two years of learning French across a range of ages.

Course components

The *Rigolo* course is based on one CD-ROM (*Rigolo 1*) and one DVD-ROM (*Rigolo 2*), for delivery primarily on an interactive whiteboard. The *Rigolo 2* DVD-ROM contains approximately 150 whiteboard activities, and 150 class activities which may be used away from the screen.

The DVD-ROM also includes several other teaching and planning tools:

- Flashcards: approximately 120 colour flashcard images with matching text captions to use either on the whiteboard or to print out and use around the class.

- Worksheets: eight worksheets for each unit (two per lesson), providing further practice in reading, writing and speaking skills, and grammar.

- Teacher's notes: notes for each of the lessons and units of *Rigolo 2* are stored on the DVD-ROM for quick reference.

- Scheme of Work plus correlation documents showing how *Rigolo 2* meets the Key Stage 2 Framework and 5–14 guidelines requirements.

- Certificates and portfolios: certificates for pupils and teachers to track their progress through *Rigolo*. There are specific *Rigolo* certificates, and also ones using the European Language Portfolio and Language Ladder 'can-do' statements.

Course structure and aims

Rigolo 2 is planned carefully so that non-specialist language teachers can easily follow a structured progression through Key Stage 2 Years 5 and 6, covering the objectives from the KS2 Framework for Modern Languages. For those teachers used to the QCA Scheme of Work for Primary Languages, *Rigolo* also covers the language from the units in the scheme. Activities, lessons and units are mapped against the 5–14 guidelines for Scotland and the levels from the Languages Ladder. Cross-curricular opportunities are also flagged throughout, so that teachers can find activities to use in other curriculum time outside the French lesson.

Rigolo 2 is divided into 12 units: six units per year, or two per term. Each unit is then divided into four lessons. The course combines whiteboard activities with class activities using the flashcards and other props for whole-class teaching, so there is a varied approach across different learning styles.

Rigolo aims to enable pupils to meet the suggested DfES target of reaching National Curriculum Level 4 by the end of Key Stage 2. *Rigolo 2* works mainly at Levels 2–3, gradually building up to Level 4 in Units 7–12. *Rigolo 2* covers Levels 1–4 in the Languages Ladder.

Rigolo storyline

Rigolo 2 continues the storyline of an English family who have moved to France, where they make new friends and learn about life in a different country. The activities and stories focus on the two English children, Jake and Polly, and their pet dragon Bof as well as their friends, Didier, Nathalie and Olivier. They continue to cross paths with Didier's aunt Madame Moulin, the cantankerous housekeeper of Château Rigolo.

A new character in *Rigolo 2* is the 20-year-old gardener, Gustave.

New in *Rigolo 2* is the video element. Each even unit starts with a video story featuring four friends: Thomas, Lucas, Chloé and Léa. We see them in a variety of situations, and the video helps to provide a strong cultural element and to give pupils a flavour of France as well as make comparisons between their own life and life in France. It also helps to address the intercultural understanding objectives of the KS2 Framework for MFL.

Teacher support

Teacher support in *Rigolo* is very thorough and provided at three levels. For non-specialists and those teachers with less knowledge of French, *Rigolo* features the unique Virtual Teacher: video clips accompanying each activity on the DVD-ROM. These present new language visually and aurally, showing correct pronunciation and gestures to reinforce understanding, and also provide instructions to pupils and a response to their answers. More specialist teachers can switch off the Virtual Teacher if they do not need this much support.

There are also short on-screen instructions in English to explain how each activity works, and to act as a quick reminder in the lesson. Finally, to back up each activity in *Rigolo*, there are detailed teaching notes explaining how to deliver these in the classroom.

For the class-based activities, there are also detailed notes and guidance in the Lesson notes on how to practise and consolidate the key language.

Delivering lessons with *Rigolo*

As mentioned above, each unit of the course contains four lessons, each designed to last approximately 45–60 minutes. The teaching notes clearly indicate how long to allow for each activity, so these can easily be broken up into shorter lessons depending on how much time you have to teach French. You can also customise the course sequence to move, remove or add activities as preferred (see *My course* below for more details on this).

Each unit is based on either an animated story or video, which introduces the new language of the unit in the context of the *Rigolo* storyline or the four friends featured in the video. You can play this in its entirety by tapping on the *Watch the whole Unit 1* (etc.) *story* button in the top corner of the lesson menu, or watch one half at a time when it is included in the lessons themselves.

Each lesson is framed by starter and plenary activities to refresh pupils' memory of language learnt previously or to reflect what has just been learnt. Most lessons proceed to introduce a set of new language – usually only five to eight short phrases – in a Language Presentation. The new language is then practised in a mixture of whiteboard and class activities, the latter using flashcards and other props where appropriate. For the class activities, detailed guidance is provided in the teaching notes.

There are also two worksheets provided for each lesson to give time for some quiet activities and to give extra practice in reading, writing and speaking skills and also grammar. The grammar is practised in a very logical, straightforward way and helps pupils understand better the structures of the language. For each unit, there are two reading, two speaking, two writing and two grammar worksheets.

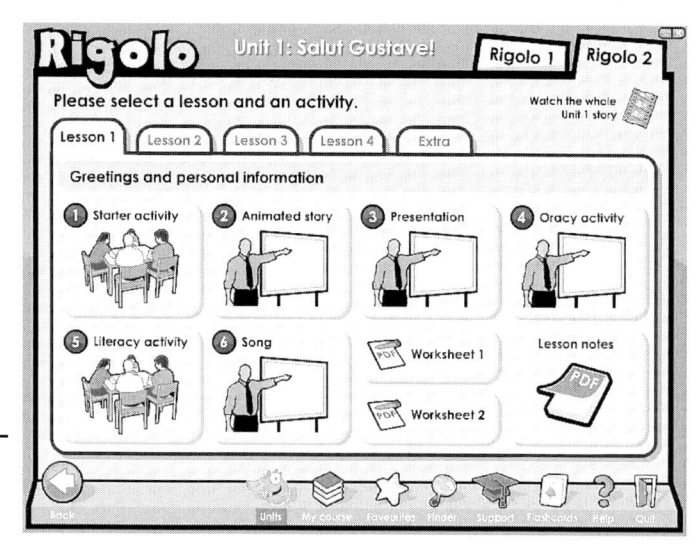

Each unit also features an *Extra!* section, containing activities to further practise the language and content. The main activity is a Project Work activity which gives the opportunity for pupils to prepare a longer piece of work such as a display, a PowerPoint presentation or an oral presentation. Often pupils have to plan and research information about France on websites and to compare what happens in their own country and in France.

Every other unit also contains a set of Sound/spelling activities focusing on French sounds encountered in the preceding two units, and a set of Assessment activities to gently test pupils' progress through Key Stage 2 (see below for more details on both Sound/spelling and Assessment).

As mentioned above, cross-curricular opportunities are clearly highlighted throughout *Rigolo*. The teaching notes on each lesson summarise the other areas of the KS2 curriculum that are covered, while teachers can use the Activity finder to search for activities or resources that cross over into other subject areas (see the *Activity finder* section below for more details on this feature).

KS2 Framework for MFL

All the activities in *Rigolo 2* are cross-referenced against the framework objectives for years 5 and 6. In the teaching notes, you will see references to framework objectives with the notes for each activity as well as National Curriculum levels. 'Knowledge about language' and 'Language learning strategies' strands run throughout the course and sections are included in the teaching notes where these are more overtly covered in a lesson.

QCA KS2 Scheme of Work for MFL

In the overview for each unit, there is a cross-reference to the units suggested in the new KS2 Scheme of Work.

Scottish 5–14 National Guidelines

In the overview for each unit, there is a grid which lists the strands and attainment targets covered in that particular unit. There is also an overview grid in the support section of the DVD-ROM showing coverage throughout *Rigolo 2*.

How to use *Rigolo* features and activities

This section explains in more detail how to use the various different types of activities and recurring features found in *Rigolo 2*.

a) Standard features

Virtual Teacher

The Virtual Teacher (VT) offers an unparalleled level of support for primary teachers who lack confidence or practice in French.

The VT panel appears in the top-right corner of the screen on every whiteboard activity. She will give brief instructions in French of what to do in the activity, so that pupils get used to hearing classroom instructions in the target language. At any other time while using the activity, you can tap on *Task* to hear the instructions one more time.

In Presentations, the VT will also pronounce each item of language when it is selected on the screen, usually giving an associated gesture at the same time. You can tap on *Replay* to play this clip again, or *Zoom* if you want to focus more closely on the teacher's mouth movements to aid pronunciation.

When pupils complete activities, the VT will also react to their answers in French, depending on whether they are right or wrong. Again, you can tap on *Replay* to repeat these clips.

While the VT is a valuable support, more experienced teachers might not want to have her enabled. To switch off this feature, tap on the *Virtual Teacher off* button in the bottom right corner of the activity screen. The next time you start an activity, the VT will then remain disabled. Tap on *Virtual Teacher on* to enable this feature again.

Text bar

In the Animated story, Video and Presentation activities, you have the option of viewing the story or new language in written form on the text bar at the bottom of the screen. To disable this, tap on the white *Turn text off* tab above the text bar. To turn it back on, tap on *Turn text on*.

Instructions

In any activity, you can tap on the *Instructions* button at any time to find out how to complete the activity. This will display short instructions in English. You can find out more details on how to use the activity in the classroom in the teaching notes. Tap on the cross to close this window.

Allez, *Encore* and *Continuez* buttons

To start most activities, tap on the *Allez* green light icon. Tap on *Allez* again to move from one question to the next. This will flash every few seconds until it is tapped.

In listening activities, you can tap on the *Encore* button to hear the audio again. In some activities, you can also tap on *Encore* to see the animation when pupils have got an answer right.

In some Presentations, when you select an object the display will 'zoom in' to a particular part of the screen to show more detail. As above, you can use *Encore* to hear the new language again. A *Continuez* button will appear to enable a return to the initial display.

Random order

Each time you use any activity, questions will appear in a different, random order.

Back button

Tap on the *Back* button at any time to return to the Lesson menu.

b) Whiteboard activities

Animated stories and Videos

There is one Animated story or Video in each unit of *Rigolo 2*, which introduces the new language of the unit in the context of a short narrative featuring the characters from the *Rigolo* storyline or the four friends from the video.

The story as a whole is approximately two minutes long, and can be watched in its entirety by tapping the *Watch the whole Unit 1* (etc.) *story* button in the top corner of the Lesson menu.

Each story has two distinct halves with discrete new language, and you can watch these shorter clips as part of two of the lessons of the unit, so that pupils see the language in action that they are about to study. These clips appear as the *Animated story/Video* buttons in the lesson folder in all four lessons.

When you start the story, you will firstly see the instructions in French and the Virtual Teacher, if activated, reading these out. Tap on the cross button in the corner of this panel to close this. The *Play* button will flash at the bottom of the screen to start the story.

Use the *Forward* and *Rewind* buttons to move through the story more quickly to a particular spot. Selecting *Pause* will pause the story at the current point until you tap *Play* to restart. If you tap on *Stop* the story goes back to the beginning.

Record

The *Record* button gives you the option to record and play back your own audio for the Animated story or Video. You can get your pupils to act out the story, recording their own versions using a microphone. To use this feature, firstly tap on *Record* to open the separate recording control panel. Tap on *Record* again to start your recording from the beginning of the story. You can pause your recording using the *Pause* button, or tap *Stop* to end the recording (note that once you stop the recording, you will not be able to change this recording and can only start again from the beginning).

Once you have recorded your own audio version, close the recording control panel by tapping on the cross. You can then play back the story with your own audio by pressing *Play*. You can toggle between your own audio and the pre-recorded story audio by tapping on the *Own audio/Rigolo audio* button on the bottom toolbar. You can record again at any time by tapping on the *Record* button.

Presentations

Most lessons in **Rigolo** are centred on a Presentation which introduces the core new language that is then practised in the accompanying activities. The Presentations are some of the most versatile teaching tools in **Rigolo**: they allow pupils to hear and see the new language pronounced by the Virtual Teacher, and also to see it illustrated in a fun, animated context where they (and the teacher) choose which language they want to discover.

You will firstly see the instructions given in French on screen and by the Virtual Teacher, if enabled. Close this panel by tapping on the cross.

There will always be around five to eight language items or short phrases in each Presentation, represented by tappable icons or images in the display. These work like interactive, animated flashcards. The images will flash automatically soon after you start the activity, and when you hover over them the cursor will change to a pointing finger. When you select an item it will be animated, and you will then hear the word spoken either by the Virtual Teacher, or by the voiceover if the VT is not enabled. Wherever appropriate, the VT will give a gesture to accompany each word to reinforce understanding. Pupils should be encouraged to repeat this gesture to help them remember the new language.

In some of the Presentations in the later units, longer texts are built up to enable pupils to see more than just single phrases. They are introduced one line at a time to make it accessible to all pupils.

Tap on the same image again to repeat the sequence above, or *Replay* on the VT panel just to hear her repeat the word(s).

There are several other options on the Presentation to further explore the new language, as below.

Record

Pupils can record themselves with an attached microphone practising the new language, then compare their pronunciation to the audio or the Virtual Teacher, making this ideal for Assessment for Learning purposes.

To use this feature, firstly tap on *Record* to open the separate recording control panel. Tap on *Record* again to start recording your own version of the audio for any particular language item on screen, and tap on *Stop* when you have finished.

You can then play back your recording using the *Play* button. You can compare this with the model pronunciation by tapping on the item again on-screen to hear the audio, or the *Replay* button on the VT panel to hear and see her pronounce the word(s). Close the recording control panel by tapping on the cross, or by selecting another object in the display.

Spell

Some presentations which are introducing single words have the *Spell* feature. To hear and see the new words spelt out, tap on the *Spell* button once you have selected an item in the main display. The relevant letters will be highlighted as they are spoken, to reinforce knowledge of the alphabet.

Sound

In most Presentations, you can focus on sound/spelling links and improve pupils' pronunciation using this feature. After selecting a word, tap on the *Sound* button and relevant sounds will be highlighted in red.

Tap on one of the sounds to hear and see the Virtual Teacher pronounce this in isolation, then ask pupils to repeat the sound, imitating her mouth movements. Pupils will recognise many of the common sounds as they recur through the Presentations, and are practised further in the separate Sound/spelling activities.

Word

This feature helps focus on grammar terms and word classes. After selecting a word, tap on the *Word* button to see and hear the Virtual Teacher describe what word class it falls into (noun, verb, adjective, etc.), together with an accompanying gesture corresponding to those recommended for KS2 Literacy.

Please note that the above options are not enabled for those language items where they are not appropriate. You cannot use the spelling feature for whole phrases, for example, and some words do not have relevant sounds to highlight.

Oracy activities

Oracy activities separately practise either speaking or listening skills.

The speaking activities in **Rigolo** are designed to practise pupils' understanding and pronunciation of new language. In each activity pupils are given visual prompts for a particular word or phrase.

To start these activities or move between questions, tap on the *Allez* button.

You can check pupils' answers by tapping on the audio check icon in the speech bubble (as above) that will appear. If pupils have given the correct answer, tap on the tick, or tap on the cross if not. If possible, it is better to give your own immediate feedback to pupils' answers and wait before tapping on the audio icon to reveal the answer, so that the activity can last longer.

Listening activities in **Rigolo** practise pupils' understanding of new language and their skills in listening for specific information. Pupils will hear various audio prompts, and have to select the relevant image on-screen to demonstrate their comprehension.

Tap on the *Allez* button to start the activity and move between questions, and on *Encore* to hear any audio line repeated. In later units of **Rigolo 2**, pupils hear longer dialogues in some of the listening activities but only have to pick out the key words/phrases they have learnt. This gives them the opportunity to hear more 'real' French and prepares them better for listening to native speakers.

In some cases pupils will have three 'lives', represented by hearts. They will 'lose a life' for any incorrect answer, and the game ends once all three hearts have disappeared.

Literacy activities

The whiteboard Literacy activities mainly focus on reading skills, with (hand)writing skills practised largely on the Worksheets.

As elsewhere, tap on the *Allez* button to start most of the activities or to move between questions. Pupils will see a visual prompt of either text or pictures, and have to select or drag and drop the corresponding text or image. As with Oracy activities, occasionally Literacy activities will also feature 'lives', to make activities more fun.

The exceptions to this are the regular animated sentence activities, which practise word order in short phrases and are a useful way to model the writing process.

In the animated sentence activities (see below), pupils can experiment with building sentences or short phrases. To do this they drag the various words into the machine and tap on the *Fini* button to see their meaning animated, if they are in the correct order. If not, then the machine will 'malfunction' and produce smoke. Once they have created a first sentence, pupils can drag and drop different words into position to produce new meanings.

Again, in the later units, pupils are exposed to longer reading texts, in line with the Year 6 Framework objectives. Sometimes they do gap-fill exercises with longer texts or put lines/words of the text into the correct order.

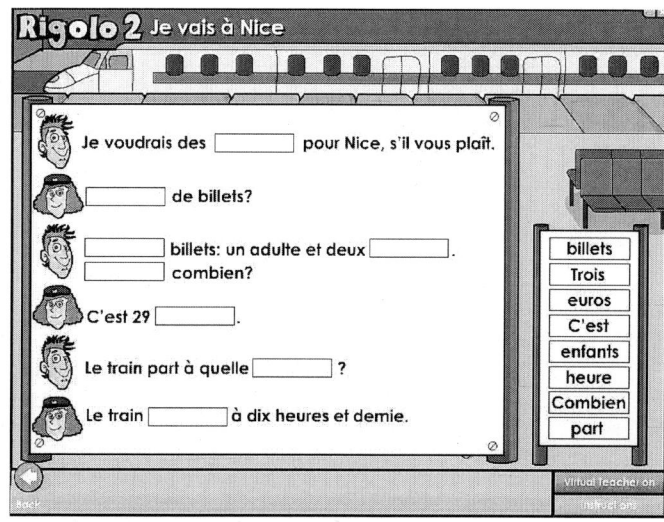

Songs

There is one song in every even unit of **Rigolo 2** (six songs in all) which revisits some or all of the language from the unit with music and movement, to reinforce learning and understanding. The songs feature a unique set of 'karaoke' controls, so that pupils can sing along to the music on its own or listen to the words without the backing music instead.

The animations that accompany the **Rigolo** songs also feature movement and animations to illustrate the meaning of the songs. Pupils should be encouraged to mimic the mimes in time with the song, wherever appropriate, thereby reinforcing their understanding of the language via kinaesthetic learning.

Each song can be used in either *Practice* or *Sing* mode. In *Practice* mode, you can play and practise one or two lines of the song in isolation, advancing to the next line(s) once pupils are ready. Tap on *Show full lyrics* to see a whole verse at a time without the animation in the background. In *Sing* mode you can hear and see the song and animation all the way through.

The controls at the bottom of the screen operate in a similar way to those in the Animated story: *Play* starts the song; *Pause* halts it (*Play* starts it again); *Rewind* and *Forward* move quickly back or ahead; and *Stop* returns to the beginning. In *Practice* mode, *Previous* and *Next* move forward or back line by line.

To allow pupils to sing along to the music without hearing the words, tap on the *Lyrics on/off* button. Tap on it again to turn the words back on again. Similarly, to focus on the words in isolation, you can turn the backing music on and off using the *Music on/off* button.

Finally, pupils can also record their own version of the song with their vocals over the backing track. The record function here works the same as in the Animated stories (see above). To switch between your own audio, the **Rigolo** lyrics and none at all, toggle on the *Own lyrics on/Lyrics on/Lyrics off* button after you have finished recording.

Further suggestions for exploiting the songs are made in the teaching notes for each unit and may include: writing their own version; completing a gapped version as they listen; re-ordering the lines of the song as they listen; memorising the words.

Sound/spelling activities

After every even unit there is a Sound/spelling activity, to practise pronunciation and recognition of some key sounds that have been met in the preceding two units.

These activities are each made up of two sections: the first (*Practice*) to practise the sound(s) in question, and the second (*Activities*) to practise recognition aurally and in writing.

Firstly select which section of the activity you want to use. In the *Practice* section, listen and watch the Virtual Teacher (if enabled) pronounce the particular sounds. You will hear the sounds firstly in isolation, and then used in several familiar words from the preceding units. This section also includes a *Record* function for pupils to compare their pronunciation with the model audio and video, which works in the same way as in the Presentations (see above).

The activities are all slightly different, but are based on listening out for the relevant sounds in the audio and matching them to the text on-screen.

Project work

As mentioned above, a short project is suggested in the *Extra!* section for each unit, and the Teacher's notes provide extra guidance and support. The project can take as little or as much time as you wish but can provide pupils with opportunities to:

- use the internet to research an aspect of French life
- learn about aspects of French life and compare them to their own
- work at their own level and work collaboratively
- produce longer pieces of written or spoken work
- use IT to present their work (i.e. PowerPoint display)
- show off their French and reuse language from previous units
- perform to the rest of the class (or to another group)
- do some cross-curricular work.

Class activities

Around three activities for each lesson are class activities including a starter, a plenary and extra oracy and literacy activities. Detailed guidance for these activities is given in the Teacher's notes. Activities with flashcards, captions and various other props are suggested. These activities are often aimed at practising further and consolidating the language which has been presented in the Presentation. Ideas are also often suggested for extension and support for pupils of different abilities.

The support ideas include suggestions to make the activities more accessible to less able pupils and the extension activities suggest ways in which more able pupils can be challenged.

The aim in **Rigolo 2** is not to teach 'chunks' of language that can only be used in one context, but to teach pupils that language is transferable and can be adapted and changed to suit different situations. The class activities, as well as practising specific language, encourage pupils to use language from different topics and to combine known language in different ways.

c) Worksheets

As mentioned above, there are two worksheets per lesson (eight worksheets in each unit), providing further practice of the new language. They cover speaking, reading and writing skills and also grammar (two of each per unit).

They are particularly helpful in providing quiet time for individual work and to give the opportunity to consolidate language learnt by doing some writing practice, which is not easy to provide on the whiteboard.

Grammar worksheets feature for the first time in *Rigolo 2* and take a very logical, straightforward approach. They provide further practice in some of the main structures introduced in *Rigolo 2* and help pupils understand the patterns of the language. They are not aimed at a high level and most pupils should be able to attempt them, with some explanations from the teacher.

Some of the reading worksheets in the later units contain some authentic French texts.

The reading, writing and grammar worksheets may be used to allow some quiet time away from the whiteboard, set as homework tasks, or used in a cover lesson. In mixed year groups you can also give one half of the class some worksheets to complete while you use different whiteboard activities with the other half.

How to use the *Rigolo* teacher tools

Along the bottom of the main *Rigolo* interface are links to the five main 'teacher tool' sections of the course:

- My course
- Favourites
- Finder
- Support
- Flashcards

To read detailed instructions on how to use each of these tools, open the relevant section by tapping on the icon on the toolbar, then tap on the *Help* icon on the right-hand end of the toolbar. This will display detailed instructions on how to use that particular section.

Below, however, is a quick overview of what each section provides:

My course

This section allows you to explore *Rigolo* in more depth, or customise the course to meet your precise teaching requirements.

Tap on the *Customise course* button to create your own version of *Rigolo*. Once you have done this you can change the sequence of activities within a lesson, or even change the sequence of lessons and units. You can add new activities to lessons from other parts of *Rigolo*, or add other activities of your own so you can launch them from *Rigolo*.

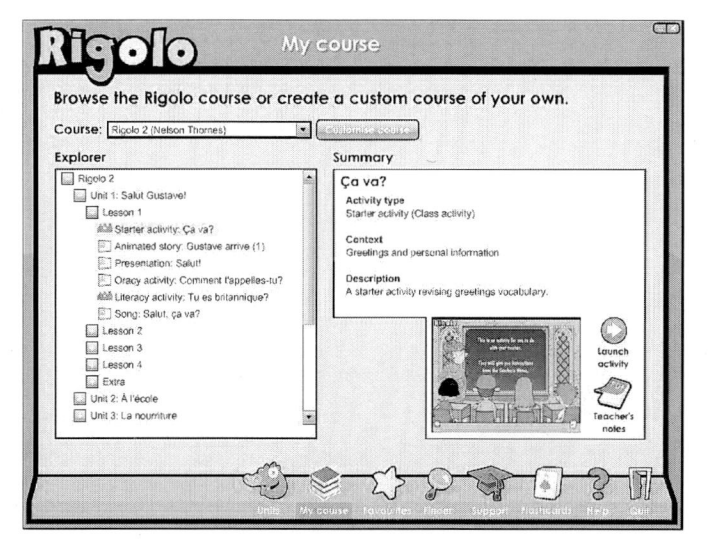

The *Summary* box on the right-hand side of the screen displays all relevant information about any activity so you can keep track of all the different resources in the course.

Favourites

This section works in a very similar fashion to 'Favourites' in Microsoft Windows. You can browse through the *Rigolo* content to add activities to the Favourites list, and then delete them or edit their details at a later point. You can also add activities to Favourites from the Activity finder (see below).

Activity finder

The Activity finder allows you to search for a particular activity to match your teaching requirements at any particular moment. You can search through the content of *Rigolo*, and any other activities you have added to the course, in several different ways.

Use the *Filter by* drop-down menu to display activities matching a particular Key Stage 2 Framework objective, at a particular National Curriculum or Languages Ladder level, or matching several other criteria. Alternatively, type in a particular search term as if you were using an internet search engine, and the Finder will display all the related activities in *Rigolo*.

When you have found an activity you can launch it straight from the list, or add it to your favourites for easy access in the classroom. You can also import activities into *Rigolo* using this screen, delete them or edit their details.

Teacher support

This section provides various levels of support for teachers using *Rigolo 2*.

The Interactive glossary allows teachers to revise the language that is covered in the different units and lessons of *Rigolo*, using the Virtual Teacher to check pronunciation.

From the *Teacher support* area you can also display or print off any unit from the Teacher's Notes, or a unit's worth of Worksheets. You will also find Mapping grids, and copies of certificates and language portfolios to mark pupils' progress through *Rigolo*.

Flashcards

There are numerous Class activities in *Rigolo* which use the supplied Flashcards as visual prompts for pupils to practise the new language in the course. You can display accompanying Flashcards for a particular activity by tapping on the link in the Class activity screen that appears when you launch the activity from the Lesson menu.

To print off the Flashcards, however, it is easier to use the Flashcards tool from the main interface. Once you have launched this section, you can choose the unit and group of flashcards you require – for example, *Unit 2/School subjects* – and then select which cards you want to print off.

Each Flashcard consists of a picture and separate card with the accompanying word or phrase. You can choose to print off either the picture card on its own, or the word card at the same time.

Using *Rigolo* to measure pupils' progress

As mentioned above, ***Rigolo*** as a whole covers National Curriculum levels and Language Ladder Grades 1–4. There are various ways in which you can measure how pupils progress through Key Stage 2.

Assessment activities

There is a group of assessment activities after every even unit in ***Rigolo***, launched from the *Extra!* section of the Lesson menu. This consists of four worksheets, one focusing on each of the four main skills: listening, speaking, reading and writing. Each worksheet contains three or four individual activities.

The activities move through a graded progression: for example, in the first half of ***Rigolo 2***, the first activity works towards National Curriculum Levels/Languages Ladder Grades 1–2, with the second working towards Levels/Grades 3–4. For more information, see the teaching notes on these activities. Assessment in Key Stage 2 is best kept fairly informal, without focusing pupils' attention on the levels at which they are working. Please note that these assessment tasks are not intended to certify that pupils have reached a certain level, but rather that they are working towards this point. However, for transition to Key Stage 3, it could well be useful to have a record of which levels pupils have reached using ***Rigolo***.

Assessment for Learning opportunities

There are numerous ways to address Assessment for Learning (AfL), or Formative assessment, using ***Rigolo***. AfL provides feedback to pupils on what has been achieved and also on which areas need further work, and can be used to inform your lesson planning. Below are several ways you can regularly incorporate this into teaching with ***Rigolo***:

- Share the objectives of each unit and lesson with pupils before you start teaching, so that they are aware of the nature and purpose of the work they will be doing. At the end of the lesson, you can review with pupils whether they feel they have achieved these objectives and what they feel unsure about.

- Use the Presentations (and the *Record* facility in particular) to allow pupils to compare their pronunciation with the model audio and video.

- Similarly, pupils can compare their pronunciation in the Songs, Animated stories and Videos.

- Use the Worksheets to measure pupils' progress, discussing the answers to each activity in class so that pupils are aware of where they have made mistakes and how they could improve. This acts as useful preparation for the Assessment worksheets at the end of every other unit.

Certificates and portfolio information

Pupils can keep track of their own progress using the supplied ***Rigolo*** certificates, accessible in the Teacher support area of the DVD-ROM. These come at the end of every two units, roughly every term. Pupils can check off the various can-do statements listing the skills and language that they should be able to produce at this point. There is also a column for their partner, so that they are encouraged to discuss their progress and level of ability.

Rigolo also provides checklists to use with the national Languages Ladder or the European Languages Portfolio (ELP). The former provides a list of the can-do statements for the first four grades of the ladder, which pupils can keep to mark their progress at the end of each year of the course. The latter provides a copy of the relevant ELP can-do statements for the two stages of ***Rigolo***. This can be used more frequently for pupils to track their progress, although please note that it does not tie into specific units of ***Rigolo***.

Transition to Key Stage 3

Planning transition between primary and secondary French lessons requires careful co-ordination between schools in a local area. ***Rigolo*** aims to ease this process by providing the means to record each pupil's progress using the certificates, portfolios and assessment materials listed above.

Erratum: For 'CD-ROM' in the Teacher's Notes, please read 'DVD-ROM'.

Rigolo 2 Unit 1: Salut Gustave!

National criteria

KS2 Framework objectives

O5.1	Prepare and practise a simple conversation, re-using familiar vocabulary and structures in new contexts
O5.3	Listen attentively and understand more complex phrases and sentences
O5.4	Prepare a short presentation on a familiar topic
L5.1	Re-read frequently a variety of short texts
L5.2	Make simple sentences and short texts
L5.3	Write words, phrases and short sentences, using a reference source
IU5.1	Look at further aspects of their everyday lives from the perspective of someone from another country
IU5.2	Recognise similarities and differences between places

QCA Scheme of Work

Unit 1 Moi
Unit 4 Portraits
Unit 8 L'argent de poche
Unit 21 Le passé et le présent

National Curriculum attainment levels

AT1.1–3, AT2.1–3, AT3.2–3, AT4.2–3

Language ladder levels

Listening: Breakthrough, Grades 1–3
Reading: Breakthrough, Grades 1–3
Speaking: Breakthrough, Grades 1–3
Writing: Breakthrough, Grades 2–3

5–14 guideline strands   Levels A–C

Listening
Listening for information and instructions   A, B, C
Listening and reacting to others   A, B, C

Speaking
Speaking to convey information   A, B, C
Speaking and interacting with others   A, B, C
Speaking about experiences, feelings and opinions A, B, C

Reading
Reading for information and instructions   A, B, C
Reading aloud   A, B, C

Writing
Writing to exchange information and ideas   A, B, C
Writing to establish and maintain personal contact A, B
Writing imaginatively to entertain   A, B, C

Unit objectives

- Greet people and give personal information
- Ask and talk about sisters and brothers
- Say what people have and have not using 3rd person *avoir*
- Say what people are like using 3rd person *être* including negatives.

Key language

- *Bonjour, Salut*
  Comment t'appelles-tu? Je m'appelle…
  Ça va? Oui, ça va bien/Non, ça ne va pas/Comme ci comme ça
  Tu es français(e)/britannique? Oui/Non, je suis…
  Quel âge as-tu? J'ai… ans
- *Tu as des frères ou des sœurs?*
  J'ai un(e)/deux/trois… frères/sœurs
  Je n'ai pas de frères ou de sœurs
- *il/elle a… il/elle n'a pas de…* + revised nouns: *une sœur, un frère, un pantalon, un vélo, une guitare*
- *il/elle est… /il/elle n'est pas… drôle, sportif(ve), sympa, timide, beau/belle, sévère, grand(e), petit (e), intelligent(e) français (e), britannique*

Grammar and skills

- Ask and answer questions
- Recognise and use plural nouns
- Understand and use *avoir* and *être* in 1st, 2nd and 3rd person
- Understand and use negatives with *avoir* and *être*
- Understand agreement of adjectives (feminine singular)
- Manipulate language by changing an element in a sentence
- Recognise patterns in simple sentences

Unit outcomes

Most children will be able to:

- Use spoken French to greet people and say their name, age and how they are
- Ask and say how many brothers and sisters they have
- Say what someone else has and hasn't got
- Say what someone is like

Some children will also be able to:

- Take part in short conversations, giving appropriate answers and asking questions
- Use plural forms accurately when talking about sisters and brothers
- Manipulate sentences by changing an element
- Use negatives in spoken and written French with *avoir* and *être*

Unit 1 — Lesson 1

Lesson summary

Context
Greetings and personal information

National criteria
KS2 framework: O5.1, O5.3, L5.1, L5.2, L5.3, IU5.1
Attainment levels: AT1.2–3, AT2.1–3, AT3.2–3, AT4.2–3
Language ladder levels:
  Listening: **Grades 1–3**; Speaking: **Grades 1–3**;
  Reading: **Grades 2–3**; Writing: **Grades 2–3**

Cross-curricular links
Geography (nationalities); music

Language structures and outcomes
Bonjour/Salut! Comment t'appelles-tu? Je m'appelle…
Ça va? Oui, ça va bien/Non, ça ne va pas/Comme ci comme ça
Tu es français(e)/britannique? Oui/Non, je suis…
Quel âge as-tu? J'ai… ans

---

1. Starter activity: Ça va?
5–10 mins — AT2.1–2 O5.1 IU 5.1

Materials
Flashcards or puppets (optional). You may wish to use the following flashcards from *Rigolo 1*: Unit 1: Polly, Jake, Bof, Nathalie, Didier, M. Mills, Mme Moulin; Unit 4: Mme Chanson; Unit 7: Olivier, Nathalie, Marine, Bernard; Unit 8: M. Mills; Unit 11: Mme Mills.

Description
Starter game to revise greetings and basic questions and answers used when first meeting someone.

Delivery
- Greet the class by asking *Ça va?* and highlighting the variety of possible answers from individuals.
- Invite a pupil to the front and model a dialogue which incorporates the key greetings and expressions.
- Using the flashcards listed above, hand out cards to pupils and invite them to come to the front of the class, in pairs, to act out a mini-dialogue using the model you have just provided.

Intercultural understanding
This is a good opportunity to discuss the differences between the ways in which the French and other nationalities/cultures greet each other. For example, kissing on the cheeks two, three or four times (depending on what part of France you're in) when arriving and departing, boys and men shaking hands when greeting and leaving each other (not just on a first meeting).

2. Animated story: Gustave arrive (1)
5–10 mins — AT1.2–3 O5.3 AT3.2–3 L5.1 IU5.1

Materials
CD-ROM, whiteboard.

Description
Watch and listen to this interactive story presenting the language for Lessons 1 and 2. You can pause and rewind the story at any point, or record your own version too.

Delivery
- You may wish to use flashcards to re-introduce characters appearing in this cartoon: Gustave Cointreau (new to *Rigolo 2*), Mme Moulin, Polly, Jake, Bof.
- Ask pupils to watch the animated story and listen out for as many greetings and questions as possible.
- Play the scene through.
- Ask pupils to tell you the expressions they recognised at the end of the viewing. You don't need to correct or develop their answers at this stage as they will be covered in the next activity.
- Play the animated story through once more.

Support
For less confident pupils, pause each frame and ask comprehension questions.

Language learning strategies
Each time pupils view an animated story or video, encourage them to look and listen for visual and aural clues. Even if they do not understand everything, they should be able to understand the gist from what they see and from what they do understand. Encourage them to use the context of the story to help understanding.

3. Presentation: Salut!
5–10 mins — AT1.2 O5.1 AT2.2 L5.1 AT3.2

Materials
CD-ROM, whiteboard.

Description
Tap on the symbols to hear the greeting or question, then tap on each character in turn to hear their answer. Use the additional features to practise sound/spelling links, or to record your own version of each word.

Delivery
- The whole class repeats the greeting/question and the response heard.
- Continue for all five symbols and for both characters. Repeat if necessary.

Record
You can use the *Record* function to compare pupils' pronunciation with the model version here.

Sound
To further reinforce accurate pronunciation:
- Point to each phrase on the text bar and ask the class to say the phrase.

- Click on the *Sound* icon and click on the different highlighted sounds to hear the Virtual Teacher say them.
- Repeat all together.

NB: if the *Sound* icon is not illuminated when the text is shown, this means it is not available for a particular word.

Extension
Invite pairs of pupils to the front of the class to re-enact the dialogues presented in this activity.

4 Oracy activity: Comment t'appelles-tu?
5–10 mins — AT1.2 O5.1, AT2.2 O5.3, IU5.1

Materials
CD-ROM, whiteboard.

Description
Tap on *Allez*. Listen to the question, and choose the picture that illustrates the best answer and reply. Then check your answer.

Delivery
- The class will hear a question and see two images, only one of which illustrates the correct answer. Pupils must point to (not tap) the correct image and predict the answer to the question, then tap on the audio icon to hear the correct version.
- If their prediction was correct, they tap on the tick button. Otherwise, they tap on the cross.

Support
Give pupils two alternative answers before they reply. They must choose the correct alternative.

Worksheet 1: *Lisez!* may be used from this point onwards.

5 Literacy activity: Tu es britannique?
5–10 mins — AT2.2 O5.1, AT3.2 L5.2

Materials
Card and markers (or PC and printer).

Description
Pupils read and match questions and answers to practise language from this lesson

Delivery
- Prepare three sets of each of the five questions/greetings and answers presented in Activity 3 of this lesson. The questions and answers should be on separate cards.
- Hand out the cards to each pupil. Pupils should then move around the room saying (or reading) what is on their card until they find a partner with a corresponding greeting or answer.
- If time allows, each pair can then 'perform' their dialogue in front of the class.

Worksheet 2: *Écrivez!* may be used from this point onwards.

6 Plenary activity: Salut, ça va?
5–10 mins — AT1.2 O5.3, AT2.2 L5.1, AT3.2 IU5.1

Materials
CD-ROM, whiteboard.

Description
Watch and listen to the interactive karaoke song (already met in *Rigolo 1* Unit 1, Lesson 3, so it will be familiar to most pupils).

Delivery
- Ask pupils to listen out for the greetings used in the song. Play the song straight through once, in *Sing* mode.
- Ask pupils to tell you as many of the greetings and questions as they can remember.

Extension
Organise a karaoke competition between smaller groups, using the recording feature. Pupils can adapt the words from the song to make their own version to perform.

Worksheet 2: *Écrivez!* may be used from this point onwards.

Worksheet 1: Lisez!
AT2.2 O5.1, AT3.2 L5.1, 10 mins

Description
Worksheet to give further reading practice in the questions and answers covered in Lesson 1. It may be used at any point after Activity 4.

Answers
1 Comment t'appelles-tu?
   f Je m'appelle Gustave (G)   h Je m'appelle Polly (P)
2 Quel âge as-tu?
   e J'ai vingt ans (G)   j J'ai dix ans (P)
3 Tu es britannique?
   b Non, je suis français (G) i Oui, je suis britannique (P)
4 Ça va?
   d Oui, ça va bien (P)   g Comme ci, comme ça (G)
5 Salut!
   a Salut Bof! (P)   c Bonjour Bof! (G)

Worksheet 2: Écrivez!
5–10 mins — AT2.2–3 O5.1, AT3.2–3 L5.2, AT4.2–3 L5.3

Description
The worksheet provides further writing practice in the questions and answers covered in this lesson. It may be used at any point after Activity 5.

Answers
1 – Bonjour!
   – Euh… bonjour, Madame.
   – Ça va?
   – Comme ci, comme ça…
   – Comment t'appelles-tu?
   – Je m'appelle Gustave Cointreau.
   – Tu es français?
   – Ah oui, je suis français.
   – Quel âge as-tu?
   – J'ai vingt ans, Madame.

3 *Suggestion only:*
   – Bonjour, Madame.
   – Euh, bonjour, Monsieur.
   – Ça va?
   – Non, ça ne va pas.
   – Comment t'appelles-tu?
   – Je m'appelle Madame Moulin.
   – Tu es française?
   – Ah oui, je suis française.
   – Quel âge as-tu?
   – Euh, j'ai vingt ans, Monsieur.

Unit 1   Lesson 2

Lesson summary

Context
Talking about sisters and brothers

National criteria
KS2 Framework: O5.1, O5.3, L5.1, L5.2, L5.3, IU5.1
Attainment levels: AT1.2–3, AT2.1–2, AT3.2–3, AT4.2
Language ladder levels:
  Listening: **Grades 2–3**; Speaking: **Grades 1–2**;
  Reading: **Grades 2–3**; Writing: **Grade 2**

Cross-curricular links
Numeracy (conducting a questionnaire and charting the results); Literacy (negatives)

Language structures and outcomes
Tu as des frères ou des sœurs?
J'ai un(e)/deux/trois frères/sœurs
Je n'ai pas de frères ou de sœurs

---

1. Starter activity: Quel âge as-tu?
5–10 mins   AT2.1–2 O5.1

Materials
CD-ROM, whiteboard (optional, to re-use presentation on ages from *Rigolo 1*, Unit 2 Lesson 3).

Description
Starter activity in which pupils ask and answers questions about each other's age.

Delivery
- If necessary, you may wish to start with the whiteboard presentation referred to above.
- Ask a few pupils the question *Quel âge as-tu?* before asking pupils to ask the same question to two pupils sitting nearby.

Extension
To provide more variety in the numbers used in answers, hand out cards displaying numbers 1–20 to each pupil. When asked how old they are, they must say the age on their card and their partner writes down the age they hear.

2. Animated story: Gustave arrive (1)
5 mins   AT1.2–3 O5.3, AT3.2–3 L5.1, IU5.1

Materials
CD-ROM, whiteboard.

Description
Watch and listen again to this interactive story presenting the language for Lessons 1 and 2. You can pause and rewind the story at any point, or record your own version too.

Delivery
- Pupils watch the animated story again and note who asks and who answers the question about age.
- In pairs, pupils can re-enact the scene between Gustave and Bof.

3. Presentation: Tu as des frères ou des sœurs?
5–10 mins   AT1.2 O5.1, AT2.2 O5.3, AT3.2

Materials
CD-ROM, whiteboard; possibly flashcards of the characters in the presentation (Polly, Jake, Gustave, Mme Mills, Bof, Bernard) in the role-play activity, or Unit 1 Flashcards (Sisters and brothers).

Description:
Tap on the portraits to hear each character's answer to the question. Use the additional features to practise sound/spelling links and word classes, or to record your own version of each word.

Delivery
- The whole class repeats each phrase as they hear it. Make sure their pronunciation is accurate.
- Continue until all six portraits have been covered.
- If time allows, invite pairs of pupils to the front of the class to re-enact the dialogues presented in this activity using Unit 1 Flashcards (Sisters and brothers).

Record
You can use the *Record* function to compare pupils' pronunciation to the model version here.

Sound
To further reinforce accurate pronunciation:
- Point to each phrase on the text bar and ask the class to say the phrase.
- Click on the *Sound* icon and click on the different highlighted sounds to hear the Virtual Teacher say them.
- Repeat all together.

NB: if the *Sound* icon is not illuminated when the text is shown, this means it is not available for a particular word.

Word
This feature helps focus on grammar terms and word classes. After selecting a word, click on the *Word* button to see and hear the virtual teacher describe what word class it falls into (noun, verb, adjective, pronoun, preposition).

Support
Ask the whole class initially to repeat both questions and answers before running the activity again as described above in 'Delivery'.

Knowledge about language

This is the first time in *Rigolo 2* that pupils have met the negative form. They will also meet more negatives in Lessons 3 and 4.
- Ask them to deduce which words make the sentence negative (i.e. *n'* and *pas*) and show them that you can use *Je n'ai pas de…* with other nouns.
- Draw comparisons with how they make English sentences negative.

4. Oracy activity: Je n'ai pas de frères
10 mins — AT1.2 O5.1, AT2.2 O5.3

Materials
Unit 1 Flashcards (Sister and brothers and Adjectives and negatives), plus flashcards of the characters from *Rigolo 1*, as before.

Description
Class-based speaking practice of questions and answers about bothers and sisters.

Delivery
- Hand out Unit 1 Flashcards (Sisters and brothers) or, alternatively, the *Rigolo 1* flashcards of the characters.
- Ask pupils with cards the question *Tu as des frères ou des sœurs?*
- Pupils answer according to their flashcard, or as though they are the character. If you use the character flashcards, if necessary put the details of the characters' bothers and sisters, as below, on the board or on a piece of paper.
- Invite pairs of pupils to the front of the class. One pupil holds a flashcard; the other asks them the target question.
- Character siblings are as follows: Polly (one brother), Jake (one sister), Olivier (one sister), Nathalie (one brother), Didier (no siblings), Bof (no siblings), Bernard (two sisters, three brothers), Marine (no siblings).

Extension
If your pupils are confident enough at this stage, they can practise asking and answering real questions about their siblings.

Support
Note possible answers on the whiteboard, from which pupils select as appropriate.

Worksheet 3: *Parlez!* may be used from this point onwards.

5. Literacy activity: J'ai un frère
5–10 mins — AT3.2 L5.2, AT4.2

Materials
CD-ROM, whiteboard.

Description
Tap on *Allez*. Drag the words into the correct order to match the sentence you hear. Tap on *Fini* when you have finished.

Delivery
- Pupils drag and drop the relevant word tiles to make the sentence they hear (e.g. *J'ai une sœur*). If their sentence is correct, the matching picture is shown in the picture frame.
- In the case of a wrong answer, pupils are invited to try again.
- Ask pupils what they notice about the endings of the nouns where there is more than one brother or sister (i.e. *frère* and *sœur* both add an 's') and compare with plurals in English.

Worksheet 4: *Grammaire* may be used from this point onwards.

6. Plenary activity: C'est qui?
5–10 mins — AT1.2 O5.1, AT2.2 O5.3

Materials
Character flashcards from *Rigolo 1*: Unit 1: Polly, Jake, Bof, Nathalie, Didier, M. Mills, Mme Moulin; Unit 4: Mme Chanson; Unit 7: Olivier, Nathalie, Marine, Bernard; Unit 8: M. Mills; Unit 11: Mme Mills

Description
Pupils identify characters from a description of their siblings.

Delivery
- Display the character flashcards at the front of the class and divide the class into two teams.
- Ask different pupils to ask you *Tu as des frères ou des sœurs?* to prompt your answer (e.g. *Je n'ai pas de frères ou de sœurs*).
- The first team to shout out the name of the character to whom you are referring wins a point.
- Continue until you have covered all the characters and ask the pupils to add up their points in French.

Worksheet 3: Parlez!
5–10 mins — AT2.2 O5.1

Description
Worksheet to give further speaking practice in asking and answering about bothers and sisters. It may be used at any point after Activity 4.

Worksheet 4: Grammaire
5–10 mins — AT2.2 L5.2, AT4.2 L5.3

Description
Worksheet to give further writing and speaking practice in changing sentences from positive to negative and vice versa. It may be used at any point after Activity 5.

Delivery
- If you have not already focused on negatives, do so here. Put the following phrase on the whiteboard: *Je n'ai pas de sœurs*. Establish which two parts of the sentences make it negative i.e. *n'* and *pas*. Explain that you can put other nouns at the end of this sentence instead of *sœurs*. Give some examples.

Answers

Didier:	Jake:
1 J'ai un livre.	Je n'ai pas de livre.
2 J'ai un stylo.	Je n'ai pas de stylo.
3 J'ai un vélo.	Je n'ai pas de vélo.
4 J'ai un lapin.	Je n'ai pas de lapin.
5 J'ai une banane.	Je n'ai pas de banane.
6 J'ai un t-shirt.	Je n'ai pas de t-shirt.
7 J'ai une pizza.	Je n'ai pas de pizza.
8 J'ai une souris.	Je n'ai pas de souris.
9 J'ai un pantalon noir.	Je n'ai pas de pantalon noir.
10 J'ai une guitare.	Je n'ai pas de guitare.

Unit 1 — Lesson 3

Lesson summary

Context
Saying what people have and don't have using *avoir* in the 3rd person

National criteria
KS2 Framework: O5.1, O5.3, O5.4, L5.1, L5.2, L5.3, IU5.1
Attainment levels: AT1.1–3, AT2.2–3, AT3.2–3, AT4.2–3
Language ladder levels:
  Listening: **Grades 2–3**; Speaking: **Grades 2–3**;
  Reading: **Grades 2–3**; Writing: **Grades 2–3**

Cross-curricular links
Literacy (concept of negatives)

Key vocabulary
Revised nouns: *une sœur, un frère, un vélo, une guitare*

Language structures and outcomes
Il a/Elle a… Il/Elle n'a pas de…

---

1. Starter activity: Coco le Clown — 5–10 mins — AT2.2 O5.3 / AT3.2 L5.1

Materials
CD-ROM, whiteboard; possibly flashcards from *Rigolo 1* Unit 12 (clothes) and Unit 2 (colours).

Description
Song to practise the 3rd person singular of *avoir* and revise clothes and colours/size previously covered in *Rigolo 1*.

Delivery
- If necessary, use the *Rigolo 1* flashcards to revise key vocabulary.
- Freeze the first frame showing Coco le Clown and ask the class to describe what he is wearing using *Il a* + clothes/colours. Play the first verse through and ask pupils to listen to check if their answers were correct.
- Freeze the next frame with Jojo le Clown, and proceed as above. Repeat the activity for Doudou and verse 3.

Extension
More confident pupils could write another verse about an imaginary clown; this could be done as a whole class, or in pairs/mini-groups.

Support
For less confident pupils, let them listen and watch each verse before asking them to describe the clowns, then play the scenes again to check their answers.

2. Animated story: Gustave arrive (2) — 10 mins — AT1.2–3 O5.3 / AT3.2–3 L5.1 / IU5.1

Materials
CD-ROM, whiteboard.

Description
- Watch and listen to this interactive story presenting the language for Lessons 3 and 4. You can pause and rewind the story at any point, or record your own version too.

Delivery
- Watch scene 1 (from Gustave standing at the door with the letter to just before Mme Moulin opens the door) right through and ask pupils to summarise what they have understood.
- Freeze the shot of Mme Moulin opening the door and ask pupils to predict what will happen in the second scene.
- Check general comprehension of this scene then play both scenes right through again, this time without pausing.

Support
Pause the cartoon after each character has spoken to check comprehension, before letting them enjoy watching the animated story right through.

3. Presentation: Il a un vélo — 5–10 mins — AT1.2 O5.1 / AT2.2 O5.3 / AT3.2

Materials
CD-ROM, whiteboard.

Description
Tap on the magic mirrors to hear the positive/negative sentences. Use the additional features to practise sound/spelling links and word classes, or to record your own version of each word.

Delivery
- Pupils listen to/read the sentence, and repeat.
- Select another pupil to tap on *Continuez* to see and hear a negative sentence.
- Continue until both scenarios for all four mirrors have been covered.
- You may wish to focus on the differences between the positive and negative sentences, i.e. the use of *Il/Elle n'a pas de…*

Refer to the Introduction for notes on the *Record*, *Sound* and *Word* features.

4. Oracy activity: Il a un chat — 10 mins — AT1.2 O5.1 / AT2.2 O5.3

Materials
Selection of relevant 'realia' (e.g. toy dog/cat, pen, bag, hat, football, recorder, drum, banana, apple, guitar). Alternatively, use flashcards from *Rigolo 1*, Units 1, 2, 4, 5.

Description
Class-based oracy activity (listening and speaking), practising sentences using *Il/Elle a* and *Il/Elle n'a pas de…*

Delivery
- Model a few sentences as follows: invite four pupils (two boys and two girls) to the front of the class. Give one boy and one girl

the same object (e.g. a pen). Point to the girl with the pen and say *Elle a [un stylo]*. Point to the girl with no pen and elicit *Elle n'a pas de [stylo]*. Repeat for the boys using *Il a/Il n'a pas...*

● Invite another four pupils to the front; give one boy and one girl an object and ask the class to make the four relevant sentences.

● If time allows, you could make this into a team game by dividing the class into two teams and awarding a point for each correct sentence made.

Support
Write some negative sentences on the whiteboard from which pupils select as appropriate.

Worksheet 5: *Parlez!* may be used from this point onwards.

Knowledge about language

● Make pupils aware that they can say many more things in French by changing one element in a sentence, e.g. changing the noun after *Il/Elle a* and *Il/Elle n'a pas de...*

● It is important that pupils realise that they have some control over what they can say and that the phrases they learn are not 'static'. They will make more progress in French if they are actively aware that they can expand their own language.

● Set them a challenge. Ask them to work in groups of four–six and give them five minutes to brainstorm how many endings they can find for the phrase *il n'a pas de...* Which group has the most words?

5. Literacy: Il n'a pas de guitare
5–10 mins   AT3.2 L5.2   AT4.2

Materials
CD-ROM, whiteboard.

Description
Tap on *Allez*. Read the text options at the bottom of the screen. Drag the text into the correct order to match the character's thought bubble. Tap on *Fini* when you have finished.

Delivery
● If the pupil's sentence is correct, the character becomes animated. In the case of an incorrect answer, one of three 'lives' is lost and pupils can try again.

● If all three 'lives' are lost pupils can opt to start the game again.

Worksheet 6: *Écrivez!* may be used from this point onwards.

6. Plenary activity: Elle a un stylo
5–10 mins   AT2.2 O5.1   AT1.1 O5.3

Materials
Realia and items used in Activity 4 of this lesson (or alternatively, flashcards of any known nouns from *Rigolo 1*).

Description
Identification game where pupils identify who is being described by the teacher using *Il/Elle a...* and *Il/Elle n'a pas de...*

Delivery
● Invite four boys and four girls to stand at the front of the class. Hand out the objects to these pupils, ensuring that any duplicates are given to a boy and a girl.

● Divide the rest of the class into two teams.

● Say a sentence, e.g. *Il a un chien*. The first team to shout out the name of the pupil to whom you are referring wins a point.

● If a team identifies the wrong pupil, they lose a point.

● At the end, ask pupils to remind you how you say 'He/She has…' and 'He/She has not…'.

Worksheet 5: Parlez!
5–10 mins   AT2.2 O5.1

Description:
'Spot the difference' picture game, in pairs, using positive and negative sentences. It may be used at any point after Activity 4.

Delivery
● Pupils work in pairs. Cut the sheet in two halves and give each partner one half. Revise the vocabulary and model the pronunciation.

● Without looking at each other's picture, pupils take it in turn to make sentences about what they can see in their picture. They must circle any differences they find.

● When they have found seven differences they can look at each other's picture to check their answers.

● Go through the seven answers verbally at the end of the activity.

Answers
Partner A:
Mme Moulin a une pizza.
Mme Moulin a une jupe blanche./Non, Mme Moulin n'a pas de jupe noire.
Jake a un piano./Non, Jake n'a pas de sandwich
Polly a un vélo./Non, Polly n'a pas de CD.
Nathalie a un chien./Non, Nathalie n'a pas de guitare.
Olivier a une banane./Non, Olivier n'a pas de sac.
Polly a une jupe noire./Non, Polly n'a pas de jupe blanche.

Partner B:
Non, Mme Moulin n'a pas de pizza.
Non, Mme Moulin n'a pas de jupe blanche./Mme Moulin a une jupe noire.
Non, Jake n'a pas de piano./Jake a un sandwich.
Non, Polly n'a pas de vélo./Polly a un CD.
Non, Nathalie n'a pas de chien./Nathalie a une guitare.
Non, Olivier n'a pas de banane./Olivier a un sac.
Non, Polly n'a pas de jupe noire./Polly a une jupe blanche.

Worksheet 6: Écrivez!
10 mins   AT2.2–3 O5.4   AT4.2–3 L5.2

Description
Pupils build up sentences to describe a friend or a family member. The worksheet may be used at any point after Activity 5.

Delivery
● The writing produced from this worksheet could be combined with a picture or photo and made into a display, or used as the basis for a mini-presentation.

Unit 1 — Lesson 4

Lesson summary

Context
Saying what people are like using the 3rd person of *être*, including negatives

National criteria
KS2 framework: **O5.1, O5.3, O5.4, L5.1, L5.2, L5.3, IU5.1**
Attainment levels: **AT1.2–3, AT2.2, AT3.2–3, AT4.2–3**
Language ladder levels:
  Listening: **Grades 2–3**; Speaking: **Grade 2**;
  Reading: **Grades 2–3**; Writing: **Grades 2–3**

Cross-curricular links
PSHE, literacy, ICT and DT (project work)

Key vocabulary
drôle, sportif(ve), sympa, timide, beau/belle, sévère, grand(e), petit(e), intelligent(e) français(e), britannique (all revised apart from *beau/belle*)

Language structures and outcomes
Il/Elle est…/Il/Elle n'est pas…

---

1. Starter activity: Il est comment? Elle est comment?
5–10 mins — AT1.2 O5.1, AT2.2 O5.3, AT3.2

Materials
CD-ROM, whiteboard.

Description
Tap on a character to hear them described in the 3rd person, using adjectives previously covered in *Rigolo 1* Unit 4 Lesson 4 presentation.

Delivery
- The class repeats the sentence, and the Virtual Teacher's gesture, each time.
- When each character has been covered a couple of times, make two teams. Ask each team, in turn, to say the phrase when you point to a character.
- Tap on the picture to check whether the answer is correct, and give a point for each right answer.

Extension
- Ask a few pupils to stand at the front, with their back to the board. Another pupil taps on a character to trigger the Virtual Teacher audio.
- Pupils must turn round and point to the relevant character on the board.

2. Animated story: Gustave arrive (2)
5–10 mins — AT1.2–3 O5.3, AT3.2–3 L5.1, IU5.1

Materials
CD-ROM, whiteboard.

Description
Watch and listen again to this interactive story presenting the language for Lessons 3 and 4. You can pause and rewind the story at any point, or record your own version too.

Delivery
- Watch scene 1 (from Gustave standing at the door with the letter to just before Mme Moulin opens the door) right through and ask pupils to tell you which adjectives they have heard.
- Watch the second scene (from Mme Moulin opening the door until the end) and again ask pupils to tell you the descriptions they have understood.
- Make a note of suggested answers on the board and play both scenes right through again to allow pupils to check their answers.

Extension
- Ask more confident pupils to 'predict' the adjectives they will hear in this cartoon, and to make full sentences rather than just give you the adjectives.

Support
Pause the cartoon after each description to double-check comprehension.

3. Presentation: Elle est belle?
5–10 mins — AT1.2 O5.1, AT2.2 O5.3, AT3.2

Materials
CD-ROM, whiteboard.

Description
Tap on the characters to hear their description. Use the additional features to practise sound/spelling links and word classes, or to record your own version of each word.

Delivery
- The whole class listens to the description and repeats, miming the gestures used by the characters.
- Continue for all eight characters and repeat if further practice is required.
- Ask pupils to say what difference there is when you say someone 'is not…' i.e. you say *Il/Elle n'est pas…* Draw similarities between this and *Il/Elle n'a pas…* from the previous lesson. Use Unit 1 Flashcards (Adjectives and negatives) to demonstrate.
- Also, if your pupils can cope, ask how the adjectives differ when describing males and females, i.e. they change: sometimes they add an 'e'; sometimes they change altogether (*beau/belle*). Draw out differences in pronunciation too.

Refer to the Introduction for notes on the *Record*, *Sound* and *Word* features.

Extension
- Additional props: two 'horror' masks.
- If you have a confident group, ask for six volunteers. Explain to them that they are going to be demonstrating different physical characteristics.
- Ask one girl and one boy to act out looking 'shy' and 'not shy'. Say e.g. *Il est timide. Elle n'est pas timide.*
- Ask another girl and boy to act out being 'sporty' and 'not sporty'. Again, say e.g. *Elle est sportive. Il n'est pas sportif.*
- Finally, give a girl and a boy horror masks or ask them to make a horrible face. Point to them in turn, saying: *Il n'est pas beau. Elle n'est pas belle.*

Unit 1: Lesson 4

- Then point to each child in turn and ask, e.g. *Il/Elle est timide?* Elicit answers of *Oui, il/elle est timide* or *Non, il/elle n'est pas timide*.
- Move on to asking *Il/Elle est comment?* and eliciting positive and negative replies as above.

4 · Oracy activity: Il n'est pas beau
10 mins — AT1.2 O5.1, AT2.2 O5.3

Materials
CD-ROM, whiteboard.

Description
Tap on *Allez*. Answer the questions, then check your answers.

Delivery
- We hear a question relating to the highlighted character on screen (e.g. *Il est beau?*). Ask pupils to answer the question, in a full sentence.
- Tap on the audio check button to confirm whether or not their suggestion was correct. If it was correct, tap on the tick button. If not, tap on the cross.
- Tap on *Allez* to go on to the next question.
- Continue for all six descriptions and repeat if further practice is needed.

Support
Provide extra prompts yourself in formulating the answers with less confident pupils. Alternatively, listen to the question, then listen to the answer straightaway and ask the class to repeat what they hear. Once you have been through all six descriptions in this way, repeat the activity as suggested in the 'Delivery' section above.

Knowledge about language
- Encourage pupils to spot patterns in sentences by displaying some positive and some negative sentences from this lesson. Can they put them into two groups and explain why?
- Also encourage them to find the patterns between feminine and masculine adjectives. Can they work out the rule?
- Encourage them to build sentences (as in Activity 5 below) where they apply these rules. Pupils are more likely to remember the rule if they discuss them and deduce them by looking at patterns.

5 · Literacy activity: Elle est sportive et timide
10 mins — AT3.2 L5.2, AT4.2

Materials
A4-size cards displaying individual words as suggested below; possibly additional magazine pictures of people displaying the characteristics below, and Unit 1 Flashcards (Adjectives and negatives).

Description
Consolidation of using *être* (positive and negative) with adjectives by building sentences using word cards.

Delivery
- Make a set of word cards, colour-coded if possible, as follows:

Il/Elle	colour 1
est/n'/pas	colour 2
beau/belle/sportif/sportive/timide	colour 3

- If you have not already done so, discuss how some adjectives differ for male/female. If necessary, draw a table on the board and show which ones change and how it affects pronunciation.
- Ask pupils to build sentences to refer to characters in the story or your magazine pictures.

Extension
Add further known adjectives, e.g. *grand(e)*, *petit(e)*, *drôle*, *sympa*, *intelligent(e)* to the list above, and add a card with *et* to encourage longer sentences.

Support
Oracy activity 3 can be re-played with or without the subtitles.

📄 Worksheet 7: *Grammaire* may be used from this point onwards.

📄 Worksheet 8: *Lisez!* may also be used from this point for more confident pupils.

6 · Plenary activity: Il n'est pas sympa
5–10 mins — AT3.2 L5.2, AT4.2 L5.3

Materials
Word cards from *Rigolo 1*, Unit 4, Lesson 4 Plenary activity (*il, elle, est* + adjectives) plus *beau* and *belle*.

Description
Pupils build sentences to describe someone in the 3rd person, using individual word cards and including negatives.

Delivery
- Give out a set of cards to each table/group.
- Allow five minutes for each group to make as many sentences as possible using the cards.
- Pupils could write out the different sentences to compare with other groups at the end.

Worksheet 7: Grammaire
10 mins — AT3.2 L5.2, AT4.2 L5.3

Description
This provides practice in making affirmative 3rd person singular sentences negative, and vice versa. It may be used at any point after Activity 5.

Answers

1. Il n'est pas sympa.
   Il n'est pas timide.
   Il n'est pas drôle.
   Il n'est pas grand.
   Il n'est pas intelligent.
   Il n'est pas sportif.
   Il n'est pas beau.

2. Elle n'est pas drôle.
   Elle est grande.
   Elle n'est pas sympa.
   Elle n'est pas intelligente.
   Elle est sportive.
   Elle n'est pas belle.
   Elle est timide.

Worksheet 8: Lisez!
10 mins — AT3.3 L5.1, AT4.3 L5.2, L5.3

Description
Pupils match descriptions with the right pictures, and try writing their own description. This worksheet may be used at any point after Activity 5, and is more suitable for more confident pupils as it concentrates on understanding longer texts.

Rigolo 2 Teacher's Notes © Nelson Thornes Ltd 2008

Answers

1. 1b 2c 3a 4d
2. Drawings should show a tall French boy, aged about 13. Short black hair, black trousers, no jacket but a hat.
3. *Suggestion:* Elle a quinze ans. Elle a une minijupe noire et un t-shirt blanc. Elle n'est pas timide. Elle n'est pas belle. Elle a un chien.

Project work: Il est comment? Elle est comment?

1–2 hours

AT3.3–3 L5.1
AT4.2–3 L5.2
L5.3
O5.4

Description
Pupils build up descriptions of people in the class or celebrities using *Il/Elle est…* and *Il/Elle n'est pas…*, *Il/Elle a* and *Il/Elle n'a pas…*, produce a display with photos and make a presentation to rest of class.

Materials
Card for displaying the profiles, magazines/photos, or access to PC/internet/printer where possible.

Delivery
- Ask pupils to choose a person (celebrity/family member/friend) as a subject for their presentation.
- Pupils must then gather a couple of pictures (from photos, magazines, or the internet if available) and write a description of that person using the structures and vocabulary practised in this unit.
- Descriptions may be handwritten or typed on a PC. Pupils then create a display which they can hold up when making their presentation to the class.

Rigolo 2 — Unit 2: À l'école

National criteria

KS2 Framework objectives

O5.1	Prepare and practise a simple conversation, re-using familiar vocabulary and structures in new contexts
O5.2	Understand and express simple opinions
O5.3	Listen attentively and understand more complex phrases and sentences
O5.4	Prepare a short presentation on a familiar topic
L5.1	Re-read frequently a variety of short texts
L5.2	Make simple sentences and short texts
L5.3	Write words, phrases and short sentences, using a reference source
IU5.1	Look at further aspects of their everyday lives from the perspective of someone from another country
IU5.2	Recognise similarities and differences between places
IU5.3	Compare symbols, objects or products which represent their own culture with those of another country

QCA Scheme of Work

Unit 2   Jeux et chansons
Unit 8   L'argent de poche
Unit 15 En route pour l'école

National Curriculum attainment levels

AT1.1–3, AT2.1–3, AT3.1–3, AT4.1–2

Language ladder levels

Listening: Breakthrough, Grades 1–3
Reading: Breakthrough, Grades 1–3
Speaking: Breakthrough, Grades 1–3
Writing: Breakthrough, Grades 1–3

5–14 guideline strands   Levels A–C

Listening
Listening for information and instructions   A, B, C
Listening and reacting to others   A, B, C

Speaking
Speaking to convey information   A, B, C
Speaking and interacting with others   A, B, C
Speaking about experiences, feelings and opinions A, B, C

Reading
Reading for information and instructions   A, B, C
Reading aloud   A, B, C

Writing
Writing to exchange information and ideas   A, B, C
Writing to establish and maintain personal contact A, B
Writing imaginatively to entertain   A, B, C

Unit objectives

- Name school subjects
- Talk about likes and dislikes at school
- Ask and say the time
- Talk about timings of the school day

Key language

- C'est… l'anglais, le français, le sport, l'histoire-géo, les sciences, les maths, la musique
- J'aime/Je n'aime pas + subjects
- C'est bien/cool/nul
- Quelle heure est-il? Il est une heure et quart/et demie/ moins le quart. Il est midi/minuit
- La récré, le déjeuner, l'école commence à… heure(s) et finit à…

Grammar and skills

- Understand and use the definite article correctly: le/la/l'/les
- Express opinions
- Use correct intonation when asking a question
- Understand that there is not always a direct equivalent to each English word in French
- Use song to help memorise language
- Form longer sentences

Unit outcomes

Most children will be able to:

- Understand and say school subjects
- Say which subjects they like and don't like
- Say the time on the hour, half-hour and quarter-hour

Some children will also be able to:

- Write accurately a range of vocabulary
- Express opinions about a range of things
- Use longer sentences in spoken and written French to talk about timings of the school day

Unit 2 — Lesson 1

Lesson summary

Context
School subjects

National criteria
KS2 Framework: **O5.1, O5.2, O5.3, L5.1, L5.3, IU5.1, IU5.2**
Attainment levels: **AT1.1–3, AT2.1, AT3.1–3, AT4.1–2**
Language ladder levels:
   Listening: **Grades 1–3**; Speaking: **Grade 1**;
   Reading: **Grades 1–3**; Writing: **Grades 1–2**

Cross-curricular links
n/a

Key vocabulary
School subjects: *l'anglais, le français, le sport, l'histoire-géo, les sciences, les maths, la musique*

Language structures and outcomes
C'est... + school subject

---

1. Starter activity: Dans la salle de classe
5–10 mins — AT1.1 O5.1, AT2.1 IU5.1

Materials
CD-ROM, whiteboard; or flashcards from *Rigolo 1*, Unit 2 (classroom objects).

Description
Class discussion about schools and revision of classroom objects.

Delivery
- Using the flashcards, or the whiteboard presentation of classroom objects from *Rigolo 1* (Unit 2, Lesson 1), quickly check that pupils have remembered the vocabulary.
- Explain to pupils that they will be looking at school life in France during this unit, and ask if they know anything about schools in France.
- Particular points of contrast could be: school holidays, length of school day, organisation of school week (e.g. in some areas there is no school on Wednesdays, but the pupils may go on a Saturday morning), no uniform (except in some private Catholic schools). Don't go into too much detail at this stage, but you may wish to whet their appetite with a few interesting facts before moving on to the next activity.

2. Video story: À l'école (1)
10 mins — AT1.2–3 O5.2, AT3.2–3 O5.3, IU5.1 L5.1, IU5.2

Materials
CD-ROM, whiteboard; school subject flashcards for the support activity.

Description
Watch and listen to this video story presenting the language for Lessons 1 and 2. You can pause and rewind the story at any point.

Delivery
- Freeze the opening scene and ask if pupils can tell whether the girl is standing in front of a French or British school. (For example, the lack of uniform could be a clue.)
- Ask pupils to watch the first scene (from Léa introducing herself to thanking Thomas) and to listen out especially for the children's names.
- Pause the film at the end of the scene; check whether pupils heard the names, and ask what they think was said by those two characters. Don't go into too much detail as you just need to check for gist understanding at this point.
- Repeat as above for the other scenes (Léa with Chloé, then Léa and Lucas).
- Ask pupils to take note of the school building and the background they can see on the video, then point out any difference they notice between this and their own school.

Support
Review the video clip at the end of the lesson: stick the subject flashcards on the wall, play the video again, this time pausing the film after each subject is mentioned. Ask a pupil to come up and point to the subject they have just heard. Encourage choral repetition.

Intercultural understanding
- Throughout this unit, use the video to look at and discuss some differences between French and English schools.
- Look at the school building and the background of the video; look at what the children are wearing.
- Ask pupils to think about how their school day and school life is different from that of pupils in France.
- If you have contact with French primary school, ask them about their school day, subjects, timings of the day, etc.
- French primary schools usually start lessons at 8 o'clock in the morning and end around 4 o'clock in the afternoon. They may have as long as two hours for lunch, and don't have to wear uniform.

3. Presentation: Les maths
5–10 mins — AT1.1 O5.1, AT2.1, AT3.1

Materials
CD-ROM, whiteboard.

Description
Tap on the objects to hear the school subjects being presented. Use the additional features to practise sound/spelling links, word classes and spelling, or to record your own version of each word.

Delivery
- The whole class listens to the school subjects being presented and repeats each one.

Unit 2: Lesson 1

- Continue for all seven subjects and repeat if further practice is required.
- By keeping the text switched on you can encourage pupils to see the similarities between the words in English and in French.

Refer to the Introduction for notes on the *Record*, *Spell*, *Sound* and *Word* features.

Support
Use Unit 2 Flashcards (School subjects) for further presentation/pronunciation practice of the school subjects.

Extension
Revise and discuss the different French words for 'the': *le/la/l'/les*

4 Oracy activity: C'est la musique
5–10 mins AT1.1 O5.1 / O5.3

Materials
CD-ROM, whiteboard.

Description
Tap on *Allez*. Listen to Mme Chanson and tap on the correct picture for each word.

Delivery
- The class will hear the name of a school subject and the pupil at the front must tap on the corresponding image.
- Tap on *Encore* to repeat, or on *Allez* to go on to the next word.
- Continue for all seven subjects and repeat if further practice is needed.

Support
Encourage less confident pupils to use the *Encore* button as much as necessary. You could also display the Unit 2 Flashcards (School subjects) during the activity as additional prompts.

Worksheet 1: *Écrivez!* may be used from this point onwards.

5 Literacy activity: C'est le français
5–10 mins AT4.1–2 L5.3

Materials
Unit 2 Flashcards (School subjects).

Description
Pupils practise writing out the school subjects learned so far.

Delivery
- Display a set of flashcards on the board.
- Give pupils two to three minutes to study the words then remove the cards.
- Call out the subjects in random order and ask pupils to write them down.
- Display the flashcards again at the end so they can check their answers.

Extension
More confident pupils could work in pairs and 'dictate' the subjects to each other by spelling them out in turn.

Support
Give copies of the words to pupils who need them. They then select the correct word from the list and try to copy it out accurately.

Worksheet 2: *Lisez!* may be used from this point onwards.

6 Plenary activity: C'est le sport
5 mins AT1.1 O5.1 / AT2.1 O5.3

Materials
Unit 2 Flashcards (School subjects), realia/objects to represent the various school subjects.

Description
A team game using realia to consolidate the school subjects covered in this lesson.

Delivery
- If necessary, use the flashcards to elicit quickly and review the school subjects.
- Place the realia/objects on a table at the front of the class. Point to each object in turn and ask the class to say what subject is represented by each one.
- Divide the class into two teams. Invite a pupil from each team to the front. Say the name of a school subject aloud. The first pupil to touch the relevant object wins a point for their team.
- Invite two new pupils to the front for each subject.
- Add up the points to see which team has won.

Worksheet 1: Écrivez!
5–10 mins AT4.1–2 L5.3

Description
This worksheet provides further practice in writing out the school subjects. It may be used at any point after Activity 4.

Answers

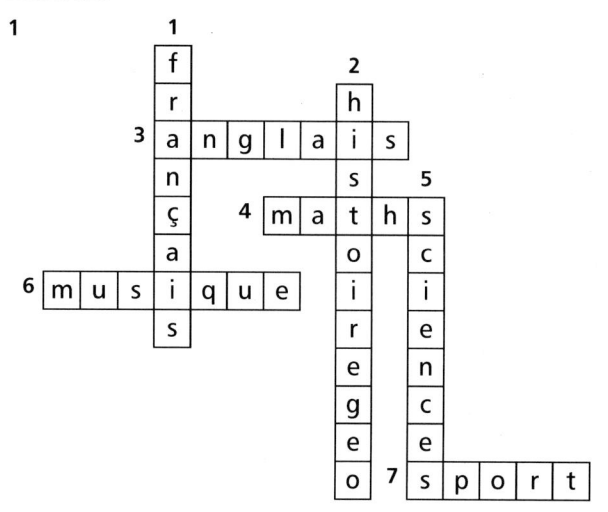

1

Crossword:
- 3 across: anglais
- 4 across: maths
- 6 across: musique
- 7 across: sport
- 1 down: français
- 2 down: histoire-géo
- 5 down: sciences

Worksheet 2: Lisez!
5–10 mins AT3.2 L5.1

Description
This worksheet provides further reading practice in school subjects. It may be used at any point after Activity 5.

Answers
1 1 F 2 V 3 F 4 V 5 F 6 F 7 F
2 1 C'est les maths.
   2 C'est le sport.
   3 C'est l'anglais.
   4 C'est le français.
   5 C'est l'histoire-géo.
   6 C'est la musique.

Unit 2 — Lesson 2

Lesson summary

Context
Talking about likes and dislikes at school

National criteria
KS2 Framework: **O5.1, O5.2, O5.3, L5.1, L5.2, L5.3, IU5.1, IU5.2**
Attainment levels: **AT1.1–3, AT2.1–2, AT3.2–3, AT4.2**
Language ladder levels:
- Listening: **Grades 1–3**; Speaking: **Grades 1–2**;
- Reading: **Grades 1–3**; Writing: **Grade 2**

Cross-curricular links
Numeracy (class survey)

Key vocabulary
School subjects (revised): *l'anglais, le français, le sport, l'histoire-géo, les sciences, les maths, la musique*

Language structures and outcomes
J'aime/Je n'aime pas + subjects
C'est bien/cool/nul

---

1. Starter activity: C'est la musique (5 mins) AT1.1 O5.1 / AT2.1 O5.3

Materials
CD-ROM, whiteboard.

Description
Repeat of Activity 4, Lesson 1: re-listen to audio prompts of school subjects and select the relevant icon.

Delivery
- Divide the class into two teams.
- In turn, a pupil from each team comes to the board to tap on *Allez*, listen to the prompt, and select the corresponding icon.
- The teams score a point for each correct answer.

2. Video story: À l'école (1) (5–10 mins) AT1.2–3 O5.2 / AT3.2–3 O5.4 / L5.1 / IU5.1 IU5.2

Materials
CD-ROM, whiteboard.

Description
Watch and listen again to this video story presenting the language for Lessons 1 and 2. You can pause and rewind the story at any point.

Delivery
- Ask pupils for the names of the seven school subjects covered so far and write a list on the board.
- Ask pupils if they can remember the names of the interviewees, then write the three names on the board (Thomas, Chloé and Lucas).
- Tell pupils they are going to listen out for who likes/dislikes which subjects.
- Watch the first scene (up to *Merci Thomas*) and ask pupils which subjects were mentioned, and whether the interviewee likes those subjects or not.
- Write the interviewee's initial next to the relevant subjects and put a tick or a cross next to the subject according to whether they liked it or not.
- Repeat as above for the other scenes (Léa with Chloé, then Léa and Lucas).
- If time allows, you may wish to play the video straight through again.

Support
Give pupils Unit 2 Flashcards (School subjects) and ask them to hold up the appropriate card each time they hear a particular subject.

3. Presentation: J'aime les sciences (10 mins) AT1.2 O5.2 / AT2.2 O5.3 / AT3.2

Materials
CD-ROM, whiteboard; Unit 2 Flashcards (School subjects and Likes/dislikes).

Description
Tap on the objects to hear how Jake feels about school subjects. Use the additional features to practise sound/spelling links and word classes, or to record your own version of each word.

Delivery
- The whole class repeats what Jake says about which subjects he likes/dislikes, using any gestures suggested by the Virtual Teacher.
- Make sure pupils are pronouncing words correctly and check that their intonation is correct.
- Continue for all seven subjects and repeat if further practice is required.

Refer to the Introduction for notes on the *Record* and *Word* features.

Support
If further reinforcement is required, use the flashcards for pupils to re-construct each of Jake's sentences on the board/wall.

Knowledge about language
- Use the language presentations in **Rigolo 2** to continue to make sure that pupils' pronunciation is accurate. Get the whole class to repeat after the audio for each phrase and use the *Record* facility to compare their pronunciation with that of the audio.
- In this lesson, also concentrate on the intonation in the question: pupils need to make sure their voices rise at the end.
- If possible, do a listening activity with them for extra practice. Say several phrases, e.g. *Tu aimes les maths?* either as a statement, or a question with your voice rising at the end. Pupils say whether it's a statement or a question. Oracy activity 4 (see below) provides specific practice of asking and answering questions.

4. Oracy activity: Tu aimes l'anglais?

⏱ 10–15 mins AT1.2 O5.1 AT2.2 O5.2

Materials
Unit 2 Flashcards (School subjects) and (Likes/dislikes).

Description
Class activity where pupils ask and answer questions about their likes/dislikes of school subjects.

Delivery
- First hold up the *J'aime/Je n'aime pas* flashcards; make appropriate positive/negative gestures as you say each one, and ask the class to repeat chorally. This is a good opportunity to reinforce pronunciation and intonation, and to emphasise the use of voice tone and gesture to help convey meaning.

- Hold up the subject flashcards and ask individual pupils *Tu aimes [la musique]?* Pupils reply with *Oui, j'aime [la musique]*, or *Non, je n'aime pas [la musique]*.

- Continue until all the subjects have been covered.

Extension
- More confident pupils can work in small groups, each with a set of flashcards, and ask each other questions about their subject preferences as per the model questions and answers in the 'Delivery' section above.

- Pupils could also add the expressions *C'est cool/bien/nul* after each sentence.

📄 Worksheet 3: *Parlez!* may be used from this point onwards.

5. Literacy activity: C'est nul ou c'est bien?

⏱ 5–10 mins AT3.2 O5.2 L5.2

Materials
CD-ROM, whiteboard.

Description
Drag the word tiles into the machine to form a sentence about likes/dislikes of school subjects and an appropriate opinion. Tap on *Fini* when you have completed each answer.

Delivery
- If the pupil's answer is correct, the machine will illustrate it. If it is incorrect, smoke appears.

- Continue until all sentence variations and opinions have been covered, and repeat if further practice is needed.

Support
Give further sentence-building practice making more, similar sentences using Unit 2 flashcards.

📄 Worksheet 4: *Grammaire* may be used from this point onwards.

6. Plenary activity: Tu aimes les maths?

⏱ 10 mins AT1.2 O5.1 AT2.2 O5.2

Materials
Worksheet 3 (if not already completed), Unit 2 Flashcards (School subjects and Likes/dislikes).

Description
Pupils conduct a class survey on attitudes to school subjects.

Delivery
- If you haven't already done Worksheet 3, you could do this as the Plenary activity itself, or in addition to the class survey suggested below.

- Make a chart on the board (or on a flip chart) with columns for subject, *j'aime, je n'aime pas* and seven rows.

- Warm up by asking individual pupils if they like various subjects and to describe how they feel about them.

- Say *J'aime les maths* and raise your hand, saying *Levez la main!* and gesturing to pupils to raise their hand if they agree with the statement.

- Count the number of hands raised in French, encouraging the pupils to count with you, and write the numbers in the chart.

- Continue through the list, then cover *Je n'aime pas...* and the various subjects in the same way.

- Discuss the results of the survey.

Extension
More confident groups could conduct this survey individually or in pairs. Results could be written up, or typed and printed on a PC, and displayed for pupils to compare the findings on each survey.

Worksheet 3: Parlez!

⏱ 10 mins AT2.2 O5.1 O5.2

Description
This provides further speaking practice in expressing opinions about school subjects. It may be used at any point after Activity 4.

Worksheet 4: Grammaire

⏱ 10 mins AT2.2 O5.1 AT3.2 O5.2 AT4.2 L5.2 L5.3

Description
This worksheet provides further practice in formulating sentences on opinions about school subjects. It may be used at any point after Activity 5.

Answers
1.
   1. Tu aimes
   2. Non, je n'aime pas
   3. Tu aimes
   4. Oui, j'aime
   5. Tu aimes
   6. Non, je n'aime pas
   7. Tu aimes
   8. Oui, j'aime

Unit 2 — Lesson 3

Lesson summary

Context
Asking and saying the time

National criteria
KS2 Framework: **O5.1, O5.2, O5.3, L5.1, L5.2, L5.3, IU5.1, IU5.2**
Attainment levels: **AT1.2–3, AT2.2, AT3.2–3, AT4.2**
Language ladder levels:
  Listening: **Grades 2–3**; Speaking: **Grade 2**;
  Reading: **Grades 2–3**; Writing: **Grade 2**

Cross-curricular links
Numeracy

Language structures and outcomes
Quelle heure est-il? Il est une heure et quart. Il est trois heures moins le quart. Il trois heures et demie. Il est midi/minuit.

---

1. Starter activity: Il est deux heures
⏱ 5 mins — AT1.2 O5.1 AT2.2

Materials
CD-ROM, whiteboard; perhaps *Rigolo 1* Unit 8 Flashcards (Telling the time), or own flashcards for numbers 1–12 and teaching clock.

Description
Revision of numbers and basic time-telling.

Delivery
- Quickly run through the Presentation activity *Quelle heure est-il?* originally met in *Rigolo 1* (Unit 8, Lesson 3), to refresh pupils' memories.
- Alternatively, using *Rigolo 1* Unit 8 Flashcards (Telling the time) or your own number flashcards and a teaching clock/clock face drawn on the board, quickly re-cap telling the time. Go through the numbers 1–12 first if necessary, then show a time (exact hours only for now) and ask *Quelle heure est-il?* to elicit *Il est [deux] heures*, etc.
- This activity could be made into a team quiz.

---

2. Video story: À l'école (2)
⏱ 10 mins — AT1.2–3 O5.2, AT3.2–3 O5.3, L5.1, IU5.1, IU5.2

Materials
CD-ROM, whiteboard, possibly Unit 2 Flashcards (*La récré* and *Le déjeuner*).

Description
Watch and listen to this video story presenting the language for Lessons 3 and 4. You can pause and rewind the story at any point.

Delivery
- The focus in this second part is on times and timings of the school day.
- Tell the class what *la récré* (break-time) is before you start.
- Ask them to watch the first scene and listen out for the school subject that is mentioned.
- Play the scene up to *Dépêche-toi!* and elicit the answer (*l'anglais*). Check that the general gist of the story has been understood, but don't go into detail as the language will be covered in depth later in this lesson.
- Freeze the screen at the beginning of the next scene (Chloé holding a musical instrument in a case and walking with Thomas) and ask pupils to guess what lesson will be featured in this scene.
- Watch the scene, elicit the answer, and check for general comprehension. If necessary, tell the pupils what *malade* and *le déjeuner* are if they haven't worked these words out.
- Play both scenes through again.

---

3. Presentation: Il est trois heures et quart
⏱ 10 mins — AT1.2 O5.1, AT2.2, AT3.2

Materials
CD-ROM, teaching clock for 'Support' activity.

Description
Tap on *Allez* to hear Jake's question and Mme Moulin's answer. Use the additional features to practise sound/spelling links and word classes, or to record your own version of each question and answer exchange.

Delivery
- The whole class listens and repeats both Jake's question, *Quelle heure est-il?* and Mme Moulin's response.
- Continue for all seven times and repeat if further practice is required.

Refer to the Introduction for notes on the *Record*, *Sound* and *Word* features.

Support
Ask other pupils to come and set the teaching clock to the same time after each presentation, then ask the whole class to repeat.

Knowledge about language

- It is useful to point out to pupils that English words do not always have a direct equivalent in French.
- For example, look at the following expressions: … *et demie* = 'half past' (literally, 'and half'), … *et quart* = 'quarter past' (literally, 'and quarter'), … *moins le quart* = 'quarter to' (literally, 'less the quarter')
- Explain the literal meaning to pupils and discuss that it's often the case in a different language that you cannot translate word for word; you have to learn some expressions by heart in order to be able to express yourself correctly in French.
- Encourage pupils to practise times for a small homework and to say times aloud to each other.
- If it appeals to pupils, they could set some times to music or rap – this will help them remember the ways of expressing times.

Unit 2: Lesson 3

4 Literacy activity: Il est midi
⏱ 10 mins 📖 AT3.2 O5.1 / AT4.2 L5.2

Materials
Teaching clock or clock faces drawn on board, plus large cards with time phrases cut up into individual words and numbers.

Description
A group activity where pupils practise making sentences about the time.

Delivery
- Prepare some time phrases on large cards and cut them up into individual words.
- Using the teaching clock/clock faces, remind pupils of the basic patterns in the time-telling covered so far and do some choral practice.
- Show a time on the teaching clock, or draw a time on the first clock face on the board and place all the cards on the front table.
- Invite between three and six pupils to the front, depending on what time you have chosen. Ask them each to select a card and put themselves in the correct order to make a phrase/sentence about the time. The rest of the class can offer assistance if required.
- When the pupils are satisfied with their sentence, ask the class to read it out and confirm that it is correct.
- Repeat with other times/groups of pupils and try to cover as many variations as possible.

Support
Do the above activity as a whole class, sticking the cards on the board to make a few sentences, before proceeding to the activity as described in 'Delivery'.

📄 Worksheet 5: *Grammaire* may be used from this point onwards.

5 Oracy activity: Il est minuit
⏱ 5–10 mins 📖 AT1.2 O5.3 / AT2.2

Materials
CD-ROM, whiteboard.

Description
Tap on *Allez*, listen to the audio and tap on the right clock for each time.

Delivery
- There is celebratory animation if the pupil's answer is correct. In the case of an incorrect answer they are invited to try again.
- You could divide the class into two groups and make it into a team game.

📄 Worksheet 6: *Écrivez!* may be used from this point onwards

6 Plenary activity: Quelle heure est-il?
⏱ 5 mins 📖 AT2.2 O5.1 / O5.3

Materials
Teaching clock(s), or clock face drawn on board.

Description
Team game to consolidate the time-telling expressions from this lesson.

Delivery
- Divide the class into two teams.
- Show one team a time and ask *Quelle heure est-il?* Award one point if their answer is correct. Show another time to the other team, and continue alternating until you have covered as many different phrases as possible.
- Add up each team's points together in French at the end.

Extension
More confident pupils could play this game in small groups: give a teaching clock to each group, or a sheet of blank clock faces. Half of each group take it in turn to display a time and ask the question, then to answer the question. Move round the groups to monitor the activity.

Worksheet 5: Grammaire
⏱ 10 mins 📖 AT4.2 L5.2 / L5.3

Description
This worksheet provides further practice in writing out sentences about the time. It may be used at any point after Activity 4.

Answers
1. 2 Il est six heures et quart.
   3 Il est sept heures et demie.
   4 Il est onze heures moins le quart.
   5 Il est six heures et demie.
   6 Il est midi/minuit moins le quart.
   7 Il est midi/minuit et quart.

Worksheet 6: Écrivez!
⏱ 10 mins 📖 AT3.2 L5.2 / AT4.2 L5.3

Description
This worksheet provides further practice in writing sentences about the time. It may be used at any point after Activity 5.

Answers
1. 2 Il est midi et demi.
   3 Il est une heure et quart.
   4 Il est midi moins le quart.
   5 Il est neuf heures et quart.
   6 Il est dix heures et demie.

Unit 2 (Lesson 4)

Lesson summary

Context
Talking about timings of the school day

National criteria
KS2 Framework: O5.1, O5.2, O5.3, O5.4, L5.1, L5.2, L5.3, IU5.1, IU5.2, IU5.3
Attainment levels: AT1.2–3, AT2.2–3, AT3.2–3, AT4.2
Language ladder levels:
　Listening: **Grades 1–3**; Speaking: **Grades 2–3**;
　Reading: **Grades 2–3**; Writing: **Grades 2–3**

Cross-curricular links
Geography, ICT, literacy, music, numeracy

Key vocabulary
la récré, le déjeuner, l'école

Language structures and outcomes
[Le déjeuner] commence à [une] heure(s). [La récré] finit à [11] heures.

---

1 Starter activity: Il est minuit — 5 mins — AT1.2 O5.1 / AT2.2 O5.3

Materials
CD-ROM, whiteboard.

Description
Repeat of Activity 5, Lesson 3. Listen to the audio and tap on the correct clock for each time.

Delivery
- Divide the class into two teams. In turn, a pupil from each team comes to the board to tap on *Allez*, listen to the time prompt, and select the corresponding clock.
- The teams score one point for each correct answer.

---

2 Video story: À l'école (2) — 5–10 mins — AT1.2–3 O5.2 / AT3.2–3 O5.3 / L5.1 / IU5.1 IU5.2

Materials
CD-ROM, whiteboard.

Description
Watch and listen again to this video story presenting the language for Lessons 3 and 4. You can pause and rewind the story at any point.

Delivery
- On this viewing, focus on the start and finish times of different subjects and activities.
- Write up on the board, and read aloud, the following sentences:

　La récré finit à 11 heures.
　L'anglais commence à 10 heures et quart.

- Check pupils understand these sentences. Tell them they are going to watch the first scene to check if these statements are true or false.
- Watch as far as *Dépêche-toi!* and check their answers.
- Do the same for Scene 2, with the following sentences:

　La musique commence à 11 heures et quart.
　Le déjeuner commence à midi.

- If time allows, play the video straight through again.

Support
If pupils find this tricky because of the number of different times that are actually mentioned, pause the video after each line and chorally repeat what has been said. Pointing to the clock on screen, or showing the time on your teaching clock may also be useful.

---

3 Presentation: La récré commence à 10 heures et demie — 10 mins — AT1.2 O5.1 / AT2.2 O5.3 / AT3.2 IU5.1

Materials
CD-ROM, whiteboard; possibly teaching clock for extension activity, and Unit 2 Flashcards (School day: *l'école, la récré,* or *le déjeuner*).

Description
Tap on an icon to hear the word. Then tap on each clock to hear when that activity starts and finishes. Use the additional features to practise sound/spelling links and word classes, or to record your own version of each expression.

Delivery
- When the pupil taps on an icon representing *l'école, la récré,* or *le déjeuner,* we hear that activity being announced. Pupils repeat the time.
- A second pupil then taps on the first clock to hear at what time that activity starts. Again, pupils repeat what they hear.
- Ask a third pupil to tap on the second clock to hear at what time that activity finishes. Again, all pupils repeat the sentence.
- Point out the use of *à* when used with time to mean 'at'.

Refer to the Introduction for notes on the *Record, Sound* and *Word* features.

Extension
Ask three confident pupils to come to the front and stand with their backs to the board during the activity described above. Without looking at the board, they must listen to what is said and respond as follows: one pupil holds up the relevant activity card (*la récré, l'école, le déjeuner*); the other two display the time heard on the teaching clock. They can then turn round to face the board and check their answers.

Support
Use Unit 2 Flashcards (School day) and the teaching clock to do further oral practice of different start and finish times.

---

4 Literacy activity: Le déjeuner commence — 10 mins — AT3.2 L5.2 / AT4.2

Materials
CD-ROM, whiteboard.

Description
Tap on *Allez*. Drag the words into the correct order. Tap on *Fini* when you have completed each answer.

18　Rigolo 2 Teacher's Notes © Nelson Thornes Ltd 2008

Unit 2: Lesson 4

Delivery
- When pupils tap on *Allez*, symbols appear to indicate a certain activity, and what time that activity starts or finishes. Pupils are congratulated if their answer is correct, or invited to try again if not.
- Repeat the activity to give more pupils the chance to practise if necessary.

Extension
More confident pupils can look at the tiles on screen and write the sentences out before the answer is revealed.

Language learning strategies

- In *Rigolo 2*, there is a song every two units. Some songs from *Rigolo 1* are also revisited.
- As well as being fun, using song is a good way to help pupils memorise language and to take language out of the classroom.
- Encourage pupils to learn the song by heart. Often saying it in rhythm, one or two lines at a time, is a good way of doing this.
- Rhymes and also actions can often aid memory, so put actions to songs if possible. Discuss and decide as a class which actions they would like to use.
- Use the text of the song to help pupils focus on matching the written word to the spoken word. Give them the text with a few words missing; they listen and complete the missing words from a selection you provide.
- Encourage able pupils to write their own version of the song, or adapt a few words to personalise it for weaker pupils.
- For confident pupils, encourage them to perform their song to the rest of the class.

5. Song: Il est huit heures
15 mins — AT1.2–3 O5.2, AT2.2–3 O5.3, AT3.2–3 L5.1

Materials
CD-ROM, whiteboard.

Description
Watch and listen to the interactive karaoke song practising school subjects, likes and times. Choose either *Practice* or *Sing* mode: *Practice* to go through the song line by line; *Sing* to sing it all the way through. Switch the music and words on or off as you prefer, or try recording your own version.

Delivery
- Ask pupils to listen out for the different times which feature in the song: they can make a note of these if they wish, but the main emphasis should be on their overall enjoyment and familiarisation with the song. Play the song, first in *Sing* mode, all the way through.
- Go through their answers, writing the suggested times on the board, then play the song through again to check answers.
- Replay the song, this time in *Practice* mode, so you can go through each line and check comprehension.
- Divide the class into four groups and assign each group a character (Mme Moulin, Jake, Polly, Nathalie). Repeat the song, each group singing the words for its character and everyone joining in the chorus.
- If time allows, swap characters and sing again.

Refer to the Introduction for more notes on the Songs.

Extension
Give pupils copies of the lyrics with a few words gapped. They listen and complete the gaps, choosing from a selection of words at the bottom of the page.

Worksheet 7: *Lisez!* may be used from this point onwards.

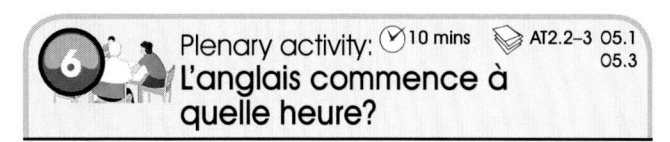

6. Plenary activity: L'anglais commence à quelle heure?
10 mins — AT2.2–3 O5.1, O5.3

Materials
Worksheet 8: *Parlez!*

Description
A pairwork information-gap activity to practise exchanging information about school timetables.

Delivery
- Give out Part A of the worksheet to one half of the class and Part B to the other half. Ask a confident pupil to model how the activity works with you at the front of the class. Model a couple of questions and answers, then go round and listen to the pupils working in pairs.
- You could display the completed timetable on the board for pupils to check their answers, or just let them check by looking at their partner's worksheet.
- Invite some pairs to the front of the class to present the timetable to the other pupils.

Worksheet 7: Lisez!
10 mins — AT3.3 L5.1, AT4.2 L5.3

Description
This worksheet provides further reading and writing practice relating to timings of the school day. It may be used at any point after Activity 5.

Answers

	commence	finit
l'école	8.45	3.30
la récré	9.45	10.30
l'histoire-géo	2.30	
l'anglais	1.15	
le déjeuner	12.15	

Worksheet 8: Parlez!
10 mins — AT2.2–3 O5.1, O5.3, O5.4

Description
An information-gap activity to practise exchanging information about school timetables. It may be used as the Plenary activity for the lesson.

Unit 2 — Extra!

Project work: L'école en France
1–3 hours · AT3.3 IU5.1 · AT4.2 IU5.2 · IU5.3

Materials
Internet access and printer if possible, library books, pupils' books from home, the Unit 2 video film, display card.

Description
Pupils work in small groups to find out more information about schools in France, and prepare a display.

Delivery
- Assign pupils to small work groups, or pairs, and ask them to think of something they would like to find out about schools in France.

- Brainstorm a few ideas to ensure pupils keep it quite simple and don't get carried away. For example, they could use a search engine to find schools in your twin town or in a town they have visited, then try to find out about school holidays, or what food they serve in French schools. Each group should work with one idea only.

- Encourage each group to display their findings, with pictures or charts where possible, on large pieces of card.

- Encourage confident pupils to use the language of the unit to write some sentences in French about their findings.

- Organise a special 'Circle Time' where each group has the chance to say what they discovered. Encourage discussions and comparisons between UK schools and French schools. Ask pupils what they think French children might make of our schools.

- If you have not already done so, this would also be a great opportunity to set up email/pen-pal links with a French school – which would of course create a very good source of information for this and other future projects.

Sound/spelling activity: Les sons 'ère' et 'ais'
10 mins · AT1.1 · AT2.1 · AT3.1

Materials
CD-ROM, whiteboard.

Description
Practice mode: Listen and practise pronouncing the 'ère' sound and the 'ais' sound on their own and then in words that have been covered in **Rigolo** so far.
Activity mode: Listen to the words as they are read out. If they contain the 'ère' sound, tap on the red button, and if they contain the 'ais' sound, tap on the green button. Listen carefully and choose your answer before the time runs out.

Delivery
- This sound/spelling activity focuses specifically on the 'ère' and 'ais' sounds.

- There are two parts to the activity: the first (*Practice*) allows pupils to familiarise themselves with the two sounds and to compare their pronunciation with the Virtual Teacher model. The second part (*Activity*) is an exercise where pupils have to listen out for the sounds within a list of French words that they have encountered so far in **Rigolo**.

- Select *Practice* and tap on *Next* to start this part. Then tap on *Allez*. The Virtual Teacher will say the 'ère' sound, first on its own then as part of four words that have been met in **Rigolo**. For each of these, get the class to repeat the words chorally several times, checking the model each time using the *Encore* button. You can also use the *Record* feature here to compare a pupil's pronunciation more closely with the model. Then either move on to *Activity* mode or tap on *Next sound* to follow suit with the 'ais' sound, for which you will hear the sound on its own then with other nouns covered in **Rigolo**.

- Once you have finished this part, tap on *Activity* to move on to test pupils' recognition of these sounds. Tap on *Allez* to start; pupils will hear eight words read out. For each word they must listen carefully and work out whether it is the 'ère' sound or the 'ais' sound, then tap on the right button before the time runs out. You can tap on *Encore* to hear the word again.

- Pupils score a point when they correctly identify the sound within the word.

- Repeat the activity if pupils need further practice.

Assessment for Units 1–2

Écoutez!

Play each audio two or three times, or more if necessary. Pause during each activity as required.
Total marks for listening: 20.

Activity 1 (AT1.1–2; O5.3)
Mark out of 5.

Answers
a1 b5 c4 d3 e2

1 – Tu as des frères ou des sœurs?
  – Oui, j'ai un frère.
2 – Tu as des frères ou des sœurs?
  – Non, je n'ai pas de frères ou de sœurs.
3 – Tu as des frères ou des sœurs?
  – Oui, j'ai deux sœurs.
4 – Tu as des frères ou des sœurs?
  – Oui, j'ai deux frères.
5 – Tu as des frères ou des sœurs?
  – Oui, j'ai une sœur.

Activity 2 (AT1.1–2; O5.3)
Mark out of 5.

Answers
1 6.30   2 1.15   3 4.15
4 9.45   5 3.30

1 – Quelle heure est-il?
  – Il est six heures et demie.
2 – Quelle heure est-il?
  – Il est une heure et quart.
3 – Quelle heure est-il?
  – Il est quatre heures et quart.
4 – Quelle heure est-il?
  – Il est dix heures moins le quart.
5 – Quelle heure est-il?
  – Il est trois heures et demie.

Activity 3
Mark out of 10.   (AT1.2–3; O5.3)

Answers

	ça va?	🇫🇷	🇬🇧	âge?
1	(✓)	(✓)		10
2	✗		✓	9
3	✓	✓		11
4	✗		✓	8

```
1  – Bonjour!
   – Salut!
   – Ça va?
   – Oui, ça va bien.
   – Tu es britannique?
   – Non, je suis français.
   – Tu as quel âge?
   – J'ai dix ans.
2  – Bonjour!
   – Salut!
   – Ça va?
   – Non, ça ne va pas.
   – Tu es britannique?
   – Oui, je suis britannique.
   – Tu as quel âge?
   – J'ai neuf ans.
3  – Salut!
   – Bonjour!
   – Ça va?
   – Oui, ça va bien.
   – Tu es français?
   – Oui, je suis français.
   – Tu as quel âge?
   – J'ai onze ans.
4  – Salut!
   – Salut!
   – Ça va?
   – Non, ça ne va pas.
   – Tu es britannique?
   – Non, je suis française.
   – Tu as quel âge?
   – J'ai huit ans.
```

Parlez!

Pupils can work in pairs for the speaking tasks. If it is not possible to assess each pair, then assess a few pairs for each assessment block and mark the rest of the class based on the spoken work they do in class.
Total marks for speaking: 10.

Activity 1
5 marks.   (AT2.1–2; O5.1)

Answers
Luc: Il a un pantalon, un vélo, un frère, deux sœurs, une guitare.
Sophie: Elle a une jupe, deux frères, une sœur, un vélo, un piano

Activity 2
5 marks.   (AT2.2–3; O5.1)

Lisez!

Total marks for reading: 20.

Activity 1   (AT3.1–2; L5.1)
Mark out of 10 (2 marks for each picture correctly matched).

Answers
2 c   3 a   4 f   5 d   6 e

Activity 2   (AT3.2–3; L5.1)
Mark out of 10.

Answers
1 j, c   2 b, f, k, d   3 h, i, a, l

Écrivez!

Total marks for writing: 20.

Activity 1   (AT4.1–2; L5.3)
Mark out of 10.

Answers
a le français   f les sciences
b la musique   g les maths
c le sport   h un vélo
d l'anglais   i une guitare
e l'histoire-géo   j un pantalon

Activity 2   (AT4.2–3; L5.2, L5.3)
Mark out of 10: three marks for each person and one for general accuracy.

Answers
a Il a un vélo. Il n'a pas de frères ou de sœurs.
b Elle a un piano. Elle n'a pas de vélo.
c Il a un frère. Il n'a pas de pantalon.

Rigolo 2 — Unit 3: La nourriture

National criteria

KS2 Framework objectives

O5.1	Prepare and practise a simple conversation, re-using familiar vocabulary and structures in new contexts
O5.2	Understand and express simple opinions
O5.3	Listen attentively and understand more complex phrases and sentences
O5.4	Prepare a short presentation on a familiar topic
L5.1	Re-read frequently a variety of short texts
L5.2	Make simple sentences and short texts
L5.3	Write words, phrases and short sentences, using a reference source
IU5.1	Look at further aspects of their everyday lives from the perspective of someone from another country

QCA Scheme of Work

Unit 6   Ça pousse!
Unit 10 Vive le sport!
Unit 13 Bon appétit, bonne santé
Unit 23 Monter un café

National Curriculum attainment levels

AT1.1–3, AT2.2–3, AT3.1–3, AT4.2–3

Language ladder levels

Listening: Breakthrough, Grades 2–3
Reading: Breakthrough, Grades 1–3
Speaking: Breakthrough, Grades 2–3
Writing: Breakthrough, Grades 2–3

5–14 guideline strands — Levels A–C

Listening
Listening for information and instructions	A, B, C
Listening and reacting to others	A, B, C

Reading
Reading for information and instructions	A, B, C
Reading aloud	A, B, C

Speaking
Speaking to convey information	A, B, C
Speaking and interacting with others	A, B, C
Speaking about experiences, feelings and opinions	A, B, C

Writing
Writing to exchange information and ideas	A, B, C
Writing to establish and maintain personal contact	A, B
Writing imaginatively to entertain	A, B, C

Unit objectives

- Ask politely for food items
- Describe how to make a sandwich
- Express opinions about food
- Talk about healthy and unhealthy food

Key language

- Je voudrais… s'il vous plaît.
  un sandwich au poulet, un sandwich au thon, un sandwich au fromage, un sandwich à la tomate
  une glace au chocolat, une glace à l'orange, une glace à la fraise, une glace à la vanille
- les tomates, le thon, le fromage, une baguette, le beurre, mangez, coupez, prenez, mettez
- J'aime/Je n'aime pas… les gâteaux, les frites, les bonbons, les pommes, les carottes, les haricots
- [Les carottes], c'est bon pour la santé/ce n'est pas bon pour la santé.

Grammar and skills

- Understand and use au/à la/à l' when referring to flavours of foods
- Give instructions in the *vous* form
- Understand and use negatives
- Use the plural form of some food vocabulary
- Use known language in a new context

Unit outcomes

Most children will be able to:
- Ask politely for sandwiches and ice-creams
- Give simple instructions to make a sandwich
- Say what foods they like/don't like
- Say which foods are healthy/unhealthy

Some children will also be able to:
- Use au/à la/à l' accurately when referring to food items
- Understand and use plural nouns in the correct context
- Use known language in a new context
- Adapt phrases to talk about different things

Unit 3 — Lesson 1

Lesson summary

Context
Asking politely for food items

National criteria
KS2 Framework: O5.1, O5.3, L5.1, L5.2, L5.3, IU5.1
Attainment levels: AT1.2–3, AT2.2, AT3.1–3, AT4.2
Language ladder levels:
  Listening: **Grades 2–3**; Speaking: **Grade 2**;
  Reading: **Grades 1–3**; Writing: **Grade 2**

Cross-curricular links
Food technology

Key vocabulary
un sandwich au poulet, un sandwich au thon, un sandwich au fromage, un sandwich à la tomate
une glace au chocolat, une glace à l'orange, une glace à la fraise, une glace à la vanille

Language structures and outcomes
Je voudrais… s'il vous plaît.

---

1. Starter activity: Je voudrais… (5–10 mins) AT1.2 O5.1 / AT2.2

Materials
CD-ROM, whiteboard possibly flashcards from *Rigolo 1*, Unit 6 (Food and drink) and Unit 11 (More food and drink).

Description
An interactive activity in which pupils tap on food items and repeat the words/sentences to revise food items met in *Rigolo 1*.

Delivery
- Use the interactive starter, which is a repeat of a presentation from *Rigolo 1* Unit 11 Lesson 1, to check that pupils have remembered the vocabulary (pupils tap on a food item to hear the word, then hear Polly politely requesting the item from the shop assistant).

- Focus this time on which words Polly uses i.e. *Je voudrais…* and *s'il vous plait*.

- If pupils seem quite confident you may wish to have a quick team quiz using all the food flashcards from *Rigolo 1*.

2. Animated story: La cuisine Rigolo (1) (10 mins) AT1.3 O5.3 / AT3.3 L5.1 / IU5.1

Materials
CD-ROM, whiteboard.

Description
Watch and listen to this interactive story presenting the language for Lessons 1 and 2. You can pause and rewind the story at any point, or record your own version too.

Delivery
- Pause the opening scene and ask pupils to tell you what items of food they can see and say in French.

- Ask them to watch the first part (up to Mme Moulin saying *Regardez les enfants. Un sandwich Rigolo*) and tell you, if possible, what sort of sandwiches Mme Moulin first offers them (answer: *au poulet/au fromage/à la tomate*).

- Watch the rest of the scene and ask pupils what was in the sandwich she actually made, and whether Didier and Polly liked it (answer: *du poulet et de la glace au chocolat* – they didn't like it).

- Replay the whole cartoon without stopping.

Support
Remind pupils not to worry about understanding everything that is said in the story, and that they will cover all the language in more detail throughout this lesson.

3. Presentation: Un sandwich au thon (5–10 mins) AT1.2 O5.1 / AT2.2 / AT3.2

Materials
CD-ROM, whiteboard.

Description
Tap on a food item on the table to hear it presented and Polly asking for it. Use the additional features to practise sound/spelling links and word classes, or to record your own version of each word.

Delivery
- The whole class listens to the food item being announced and repeats.

- We then hear Polly saying *Je voudrais* [+ food item] *s'il vous plaît*. The whole class repeats the sentence. Make sure pupils are happy about pronouncing *Je voudrais…* and *s'il vous plaît*.

- Continue for all eight food items and repeat if further practice is required.

- Point out *un/une* and make sure pupil understand the concept of why each is used (i.e. masculine and feminine words) and make sure they pronounce both correctly.

Refer to the Introduction for notes on the *Record*, *Sound* and *Word* features.

Extension
Draw pupils' attention to *au/à la/à l'* and ask why they think each is used. Worksheet 2: *Grammaire* practises this point.

Language learning strategies

- If appropriate, draw pupils' attention to the patterns *au/à la /à l'* and explain why each is used (masculine words, feminine words and words which begin with a vowel).

- Write the different types of ice-cream and sandwiches on the whiteboard and ask pupils to put them into the three pattern categories. (Worksheet 2: *Grammaire* provides further practice of this and helps pupils apply grammatical knowledge to make sentences.)

- Explain that when they learn new words that it's important also to learn whether each is masculine or feminine.

4. Oracy activity: Je voudrais une glace au chocolat
5–10 mins · AT1.2 O5.3

Materials
CD-ROM, whiteboard, Unit 3 Flashcards (Sandwiches and ice-creams) for support.

Description
Tap on *Allez*. Listen to the characters, then drag and drop the correct food onto their plate.

Delivery
- We hear Jake or Bof asking for a food item. The pupil taps on the relevant item and drags it on to their plate. The first three ask for one item and the last four ask for two items.
- The characters will say *Merci*, eat the food, and the Virtual Teacher will congratulate the pupil if the selection is correct.
- Tap on *Allez* to go on to the next question.
- Continue for all eight items and repeat if further practice is needed.

Support
- Encourage less confident pupils to use the *Encore* button as often as necessary.
- If some pupils find it difficult to listen and identify two items for the last four sentences, ask them to listen for one at a time.
- You could also display Unit 3 Flashcards (Sandwiches and ice-creams) during the activity as additional prompts.

Worksheet 1: *Lisez!* may be used from this point onwards.

5. Literacy activity: Les sandwichs
5–10 mins · AT3.1–2 L5.1

Materials
Unit 3 Flashcards (Sandwiches and ice-creams).

Description
Pupils play a game matching food pictures to the words.

Delivery
- Display the flashcards on the board – the words on one side of the board, the pictures on the other.
- Ask a pupil to come to the front and place a word card with its corresponding picture card in the centre of the board.
- Repeat for all eight items.
- You could make this into a team game by dividing the class into two teams. Invite pupils from alternate teams to match the cards and award one point for each correct pair.

Worksheet 2: *Grammaire* may be used from this point onwards.

6. Plenary activity: Je voudrais un sandwich
5–10 mins · AT1.2 O5.1 AT2.2

Materials
Unit 3 Flashcards (Sandwiches and ice-creams).

Description
A role-play game to practise polite requests for food.

Delivery
- Place the flashcards on a table at the front and ask for a volunteer to be Mme Moulin.
- Other pupils come to the table, one by one, and politely ask for a food item using *Je voudrais* [+ food item] *s'il vous plaît*. 'Mme Moulin' must pass them the appropriate card, and the pupil replies *Merci* before returning to their place.
- Continue until all the cards have been used.

Extension
You may wish to include the food flashcards from *Rigolo 1* Unit 6 (Food and drink) and Unit 11 (More food and drink) and encourage pupils to ask for two things: *Je voudrais* [*un sandwich au thon*] *et* [*un gâteau*], *s'il vous plaît*.

Worksheet 1: Lisez!
5–10 mins · AT3.2 L5.2 AT4.2 L5.3

Description
This worksheet provides further practice in reading and writing about the food items covered this lesson. It may be used at any point after Activity 4.

Answers
1a
1. un sandwich au poulet
2. un sandwich au thon
3. une glace à la fraise
4. une glace au chocolat
5. un sandwich au fromage
6. un sandwich à la tomate

1b
1. poulet, baguette
2. thon, baguette
3. fraise, glace
4. chocolat, glace
5. fromage, baguette
6. tomate, baguette

Worksheet 2: Grammaire
10–15 mins · AT3.2 L5.2 AT4.2 L5.3

Description
This worksheet provides practice in gender and *au/à la/à l'* relating to the food items covered this lesson. It may be used at any point after Activity 5.

Answers
1

feminine (f) words		masculine (m) words		words starting with a vowel: *a e i o u*	
à la	fraise tomate vanille	au	fromage chocolat thon poulet	à l'	orange

2
1. au poulet
2. au chocolat
3. à l'orange
4. à la fraise
5. au fromage

3
1. Je voudrais une glace à la vanille, s'il vous plaît.
2. Je voudrais un sandwich au fromage, s'il vous plaît.
3. Je voudrais un sandwich au thon, s'il vous plaît.
4. Je voudrais une glace à la fraise, s'il vous plaît.

Unit 3 — Lesson 2

Lesson summary

Context
Describing how to make a sandwich

National criteria
KS2 Framework: O5.1, O5.3, O5.4, L5.1, L5.2, L5.3, IU5.1
Attainment levels: AT1.2–3, AT2.2–3, AT3.2–3, AT4.2–3
Language ladder levels:
  Listening: **Grades 2–3**; Speaking: **Grades 2–3**;
  Reading: **Grades 2–3**; Writing: **Grade 2**

Cross-curricular links
Food technology

Key vocabulary
Revise: *les tomates, le thon, le fromage*
New: *une baguette, le beurre*

Language structures and outcomes
Mangez, Coupez, Prenez, Mettez

---

1. Starter activity: *Je voudrais des tomates*
5–10 mins — AT1.2 O5.1, AT2.2

Materials
Food flashcards: *Rigolo 1* Units 6 and 11, *Rigolo 2* Unit 3.

Description
Starter game using flashcards to revise food items.

Delivery
- In quick succession, hold up the picture flashcards and elicit the words from the class.
- Place the cards on a table at the front.
- Begin the game by saying *Je voudrais [des tomates]*. Go to the table, pick up the *[tomates]* card, hold it towards the class and invite a pupil to extend the sentence, e.g. *Je voudrais [des tomates] et [des fraises]*. They must then come to the front and hold up the relevant card. The next pupil will say, e.g. *Je voudrais [des tomates], [des fraises] et [un sandwich au poulet]*, before coming to the front and holding up the relevant card. Continue in this way until all the words have been used up.

Support
If pupils are having difficulty remembering all the food items, first stick all the flashcards on the board then let pupils remove them and hold them up once they have said the word.

---

2. Animated story: *La cuisine Rigolo (1)*
5–10 mins — AT1.3 O5.3, AT3.3 L5.1, IU5.1

Materials
CD-ROM, whiteboard.

Description
Watch and listen again to this interactive story presenting the language for Lessons 1 and 2. You can pause and rewind the story at any point, or record your own version too.

Delivery
- In this second viewing, focus on the imperative language structures, e.g. *Prenez, Coupez*, etc.
- Play the story through, asking pupils to listen out for any words Mme Moulin uses when making the *sandwich Rigolo*.
- Elicit any suggestions, accompanying the verbs with actions to help reinforce learning.
- Don't dwell too long on these words as they will be covered throughout this lesson. Tell pupils that they can see the cartoon again at the end of the lesson if there is time, by which point they will be very familiar with the language.

Support
If you feel pupils are struggling to pick out any of the language and not enjoying the cartoon as a result, you could pause the film after each imperative and chorally repeat each one.

---

3. Presentation: *Mettez le beurre*
5–10 mins — AT1.2 O5.1, AT2.2, AT3.2

Materials
CD-ROM, whiteboard.

Description
Tap on each frame to hear, in order 1 to 8, the recipe instructions. Use the additional features to practise sound/spelling links and word classes, or to record your own version of each word.

Delivery
- The whole class listens to Mme Moulin giving the recipe instructions and repeats each of them, using any relevant gestures.
- Continue for all eight stages of the recipe and repeat if further practice is required.
- Point out the '-*ez*' ending to each of the instructions and make sure pupils pronounce it correctly.

Refer to the Introduction for notes on the *Record*, *Sound* and *Word* features.

Extension
Point out *le/la/les* and ensure that pupils understand the meaning and the gender that each accompanies.

Support
Discuss and decide on a mime to use for each instruction; this will help pupils understand and recall each verb.

---

4. Literacy activity: *Coupez la baguette*
10 mins — AT3.2–3 L5.2

Materials
CD-ROM, whiteboard.

Description
Tap on *Allez*. Look at each series of pictures showing instructions for making different sandwiches. Drag the text into the correct order to match each series.

Unit 3: Lesson 2

Delivery
- The pupil drags the suggested phrases into the correct order according to the sequence of images and taps on *Fini*.
- After a correct answer, another pupil comes to the front and taps on *Allez* for the next recipe prompt. In case of any incorrect answers pupils can simply try again, perhaps with some help from the rest of the class.
- Repeat for each of the five sets of instructions.

Extension
Ask more confident pupils to read out their suggested recipe before tapping on *Fini*.

Worksheet 3: *Parlez!* may be used from this point onwards.

5. Oracy activity: Préparer un sandwich
10–20 mins — AT1.2–3 O5.1, AT2.2–3 O5.3, O5.4

Materials
Food and utensils for making sandwiches: baguette/bread, butter and fillings, e.g. cheese, tuna, tomatoes.

Description
Pupils listen to and watch the teacher making a sandwich, then make a sandwich themselves.

Delivery
- Provide a commentary as you demonstrate how to make a simple sandwich, using the key words and structures which have been presented in this lesson.
- Pupils work in pairs to plan and prepare their own sandwiches in the same way. One partner could say the instructions aloud whilst the other makes the sandwich, then swap roles.

Support
Give cue cards with model instructions as support and underline or colour-code the parts that can be changed.

Worksheet 4: *Ecrivez!* may be used from this point onwards.

6. Plenary activity: Les recettes
10–15 mins — AT1.2–3 O5.1, AT2.2–3 O5.4

Materials
Worksheet 4: *Écrivez!* if not already completed.

Description
Pupils write out and present their favourite sandwich recipe to the class.

Delivery
- Give pupils some time to do the worksheet (see below), if this has not already been done.
- Each pair will then present the recipe for the sandwich they have designed, using the key phrases from this lesson. Have a vote at the end as to who designed the best sandwich!

Worksheet 3: Parlez!
10 mins — AT2.2 O5.1, AT3.2 O5.4

Description
This worksheet provides more practice in recipe instructions. It may be used at any point after Activity 4.

Delivery
- Divide the class into groups of six to eight pupils and give each group a set of cards.
- Give the groups a couple of minutes to complete the words and cut up the cards, then place them face down on the table.
- Pupils take it in turn to take a card, without revealing it to the others, and do a mime based on what is written on the card. The pupil who correctly describes the action on the card has a turn, and so on.
- You may need to monitor this activity quite closely and intervene from time to time, to ensure that all pupils have a turn.

Answers
Coupez la baguette.
Mangez un sandwich.
Mettez le beurre.
Mettez les tomates.
Prenez une baguette.
Coupez le fromage.
Mettez le thon.
Mangez les tomates.
Mangez une glace.
Prenez une glace à la fraise.
Mangez les fraises.
Coupez les tomates

Worksheet 4: Écrivez!
10 mins — AT2.2–3 O5.4, AT4.2–3 L5.2, L5.3

Description
This worksheet provides further writing practice in recipe instructions. It may be used at any point after Activity 5, or as the Plenary activity for this lesson.

Answers
1. mangez
2. prenez
3. mettez
4. coupez

Unit 3 (Lesson 3)

Lesson summary

Context
Expressing opinions about food

National criteria
KS2 Framework: O5.1, O5.2, O5.3, L5.1, L5.2, L5.3, IU5.1
Attainment levels: AT1.2–3, AT2.2, AT3.2–3, AT4.2–3
Language ladder levels:
   Listening: **Grades 2–3**; Speaking: **Grade 2**;
   Reading: **Grades 2–3**; Writing: **Grades 2–3**

Cross-curricular links
Numeracy, ICT (plenary activity), PSHE and FT (healthy eating)

Key vocabulary
les frites, les bonbons, les pommes, les carottes, les haricots, les gâteaux

Language structures and outcomes
Revised: *J'aime/Je n'aime pas [les carottes]*

---

1. Starter activity: J'aime les bananes
⏱ 5–10 mins 📄 AT1.2 O5.1 AT2.2 O5.2

Materials
Units 2 and 3 Flashcards (Sandwiches and ice-creams, and Likes/dislikes); food flashcards from *Rigolo 1* Units 6 and 11.

Description
Starter activity using flashcards to revise expressing food likes and dislikes.

Delivery
- Stick the *J'aime/Je n'aime pas* flashcards on the board, each followed by a food item card.
- Ask the class *Tu aimes [les pommes]?* and elicit the sentences depicted by the cards in order to model possible answers, e.g. *Oui, j'aime [les pommes]* or *Non, je n'aime pas [les fraises]*.
- Using other flashcards as prompts, ask individual pupils about their food likes and dislikes until you feel they are sufficiently confident.

2. Animated story: La cuisine Rigolo (2)
⏱ 10 mins 📄 AT1.3 O5.2 AT3.3 O5.3 IU5.1 L5.1

Materials
CD-ROM, whiteboard.

Description
Watch and listen to this interactive story presenting the language for Lessons 3 and 4. You can pause and rewind the story at any point, or record your own version too.

Delivery
- Ask pupils to watch the animated story and note as many different food items as possible which appear in the story.
- Ask pupils to tell you what they think happens in the story and provide some gentle guidance as to the gist, if necessary, without going into too much detail.

3. Presentation: Tu aimes les frites?
⏱ 10 mins 📄 AT1.2 O5.1 AT2.2 O5.2 AT3.2

Materials
CD-ROM, whiteboard, food flashcards as Activity 1 (see above) for Support and Extension activities.

Description
Tap on the food items to hear the question, then tap on the characters to hear their answer. Use the additional features to practise sound/spelling links, word classes and spelling, or to record your own version of each question and answer exchange.

Delivery
- We hear a question e.g. *Tu aimes [les frites]?* and responses from both characters e.g. *Oui, j'aime [les frites]* or *Non, je n'aime pas [les frites]*. The whole class repeats, making appropriate gestures (e.g. thumbs up, thumbs down).
- Continue for all 12 variations and repeat if further practice is required.

Refer to the Introduction for notes on the *Record*, *Spell*, *Sound* and *Word* functions.

Extension
- More confident pupils could take turns to stand at the front with their backs to the board. When the characters say what they like/dislike, they hold up the appropriate flashcards.
- Point out the use of the plural *les* when using *J'aime* and *Je n'aime pas* to talk about food items. Ask pupils to look at the patterns of *J'aime* and *Je n'aime pas* and to point out which parts make the sentences negative.

Support
Ask pupils to come and hold up the relevant flashcards after each presentation and ask the whole class to repeat the sentence.

Language learning strategies

Remind pupils that they have already used *J'aime* and *Je n'aime pas* in Unit 2 with school subjects; they can now use these expressions with food. It is important that pupils realise that the French language is not made up of 'set phrases' but can be flexible and change according to new situations.

4. Oracy activity: Je n'aime pas les carottes
⏱ 10 mins 📄 AT1.2 O5.1 O5.3

Materials
CD-ROM, whiteboard, food flashcards as Activity 1 (see above) for Support and Extension activities.

Unit 3: Lesson 3

Description
Tap on *Allez*. Listen to what the characters say about the food, then drag and drop the like/dislike icons to the correct food item.

Delivery
- We hear a question, e.g. *Tu aimes [les carottes]?* and a reply from one of the characters. Pupils tap on the appropriate like/dislike icon and drag it to the relevant food item.
- Continue in the same way with all six dialogues, and repeat if required.

Support
Ask pupils to hold up the relevant flashcards after each dialogue, and ask the whole class to repeat both sentences each time.

5. Literacy activity: J'aime les pommes
10 mins — AT1.2 O5.2, AT2.2 L5.2, AT3.2

Materials
Food flashcards as Activity 1 (see above); pre-prepared sentences, written on cards or on the board, expressing likes and dislikes of food items.

Description
Pupils read a sentence and select the most appropriate flashcards to illustrate it.

Delivery
- Prepare word cards with *J'aime* and *Je n'aime pas* + food items.
- Focus the class on your first sentence; ask one pupil to read out the sentence and another to select the appropriate flashcards and hold them up.
- You could make this into a team game: ask pupils from alternate teams to read and respond, awarding a point for each correct answer.

Extension
Invite more confident pupils to write some sentences of their own for other pupils to illustrate with the cards.

Worksheet 5: *Écrivez!* and Worksheet 6: *Grammaire* may be used from this point onwards.

6. Plenary: Un sondage
10 mins — AT1.2-3 O5.1, AT2.2 O5.2, O5.3

Materials
Survey chart written on board or printed on PC, food flashcards as Activity 1 (see above).

Description
A survey to consolidate language expressing opinions about food.

Delivery
- Either draw/display your chart on the board, or give out a printed survey to each group/table.
- Using flashcards to back up your statements if necessary, say *J'aime [les carottes]. Levez la main!* and raise your hand to demonstrate. Note down the number of pupils who agree with the statement or ask pupils to fill in their charts. Now say *Je n'aime pas [les carottes]. Levez la main!* and so on until all food items in the survey have been covered.
- Discuss the survey findings.

Extension
More confident pupils could devise their own food survey chart on computer.

Worksheet 5: Écrivez!
10 mins — AT4.2-3 O5.2, L5.2, L5.3

Description
This worksheet provides further practice in writing about food likes and dislikes. It may be used at any point after Activity 5.

Answers
1. 1b   2a
2.
   2. Je n'aime pas les carottes.
   3. Je n'aime pas les bonbons.
   4. Je n'aime pas les frites.
   5. J'aime les gâteaux.
   6. J'aime les haricots.

Knowledge about language
Worksheet 6: *Grammaire* gives pupils the opportunity to recognise patterns in sentences and to formulate their own rules by seeing language in context. Pupils are encouraged to work out some of the rules about plurals in French by looking at different sentences.

Worksheet 6: Grammaire
10 mins — AT3.2-3 L5.1, AT4.2 L5.2, L5.3

Description
This worksheet provides practice in looking at the language patterns of French singular and plural words. It may be used at any point after Activity 5 and is particularly suitable for more confident pupils.

Answers
1.
   1. Regardez! **Les gâteaux** au chocolat!
      Je voudrais (**le gâteau**) au chocolat s'il vous plaît.
   2. Coupez **les tomates**!
      (**La tomate**) est dans la cuisine.
   3. Mangez (**le haricot!**)
      Miam. J'aime **les haricots**.
   4. Coupez (**la carotte.**)
      Beurk! Je n'aime pas **les carottes**.
   5. J'ai (**un bonbon**) dans ma trousse.
      J'aime **les bonbons**.
   6. Je voudrais (**la pomme**) verte s'il vous plaît.
      J'aime **les pommes**.

   1. What happens to most French nouns in the plural? You add an 's'.
   2. Which word was the exception? *Les gâteaux*
   3. What happens to *le* and *la* in the plural? They become *les*.

2.
   1. les carottes   4. les tomates
   2. les haricots   5. les bonbons
   3. les pommes   6. les gâteaux

3. j'aime les pommes
   1. les carottes   4. les bonbons
   2. les gâteaux   5. les pommes
   3. les tomates   6. les haricots

Unit 3 — Lesson 4

Lesson summary

Context
Talking about healthy and unhealthy foods

National criteria
KS2 Framework: O5.1, O5.2, O5.3, O5.4, L5.1, L5.2, L5.3, IU5.1
Attainment levels: AT1.2–3, AT2.2–3, AT3.2–3, AT4.2–3
Language ladder levels:
  Listening: **Grades 2–3**; Speaking: **Grades 2–3**;
  Reading: **Grades 2–3**; Writing: **Grades 2–3**

Cross-curricular links
Numeracy, ICT (Activity 4 and Worksheet 7: *Parlez!*), PSHE and FT (healthy eating)

Key vocabulary
Food items from Lesson 3: *les frites, les bonbons, les pommes, les carottes, les haricots, les gâteaux*

Language structures and outcomes
C'est bon pour la santé. Ce n'est pas bon pour la santé.

---

1. Starter activity: *Je n'aime pas les bonbons* — 5 mins — AT1.2 O5.1 / AT2.2 O5.2

Materials
Units 2 and 3 Flashcards (Healthy/unhealthy food items, and Likes/dislikes).

Description
Starter to revise using *J'aime* and *Je n'aime pas* + plural food words.

Delivery
- Hold up two flashcards, or stick them on the board, to represent *J'aime* or *Je n'aime pas* + food item. Ask pupils to say the sentence aloud.
- Continue until all combinations have been covered.
- This activity can be done as a team game if preferred.

---

2. Animated story: *La cuisine Rigolo (2)* — 5–10 mins — AT1.3 O5.2 / AT3.3 O5.3 / IU5.1 L5.1

Materials
CD-ROM, whiteboard, Unit 3 Flashcards (Healthy/unhealthy food items).

Description
Watch and listen again to this interactive story presenting the language for Lessons 3 and 4. You can pause and rewind the story at any point, or record your own version too.

Delivery
- In this second viewing, focus on the language used to say whether a food is healthy or unhealthy.
- Draw two boxes on the board. Put a tick (✓) at the top of one box, and a cross (✗) at the top of the other.
- Ask six pupils to place one flashcard each in one of the boxes, according to whether they think it is healthy (*C'est bon pour la santé* = ✓) or unhealthy (*Ce n'est pas bon pour la santé* = ✗). Use the language subtly at this stage, with no pressure on pupils to repeat what you say.
- Ask pupils to watch the scene, and check if the characters agree with the class on which are healthy/unhealthy foods.
- Discuss answers at the end of the viewing.
- If time allows you can show the animated story again at the end of the lesson, when pupils should be able to understand more of the language.

---

3. Presentation: *C'est bon pour la santé* — 5–10 mins — AT1.2 O5.1 / AT2.2 O5.2 / AT3.2

Materials
CD-ROM, whiteboard; possibly flashcards as Activities 1 and 2 (see above).

Description
Tap on the food items to hear whether they're healthy or unhealthy. Use the additional features to practise sound/spelling links, or to record your own version of each word.

Delivery
- We hear Didier saying either *c'est bon pour la santé* or *ce n'est pas bon pour la santé* when each food item is touched. The whole class listens and repeats, giving a thumbs up or thumbs down gesture at the same time.
- Continue for all six items and repeat if further practice is required.

Refer to the Introduction for notes on the *Record* and *Sound* features.

Extension
Ask more confident pupils to come to the front and stand with their backs to the board during each activity described above. Without looking at the board, they listen to what is said and respond by selecting the appropriate flashcard and giving a thumbs up or thumbs down gesture. They can then turn round to check their answers.

Support
First break each expression into smaller chunks then get pupils to chant them, building up to the complete sentence.

---

4. Oracy activity: *La santé* — 10–20 mins — AT1.2 O5.1 / AT2.2 O5.2

Materials
Unit 3 Flashcards (Sandwiches and ice-creams, and Healthy/unhealthy food items), *Rigolo 1* Units 6 and 11 Flashcards (Food and drink), Worksheet 7.

Description
Pupils say whether a food is healthy or unhealthy.

Delivery
- Complete Worksheet 7: *Parlez!* (survey on pupil's likes/dislikes).

Unit 3: Lesson 4

- Discuss the survey findings: first look at which foods were pupils' favourites, then discuss opinions on which foods are healthy or unhealthy. (There may, of course, be some variation in opinions on certain foods, e.g. a pizza can be considered healthy or unhealthy, depending on ingredients; ice cream and chocolate can also contain foods which are good for us!)

Extension
Pupils could draw up a table, on computer or on paper, to illustrate the results of the survey.

Support
Less confident pupils could work in pairs to conduct the survey interviews.

5. Literacy activity: C'est bon ou ce n'est pas bon?
⏱ 10 mins — AT3.2 L5.2

Materials
CD-ROM, whiteboard.

Description
Tap on *Allez*. Drag the food and drink words to the correct cauldron.

Delivery
- Pupils sort the food items into cauldrons labelled *C'est bon pour la santé* or *Ce n'est pas bon pour la santé*. Discuss whether all pupils agree or disagree with the decision and, if possible, say in English why each item is healthy/unhealthy.
- Continue until all 14 items have been sorted.

Support
Display the relevant picture and word flashcards together on the board or classroom wall so they can be referred to as necessary.

Worksheet 8: *Lisez!* may be used from this point onwards.

6. Plenary activity: Ce n'est pas bon!
⏱ 5–10 mins — AT1.2 O5.1 / AT2.2 O5.2

Materials
Unit 3 Flashcards (Sandwiches and ice-creams, and Healthy/unhealthy food items), food flashcards from *Rigolo 1* Units 6 and 11.

Description
Team quiz to revise food vocabulary and expressions from this unit.

Delivery
- Divide the class into two or more teams. Each team is asked a question in turn.
- Hold up a flashcard and ask *Qu'est-ce que c'est?* Teams score one point for a correct answer. Then ask, *C'est bon pour la santé ou ce n'est pas bon pour la santé?* Teams score another point for a correct answer. Add up the points in French at the end.

Worksheet 7: Parlez!
⏱ 10 mins — AT1.2–3 O5.1 / AT2.2–3 O5.2 / AT3.2

Description
This worksheet provides further practice in talking about which foods can be considered healthy or unhealthy. It may be used at any point after Activity 3.

Answers
1. 1 les pommes ☑ C'est bon pour la santé.
   2 les frites
   3 les bananes ☑ C'est bon pour la santé.
   4 les gâteaux
   5 les carottes ☑ C'est bon pour la santé.
   6 le jus d'orange ☑ C'est bon pour la santé.
   7 la pizza
   8 les bonbons
   9 les sandwichs ☑ C'est bon pour la santé.
   10 le chocolat
   11 la glace
   12 les haricots ☑ C'est bon pour la santé.

Worksheet 8: Lisez!
⏱ 10 mins — AT3.3 L5.1 / AT4.2–3 L5.3

Description
This worksheet provides further reading and writing practice in which foods can be considered healthy or unhealthy. It may be used at any point after Activity 5.

Answers
1. 1 faux   4 vrai
   2 faux   5 vrai
   3 faux   6 faux

Language learning strategies
- When pupils are researching on the internet, reassure them that they don't need to understand all the French words in authentic texts but should try to pick out a few they do know, then perhaps use a dictionary for some words they would like to know.
- Encourage them to try to pronounce some unfamiliar words using the strategies they've learned from *Rigolo*.

Project work: Les repas français
⏱ 1–2 hours — AT1.2–3 O5.4 / AT2.2–3 L5.1 / AT3.2–3 L5.3 / AT4.2–3 IU5.1

Description
Pupils work in small groups to find out more information about what French people eat for lunch.

Materials
Internet access and printer, email correspondence with French primary school, library books, French magazines (women's or children's) including some recipes or food pictures.

Delivery
- Assign pupils to small work groups or pairs, and ask them to use the resources you have to find out about what French people eat at lunchtime. Pupils will hopefully discover that many will eat a sit-down meal at lunchtime and that most French schools have a *cantine* (= 'canteen') which serves healthy, three-course meals at a very reasonable cost. Packed lunches are quite rare amongst French primary-aged children.
- Pool the information the pupils have gathered and prepare a display. Discuss any interesting comparisons with British food. Pupils then can make short presentations about their findings, using *Les français aiment* [+ food items]' (= 'French people like [+ food items]'), then add other language covered in this unit to say whether the food is healthy or not.

Rigolo 2 — Unit 4: En ville

National criteria

KS2 Framework objectives

- O5.1 Prepare and practise a simple conversation, re-using familiar vocabulary and structures in new contexts
- O5.3 Listen attentively and understand more complex phrases and sentences
- O5.4 Prepare a short presentation on a familiar topic
- L5.1 Re-read frequently a variety of short texts
- L5.2 Make simple sentences and short texts
- L5.3 Write words, phrases and short sentences, using a reference source
- IU5.1 Look at further aspects of their everyday lives from the perspective of someone from another country
- IU5.2 Recognise similarities and differences between places
- IU5.3 Compare symbols, objects or products which represent their own culture with those of another country

QCA Scheme of Work

Unit 15 En route pour l'école
Unit 21 Le passé et le présent

National Curriculum attainment levels

AT1.1–3, AT2.1–3, AT3.1–3, AT4.1–3

Language ladder levels

Listening: Breakthrough, Grades 1–3
Reading: Breakthrough, Grades 1–3
Speaking: Breakthrough, Grades 1–3
Writing: Breakthrough, Grades 1–3

5–14 guideline strands — Levels A–C

Listening
Listening for information and instructions	A, B, C
Listening and reacting to others	A, B, C

Speaking
Speaking to convey information	A, B, C
Speaking and interacting with others	A, B, C
Speaking about experiences, feelings and opinions	A, B

Reading
Reading for information and instructions	A, B, C
Reading aloud	A, B, C

Writing
Writing to exchange information and ideas	A, B, C
Writing to establish and maintain personal contact	A, B
Writing imaginatively to entertain	A, B, C

Unit objectives

- Name places in the town
- Ask the way and give directions
- Say where you are going
- Give the time and say where you are going

Key language

- Qu'est-ce que c'est? C'est… la boulangerie, le centre sportif, le château, l'école, le jardin public, le marché, la piscine, le supermarché
- [La piscine] s'il vous plaît? Tournez à droite/à gauche. Allez tout droit. D'abord… ensuite… enfin… + directions
- Où vas-tu? Je vais au château/centre sportif/jardin public/marché/supermarché. Je vais à la boulangerie/piscine. Je vais à l'école.
- Il est [deux] heure(s). Je vais au/à la/à l' + places

Grammar and skills

- Use *le/la/l'* correctly with places
- Use sequencers *d'abord, ensuite, enfin* to say longer sentences
- Give instruction using the *vous* form
- Use prepositions *au/à la/à l'* with places
- Recognise language patterns and deduce rules
- Incorporate known language into new structures

Unit outcomes

Most children will be able to:

- Name places in a town
- Ask the way and give simple directions
- Say where they're going
- Give the time and say where they're going

Some children will also be able to:

- Say longer sentences using sequencers
- Use prepositions *au/à la/à l'* correctly with places
- Recognise patterns in language
- Incorporate known language into new structures

Unit 4 — Lesson 1

Lesson summary

Context
Places in the town

National criteria
KS2 Framework: O5.1, O5.3, L5.1, L5.3, IU5.3, IU5.2, IU5.3
Attainment levels: AT1.1–3, AT2.1–2, AT3.1–3, AT4.1–2
Language ladder levels:
  Listening: **Grades 1–3**; Speaking: **Grades 1–3**;
  Reading: **Grades 1–3**; Writing: **Grades 1–2**

Cross-curricular links
Literacy, geography

Key vocabulary
la boulangerie, le centre sportif, le château, l'école, le jardin public, le marché, la piscine, le supermarché

Language structures and outcomes
Qu'est-ce que c'est? C'est…

---

1. Starter activity: Chantez l'alphabet!
5–10 mins — AT1.2 O5.1, AT2.2 L5.3, AT3.2

Materials
CD-ROM, whiteboard.

Description
A quick revision of the alphabet using the alphabet song from *Rigolo 1* (Unit 5, Lesson 2).

Delivery
- Go through the alphabet as a choral chant to refresh everyone's memory.
- Play the karaoke alphabet song straight through in *Sing* mode, unless pupils are not very confident – in which case choose *Practice* mode first.

2. Video story: En ville (1)
10 mins — AT1.2–3 O5.3, AT3.2–3 L5.1, IU5.1 IU5.2 IU5.3

Materials
CD-ROM, whiteboard.

Description
Watch and listen to this video story presenting the language for Lessons 1 and 2. You can pause and rewind the story at any point.

Delivery
- This video features the French children from Unit 2 as they show viewers around their town.
- Before playing the video ask *Comment s'appellent-ils?* to see if pupils remember the names of the French children. Tell pupils the children are going to show us around the town and ask them to predict what places they will include. Note down suggestions on the board, in English and in French.
- Play the video through and ask pupils if their predictions were correct, or what differences there were between the predictions and the actual places shown. Amend the list on the board accordingly.
- Ask pupil to look at the buildings and anything they can see in the background in the video. Ask what differences they notice compared to buildings in their own towns. (NB: accept answers in English or French – pupils will have lots of opportunities to learn the French words during the rest of the lesson.)
- Replay the whole video without stopping for pupils to enjoy.

Support
Remind pupils not to worry about understanding everything that is said in the video at this stage; they will cover all the language in more detail throughout this lesson. You may wish to replay the video, line by line, at the end of the lesson, before letting pupils view it all the way through again.

Intercultural understanding
- The video section of this lesson should be very useful in helping pupils to recognise similarities and differences between places, and also to compare places they see in France in the video with places in their own country.
- Encourage pupils to look really carefully at the places they see on screen. Help them look at details of the buildings and the streets they see: the signs outside the shops, the shop fronts, etc. Then ask which similarities and differences they have spotted.

3. Presentation: C'est la boulangerie
5–10 mins — AT1.1 O5.1, AT2.1 IU5.1, AT3.1 IU5.2

Materials
CD-ROM, whiteboard, Unit 4 Flashcards (Places in the town).

Description
Tap on one of the pictures on the signpost to see and hear the name of the place. Use the additional features to practise sound/spelling links, word classes and spelling, or to record your own version of each word.

Delivery
- The whole class listens to each word and repeats. Pay particular attention to accurate pronunciation.
- Continue for all eight destinations and repeat if further practice is required.

Refer to the Introduction for notes on the *Record, Spell, Sound* and *Word* features.

Support
Use the flashcards for further presentation and oral practice.

Extension
Point out and revise *le/la/l'* then ask pupils what the three words mean and why each is used. Encourage pupils to try to learn the article together with the noun.

Unit 4: Lesson 1

4. Oracy activity: La piscine
5–10 mins · AT1.2 · O5.3 IU5.1 IU5.2

Materials
CD-ROM, whiteboard, possibly Unit 4 Flashcards (Places in the town).

Description
Tap on *Allez*. Listen to the audio and tap on the correct picture for each word.

Delivery
- We hear a destination being announced; the pupil at the front must tap on the relevant picture. Tap on *Encore* to hear the announcement again if necessary.
- If the selection is correct, a photo will appear. Discuss similarities/differences between the photos and the places where pupils live.
- Tap on *Continuez* to go on to the next destination.
- Continue for all eight places and repeat if further practice is needed.

Extension
Make this into a competitive game for more confident pupils: invite two pupils up to the board at a time. When they hear the audio prompt they race to be the first to tap on the correct sign.

Support
Encourage less confident pupils to use the *Encore* button as often as necessary. You could also display the flashcards during the activity as additional prompts.

Worksheet 1: *Parlez!* may be used from this point onwards.

5. Literacy activity: C'est le château
5–10 mins · AT2.1 IU5.2 AT3.1

Materials
Unit 4 Flashcards (Places in the town).

Description
Game where pupils match pictures to the captions.

Delivery
- Display a set of places flashcards on the board: the captions on one side of the board, the pictures on the other.
- Ask a pupil to come to the board and place a word card with its corresponding picture card in the centre of the board.
- Repeat for all eight items.
- You could make this into a team game by dividing the class into two teams. Invite pupils from alternate teams to match the cards and award one point for each correct pair, or see which team can match the pairs in the shortest time.

Worksheet 2: *Écrivez!* may be used from this point onwards.

6. Plenary activity: Le jeu du pendu
5–10 mins · AT2.1–2 O5.1 IU5.2

Materials
Possibly Unit 4 Flashcards (Places in the town).

Description
A game of hangman to revise the target vocabulary.

Delivery
- If necessary, use the flashcards quickly to elicit and review the vocabulary.
- Demonstrate the game by choosing a place around town and drawing a dashed line on the board, with one dash to represent each letter in your chosen word. Invite pupils to call out letters of the alphabet. If a letter appears in the word, write it in the appropriate space. For each incorrect answer draw one element (e.g. the head or an arm) of a 'stick' person on the board. Pupils must try to complete the word before you complete the drawing in order to win.

Extension
Pupils can come to the front and act as the teacher. They decide on the word and the rest of the class has to guess.

Worksheet 1: Parlez!
5–10 mins · AT1.1–2 O5.1 AT2.1–2

Description
This worksheet provides further practice in asking and answering questions about places on a town map. It may be used at any point after Activity 4.

Answers
1 = school
2 = market
3 = park
4 = castle (*missing place on both maps*)
5 = sports centre
6 = baker's
7 = swimming pool
8 = supermarket

Worksheet 2: Écrivez!
10 mins · AT4.1–2 L5.3 IU5.2

Description
This worksheet provides further writing practice in places in town, with the emphasis on spelling accuracy. It may be used at any point after Activity 5.

Answers
1 1 l'école
   2 la boulangerie
   3 le centre sportif
   4 le jardin public
   5 le château
   6 la marché
   7 le supermarché
   8 la piscine

2 1 Qu'est-ce que c'est? C'est la boulangerie.
   2 C'est le centre sportif? Non, c'est la piscine.
   3 Qu'est-ce que c'est? C'est le château.
   4 C'est le supermarché? Non, c'est le marché.
   5 C'est le jardin public? Non, c'est l'école.

Rigolo 2 Teacher's Notes © Nelson Thornes Ltd 2008

Unit 4 (Lesson 2)

Lesson summary

Context
Asking the way and giving directions

National criteria
KS2 Framework: **O5.1, O5.3, O5.4, L5.1, L5.2, L5.3, IU5.1, IU5.2, IU5.3**
Attainment levels: **AT1.2–3, AT2.2–3, AT3.2–3, AT4.3**
Language ladder levels:
  Listening: **Grades 2–3**; Speaking: **Grades 2–3**;
  Reading: **Grades 2–3**; Writing: **Grade 3**

Cross-curricular links
Literacy, geography

Key vocabulary
Places in the town from Lesson 1; *d'abord… ensuite… enfin…*

Language structures and outcomes
[La piscine] s'il vous plaît? Tournez à droite/à gauche. Allez tout droit.

---

1. Starter activity: Arrêtez!   ⏱ 5 mins   AT1.2 O5.1 / AT2.2 O5.3

Materials
CD-ROM, whiteboard, *Rigolo 1* Unit 10 Flashcards (Directions).

Description
Tap on the direction symbols to revise basic directions (this repeats a presentation from *Rigolo 1* Unit 10, Lesson 2).

Delivery
- Invite a few pupils to the board to tap on the four direction icons. The whole class listens, repeats, and makes the appropriate gesture.
- Hold up the flashcards to revise the same directions.

2. Video story: En ville (1)   ⏱ 5–10 mins   AT1.2–3 O5.3 / AT3.2–3 L5.1 / IU5.1 IU5.2 IU5.3

Materials
CD-ROM, whiteboard, Unit 4 Flashcards (Places in the town) and *Rigolo 1* Unit 10 Flashcards (Directions).

Description
Watch and listen again to this video story presenting the language for Lessons 1 and 2. You can pause and rewind the story at any point.

Delivery
- On this second viewing of the video, focus on the directions. Play the video through and ask pupils to note to which places we are given directions (sports centre and market). Ask them also to try and remember the directions to each place.
- Go through the answers and note the suggestions on the board. Play the video through a second time to confirm whether the answers were correct.

3. Presentation: La boulangerie, s'il vous plaît   ⏱ 5–10 mins   AT1.3 O5.1 / AT2.3 O5.3 / AT3.3

Materials
CD-ROM, whiteboard, Unit 4 Flashcards (Places in the town).

Description
Tap on one of the location icons to hear Mme Mills ask the way to that place, and the directions she receives. Use the additional features to record your own version of each exchange.

Delivery
- We hear first the question, then the directions.
- Pupils repeat both the question and the answer, using direction gestures to reinforce the language. If some pupils find the utterances rather long, practise them further as suggested in 'Support' below. Make sure pupils understand the words *d'abord* (first of all), *ensuite* (then) and *enfin* (finally). Encourage pupils to use these sequencing expressions from now on to join other sentences/phrases together.
- Continue for all five destinations and repeat if further practice is required.

Refer to the Introduction for notes on the *Record* feature.

Knowledge about language

- Point out to pupils how important it is to know useful 'little' words like *d'abord*, *ensuite* and *enfin* that allow them to change and manipulate phrases: combining sequences with directions enables them to express many different combinations. Once pupils understand that they can start forming their own sentences and change elements to say something slightly different, they will feel more in control of the language and their own learning.
- Set them a challenge to see how many different combinations of the phrases they can make.
- It is also important for them to see how they can incorporate known language (e.g. phrases used in giving directions from Unit 10 of *Rigolo 1*) and use them to produce more complex sentences.

Support
If some pupils find the utterances rather long, include further oral practice on single directions using direction gestures. Use Unit 4 Flashcards (Places in the town) to give pupils further practice in asking the way to places.

Unit 4: Lesson 2

4. Oracy activity: Tournez à gauche
10 mins — AT1.3 O5.1, AT2.3 O5.3

Materials
CD-ROM, whiteboard, Unit 4 Flashcards (Places in the town)

Description
Use the Activity 3 Presentation above to prompt pupils to ask for and give directions.

Delivery
- Play the Activity 3 whiteboard presentation (*La boulangerie, s'il vous plaît*) with the sound turned off.
- One pupil taps on one of the location icons. A second pupil holds up the relevant flashcard and asks for directions to that place. A third pupil taps on M. Chanson to see which direction symbols are highlighted. A fourth pupil says the appropriate directions and holds up the relevant flashcards. Turn the sound back on to hear the dialogue and ask pupils to compare with their own question/answer.
- Repeat for all five destinations.

Extension
- Ask more confident pupils to make up dialogues based on the model, using the destinations on the flashcards not featured in the presentation (*le centre sportif, le château, le marché*).

5. Literacy activity: Allez tout droit
10 mins — AT3.3 L5.2

Materials
CD-ROM, whiteboard.

Description
Tap on *Allez*. Look at the symbols and drag the text tiles into the correct order to match the symbols.

Delivery
- Pupils drag the appropriate phrases into the correct order to match the directions shown, then tap on *Fini* to see if the sentence is correct.
- We hear Mme Chanson saying the sentence if the answer is correct. One of three 'lives' is lost for each incorrect answer. If three 'lives' are lost pupils are invited to start a new game.
- Continue until all six sentences have been covered and repeat if necessary.

Support
This activity can be done as a whole-class activity: the class suggests what the sentence should be, and discusses their choices if necessary, before the pupil taps on *Fini*.

Worksheets 3: *Lisez!* and 4: *Grammaire* may be used from this point onwards.

6. Plenary activity: Le jeu du robot
5–10 mins — AT1.3 O5.1, AT2.3 O5.3, O5.4

Description
Pupils practise giving each other directions.

Delivery
- Ask a confident pupil to come to the front and tell them they are a robot and you are the controller!
- Give instructions to the pupil who must move, robot-style, in the appropriate directions.
- Invite another two pupils to the front: one is the robot, the other the controller. The controller gives instructions as before.
- You can either continue with a few more volunteers as a whole-class activity, or let pupils work in small groups whilst you circulate and listen in.

Extension
More confident pupils can give a string of directions (using *d'abord… ensuite… enfin…*) instead of just one at a time. The 'robot' must then remember to make all the movements in the correct order.

Worksheet 3: Lisez!
10 mins — AT3.3 O5.1, L5.1

Description
This worksheet provides further practice in reading directions. It may be used at any point Activity 5.

Answers
1b a = 4 (l'école)
 b = 2 (la boulangerie)
 c = 3 (le centre sportif)
 d = 1 (la piscine)

Worksheet 4: Grammaire
10 mins — AT2.3 O5.1, AT3.3 L5.2, AT4.3 L5.3

Description
This worksheet provides further practice in directions. It may be used at any point after Activity 5.

Delivery
- Activity 1 is a gap-fill activity: ask pupils to try to predict what sort of word should go into each gap, i.e. a place, a sequencer (*d'abord, ensuite, enfin*), etc. Give pupils a few minutes to complete the activity and quickly run through the answers.

Answers
1 1 – Bonjour, monsieur. Le marché, s'il vous plaît?
   – Le marché… D'abord, **tournez** à gauche, ensuite tournez à droite, enfin allez tout droit.
   – Merci, monsieur, au revoir.
  2 – Bonjour, madame. La piscine s'il vous plaît?
   – La piscine. D'abord, **allez** tout **droit**, ensuite tournez à gauche, **enfin** tournez à droite.
   – Merci, madame. Au revoir.
  3 – Bonjour, madame. Le château, s'il vous plaît?
   – D'abord tournez à droite, **ensuite** tournez à droite, enfin allez tout droit.
   – Merci, madame, **au** revoir.
  4 – Bonjour, madame. La **boulangerie**, s'il vous plaît?
   – **D'abord** tournez à droite, ensuite allez **tout** droit, enfin tournez à gauche.

Unit 4 — Lesson 3

Lesson summary

Context
Saying where you're going

National criteria
KS2 Framework: **O5.1, O5.3, L5.1, L5.2, L5.3, IU5.1, IU5.2, IU5.3**
Attainment levels: **AT1.2–3, AT2.2–3, AT3.2–3, AT4.2–3**
Language ladder levels:
  Listening: **Grades 2–3**; Speaking: **Grades 2–3**;
  Reading: **Grades 2–3**; Writing: **Grades 2–3**

Cross-curricular links
Geography, literacy

Key vocabulary
Places in the town from Lesson 1

Language structures and outcomes
Où vas-tu? Je vais…
au château/centre sportif/jardin public/marché/supermarché
à la boulangerie/piscine
à l'école

---

1. Starter activity: C'est le marché?
⏱ 5 mins — AT1.2 O5.1, AT2.2 O5.3

Materials
Unit 4 Flashcards (Places in the town).

Description
Quick revision of places in the town using flashcards.

Delivery
- Hold up the flashcards one by one to elicit the various place names.
- Stick the cards on the board. Divide the class into two teams. Invite two pupils (one from each team) to the front. Call out a place name; pupils race to be the first to touch the correct card. Continue with different pupils until you have covered all the places on the cards.

---

2. Video: En ville (2)
⏱ 10 mins — AT1.3 O5.3, AT3.3 L5.1, IU5.1 IU5.2, IU5.3

Materials
CD-ROM, whiteboard, possibly Unit 4 Flashcards (Places in the town).

Description
Watch and listen to this video story presenting the language for Lessons 3 and 4. You can pause and rewind the story at any point.

Delivery
- The second part of the video introduces the target structure for this lesson (Je vais au/à la/à l' [+ place name]). Pupils note the places and times that are mentioned.
- Play the film through one more time to check/discuss answers. Again, ask pupils to look and note differences between buildings and streets in France compared to those they see in their own town.

Support
Pause the video after each place name is mentioned, ask pupils to say the place name, then stick the relevant flashcard on the board. Pause the video after the times are mentioned also and write the times on the board.

---

3. Presentation: Où vas-tu?
⏱ 10 mins — AT1.2 O5.1, AT2.2 O5.3, AT3.2 IU5.2

Materials
CD-ROM, whiteboard, possibly Unit 4 Flashcards (Places in the town).

Description
Tap on the characters, in turn, to hear the question and answer. Use the additional features to practise sound/spelling links and word classes, or to record your own version of each question and answer exchange.

Delivery
- We hear the question Où vas-tu? and an answer, e.g. Je vais à la boulangerie, illustrated by a photo. The whole class repeats both. Ask if they remember what tu means. Point out that it means 'you' when you know someone well and you would normally use it when addressing someone you know.
- Continue for all five sentences and repeat if further practice is required.

Refer to the Introduction for notes on the Record, Sound and Word features.

Extension
More confident pupils could take turns to stand at the front with their backs to the board. When the characters say where they are going, pupils must hold up the appropriate flashcards.

Support
Stick all the flashcards (words and pictures) on the board. After each presentation, ask pupils to come and hold up the relevant flashcards, then ask the whole class to repeat the sentence.

Knowledge about language

- Use the prepositions au/à la/à l' to encourage pupil to recognise language patterns. Write the places with à la/au/à l' on the whiteboard and ask pupils to put the places into three categories; hopefully they will categorise them according to the preposition (au/à la/à l'). Elicit what the three categories are (pupils have met them before in Unit 3 when talking about different sandwiches and ice-creams so they may remember) i.e. feminine places, masculine places and places which start with a vowel.

- There is further practice on this grammar point in Worksheets 5: Grammaire and 6: Écrivez!

4. Oracy activity: Je vais au jardin public
10 mins — AT1.2 O5.1, AT2.2 O5.3, IU5.1 IU5.2

Materials
CD-ROM, whiteboard, Unit 4 Flashcards (Places in the town) for Support activity.

Description
Tap on *Allez*. Answer each of Gustave's questions, then check your answers.

Delivery
- Encourage pupils to repeat Gustave's questions chorally and ask them to use the visual clues to predict each character's answer.
- Pupils then tap on the audio check button each time, to hear the model answer and compare it with their own. They tap on the tick button if correct and on the cross if incorrect.
- By dividing the class into two groups you could make this into a team game, awarding one point for each correct answer.

Extension
Ensure accurate use of *au/à la/à l'*.

Support
Ask pupils to hold up the relevant flashcards after each dialogue, then ask the whole class to repeat both sentences each time.

5. Literacy activity: Le jeu de mots
5–10 mins — AT3.2–3 L5.2

Materials
Unit 4 Flashcards (Places in the town).

Description
Pupils complete sentences using *au/à la/à l'*.

Delivery
- Write *au...*, *à la...* and *à l'...*, on the board, or prepare a large card for each. Below this write *Je vais...* Stick a place flashcard after the gap.
- Complete the sentence together orally, pointing to the missing words or holding up the relevant flashcards. Repeat for each place name, gradually providing less and less assistance.
- You could make this into a team game: ask pupils from alternate teams to complete the sentence and award a point for each correct answer.

Extension
Invite more confident pupils to write out complete sentences based on the flashcard prompts.

Worksheets 5: *Grammaire* and 6: *Écrivez!* may be used from this point onwards.

6. Plenary activity: D'abord, je vais à la boulangerie
5–10 mins — AT1.3 O5.1, AT2.3 O5.3

Materials
Possibly Unit 4 Flashcards (Places in the town).

Description
A 'chain-story' game to revise the target structures.

Delivery
- Demonstrate how the game works by giving three sample sentences, e.g. *D'abord, je vais à la boulangerie... ensuite je vais au marché... enfin je vais à la piscine...*
- One pupil starts the story with the first sentence. A second pupil continues the story by repeating the first sentence and adding a second sentence. The third pupil repeats the first two sentences before adding a third, and so on until all the place names have been used.

Extension
More confident pupils can do this in small groups.

Support
Use flashcards as prompts if necessary.

Worksheet 5: Grammaire
10 mins — AT3.2 L5.3

Description
This worksheet provides further practice in using *au/à la/à l'*. It may be used at any point after Activity 5.

Answers
1. 1. Je vais au **supermarché**
   2. Tu vas à l'**école**?
   3. On va à la **boulangerie**.
   4. Moi, je vais **au** centre sportif.
   5. Allez tout droit **à la** piscine.
   6. Allez **au** marché!
   7. On va **au** jardin public?
   8. Je vais **au** château.

Worksheet 6: Écrivez!
10 mins — AT2.2–3 O5.1, AT4.2–3 L5.3

Description
This worksheet provides further practice in writing sentences with prepositions and places. It may be used at any point after Activity 5.

Answers
1. 1. Je vais au supermarché.
   2. Je vais à la boulangerie.
   3. Je vais à l'école.
   4. Je vais au centre sportif.
   5. Je vais au château.
   6. Je vais au marché.

2/3. 2. D'abord, je vais au marché. Ensuite, je vais au jardin public et enfin je vais au centre sportif.
   3. D'abord, je vais au château. Ensuite, je vais à la boulangerie et enfin je vais à l'école,
   4. D'abord, je vais au marché. Ensuite, je vais au supermarché et enfin je vais à la boulangerie.
   5. D'abord, je vais au jardin public. Ensuite, je vais à la piscine et enfin je vais au centre sportif.
   6. D'abord, je vais a la piscine. Ensuite, je vais à l'école et enfin je vais au jardin public.

Unit 4 (Lesson 4)

Lesson summary

Context
Giving the time and saying where you're going

National criteria
KS2 Framework: O5.1, O5.3, O5.4, L5.1, L5.2, L5.3, IU5.1, IU5.2, IU5.3
Attainment levels: AT1.2–3, AT2.2–3, AT3.2–3, AT4.3
Language ladder levels:
   Listening: **Grades 2–3**; Speaking: **Grades 2–3**;
   Reading: **Grades 2–3**; Writing: **Grades 2–3**

Cross-curricular links
Literacy, numeracy, geography, music

Key vocabulary
Places in the town from Lesson 1

Language structures and outcomes
Il est [deux] heures.
Je vais au/à la/à l' [+ places].

---

1. Starter activity: *Je vais à la piscine* — 5 mins — AT1.2–3 O5.1, AT2.2–3 O5.3

Materials
Teaching clock, Unit 4 Flashcards (Places in the town).

Description
Starter activity to revise saying the time and saying where you're going.

Delivery
- Hold up the teaching clock and one of the place flashcards, and chorally make two sentences, e.g. *Il est [deux heures]. Je vais à [la piscine]*.
- Repeat with a different time and flashcard, and ask pupils to say the sentence aloud.
- Continue for a few minutes until you feel the class is sufficiently warmed up!

Extension
For more confident pupils, set the clock to more complex times, using 'quarter past', 'quarter to', etc.

---

2. Video story: *En ville (2)* — 5–10 mins — AT1.3 O5.3, AT3.3 L5.1, IU5.1 IU5.2 IU5.3

Materials
CD-ROM, whiteboard.

Description
Watch and listen again to this video story presenting the language for Lessons 3 and 4. You can pause and rewind the story at any point.

Delivery
- On this second viewing of the video, focus on the language of what time the characters go to different places.
- Write the following names on the board: Chloé, Lucas, Thomas.
- Ask pupils to listen out for the times mentioned and the places the three characters are going to.
- Play the film through. Ask pupils to produce two sentences that each character could say, based on the information in the film, e.g. Lucas: *Il est midi. Je vais au marché*.
- Write the three sentences on the board and play the film through again if necessary.

---

3. Presentation: *Quelle heure est-il? Où vas-tu?* — 10–15 mins — AT1.2–3 O5.1, AT2.2–3 O5.3, AT3.2–3

Materials
Teaching clock, Unit 4 Flashcards (Places in the town), Worksheet 7: *Parlez!*

Description
Pupils use the cards from Worksheet 7: *Parlez!* as prompts for making sentences.

Delivery
- Quickly revise times using the teaching clock if necessary, asking *Quelle heure est-il?* each time.
- Ask *Où vas-tu?* and hold up the place flashcards to elicit sentences as before, e.g. *Je vais au marché*.
- Combine a time and a place flashcard, asking both questions together (*Quelle heure est-il? Où vas-tu?*) to elicit *Il est [douze heures]. Je vais [au marché]*.
- In pairs, pupils make sentences based on the picture and time cards in Worksheet 7: *Parlez!*

Extension
Again, you can use more complex times to stretch more confident pupils.

Support
Provide cue cards with sentences, e.g. *Je vais à la boulangerie*, etc. for pupils who need more support.

---

4. Song: *Où vas-tu, Olivier?* — 10–15 mins — AT1.3 O5.3, AT2.3 L5.2, AT3.3

Materials
CD-ROM, whiteboard, possibly Unit 4 Flashcards (Places in the town).

Description
Watch and listen to the interactive karaoke song practising directions and places in the town. Choose either *Practice* or *Sing* mode: *Practice* to go through the song line by line; *Sing* to sing it all the way through. Switch the music and words on or off as you prefer, or try recording your own version.

Delivery
- Write the names of the four characters from the song on the board: Olivier, Marine, Didier, Polly. Ask pupils to listen to and watch the song, and to note which character is going where.

- Play the song straight through without stopping in *Sing* mode, then go through the answers.

- Go through the song line by line in *Practice* mode, checking comprehension and adding actions where appropriate, e.g. for the directions.

- Divide the class into four groups and assign a character to each group.

- Go through the song again in *Sing* mode; this time each group sings the line sung by 'their' character and the rest of the class sings the question. All pupils join in with the chorus.

Extension
- More confident pupils could invent another verse, following the pattern of the previous verses, and perform it for the rest of the class.

- Do a gapped exercise with the song. Give pupils a version with some words missing; they listen and try to complete the missing words.

Support
- Stick the relevant flashcards on the board as you go through the song in *Practice* mode to provide additional support if required.

- You could also distribute the flashcards around the class and pupils hold up their flashcard when they hear that place mentioned.

5. Literacy activity: Il est onze heures
10 mins — AT3.3 L5.2

Materials
CD-ROM, whiteboard.

Description
Tap on *Allez*. Look at the two symbols showing what the time is and where Bof and Polly want to go. Read the options at the bottom of the screen. Drag the text into the correct order at the top.

Delivery
- Pupils press *Fini* when they have completed their sentence. Polly or Bof will read out the sentence if it is correct; if the sentence is wrong, a 'life' will be lost and pupils can try again. This provides good practice in recognising word order in sentences and also in producing longer sentences.

- The game ends when all six sentences have been completed, or if all three 'lives' are lost. Pupils are invited to start another game if they wish.

Extension
Encourage pupils to form similar sentences of their own after completing the interactive activity.

Support
For less confident pupils, you may wish to do the activity as a whole class. Alternatively, as a team activity, two or three pupils at a time could go to the board and make the sentence.

Worksheet 8: *Lisez!* may be used from this point onwards.

6. Plenary activity: Tout droit!
5–10 mins — AT1.3 O5.1 / AT2.3 O5.3 / AT3.3 L5.2 / AT4.3 L5.3

Materials
CD-ROM (karaoke song from Activity 4 above), Unit 4 Flashcards (Places in the town).

Description
Pupils adapt the karaoke song to include names of pupils in the class.

Delivery
- Ask pupils to suggest a few names from the class which could be substituted for the characters' names in the song.

- Write the suggested verses on the board, e.g. *Où vas-tu, Chloe? Je vais au marché.*

- Turn the lyrics and text off, and play the song through in *Sing* mode, incorporating the new verses.

Extension
Encourage more confident classes to add some different locations to the song.

Worksheet 7: Parlez!
10 mins — AT2.2–3 O5.1

Description
This worksheet provides further practice in saying times and where you're going. It may be used at any point after Activity 2.

Worksheet 8: Lisez!
10 mins — AT3.3 L5.1

Description
This worksheet provides further reading and writing practice in times, directions and places in the town. It may be used at any point after Activity 5.

Delivery
Ask pupils to read aloud the various captions. Check pronunciation and general comprehension.

Answers
1 1d 2b 3c 4e 5a

Unit 4 — Extra!

Language learning strategies

The Project work in *Rigolo 2* encourages pupils to plan and prepare for a longer task and analyse what needs to be done to carry it out. In the project below, encourage pupils, in pairs or groups, to think and plan what they have to do to get relevant information. They then need to think about what they are going to do with that information, i.e. write a few sentences; put pictures into a display with captions; make a PowerPoint presentation, etc.

Project work: En ville — 1–2 hours
AT2.2–3 O5.1
AT3.2–3 O5.4
AT4.2–3 L5.1
IU5.1   L5.3
IU5.2   IU5.3

Description
Pupils research pictures and maps of a French town and prepare a display.

Materials
Internet access and printer if possible, email correspondence with French primary school if possible, leaflets and maps of a French town (from relevant tourist office or from school links), card and paper to display the leaflets and maps in the classroom.

Delivery
- Choose between one and four French towns for pupils to research. If you decide to research more than one town, divide the class into groups and assign a different town to each group. Try to include your French twin town if possible.

- Ask pupils how they think they can obtain information, leaflets, maps, etc. (e.g. internet research, writing to the local tourist office, sending an email to a partner school to request information) and encourage pupils to follow their ideas through where feasible.

- Pupils can then prepare a display in which they label the place names they have learned in this lesson, and highlight those places on town maps. If facilities are available they could make a PowerPoint presentation with their findings.

Sound/spelling activity — 5–10 mins
AT1.1
AT2.1
Les sons 'un' et 'une'

Materials
CD-ROM, whiteboard.

Description
Practice mode: Listen and practise pronouncing *un* and *une* on their own and then with words that have been covered in *Rigolo* so far.

Activity mode: Listen to the short phrases as they are read out. If they contain *un*, tap on the green button. If they don't contain *un*, tap on the red cross button. Repeat the process for *une*. Listen carefully and choose your answer before the time runs out!

Delivery
- There are two parts to the activity: the first (*Practice*) allows pupil to familiarise themselves with the two sounds and to compare their pronunciation with the Virtual Teacher model. The second part (*Activities*) contains two exercises: Activity 1, where pupils have to tap on a green button if they hear *un* and a red cross if they don't, and Activity 2, where pupil do the same for *une*.

- Select *Practice* and tap on *Next sound* to start this part. Then tap on *Allez*. The Virtual Teacher will say *un* and *une*, first on their own then with words that have been covered so far in *Rigolo*. Get the class to repeat the words chorally several times, checking the model each time using the *Encore* button. You can also use the *Record* feature here to compare a pupil's pronunciation more closely with the model. Move on to *Activities* or tap on *Next sound* to follow suit with *une*.

- Tap on *Activities* to start Activity 1. Pupils will hear a list of words read out in random order and must tap on the green button if they hear *un* or on the red cross if they don't (they can tap on the *Example* button first, to see and hear how it works). Pupils score one point when they correctly identify a word with *un* within the time allowed. They can tap on *Encore* to hear the word again.

- Finally, in Activity 2, pupils proceed as above, this time listening out for words with *une*.

- Repeat the activity if pupils need further practice.

Assessment Units 3–4

Écoutez!

Play each recording two or three times, or more if necessary. Pause during each activity as required.

Total marks for listening: 20.

Activity 1 (AT1.2; O5.3)
Mark out of 5.

Answers
2 b   3 d   4 e   5 c   6 a

Activity 2 (AT1.2; O5.3)
Mark out of 5.

Answers
2 g (or i)   3 h   4 l   5 i (or g)   6 j

> 1 Il est trois heures. Je vais au château.
> 2 Il est huit heures. Je vais à la boulangerie.
> 3 Il est deux heures et demie. Je vais à la piscine.
> 4 Il est cinq heures et demie. Je vais au jardin public.
> 5 Il est huit heures. Je vais à l'école.
> 6 Il est neuf heures et quart. Je vais au marché.

Activity 3 (AT1.2–3; O5.3)
Mark out of 10.

Answers
1 1 b   2 e   3 a   4 c   5 d
2 1 i   2 g   3 h   4 f   5 j

> 1 Coupez la baguette.
>   Mettez le beurre.
>   Coupez le fromage.
>   Mettez le fromage.
>   Mangez!
>
> 2 Prenez la baguette.
>   Coupez le poulet.
>   Mettez le poulet.
>   Mettez les tomates.
>   Mangez!

— Unit 4: Extra! —

Parlez!

Pupils can work in pairs for the speaking tasks. If it is not possible to assess each pair, then assess a few pairs for each assessment block and mark the rest of the class based on the spoken work they do in class.

Total marks for speaking: 10.

Activity 1 (AT2.2; O5.1, O5.2)
Mark out of 5.

Answers
(*any 5:*)
J'aime les bonbons.
Je n'aime pas les pommes.
J'aime les carottes.
Je n'aime pas les frites.
J'aime les haricots.
Je n'aime pas les gâteaux.

Activity 2 (AT2.2–3; O5.1)
Mark out of 5 (maximum =1 mark for each sentence).

Answers
1 La boulangerie s'il vous plaît?
  D'abord, tournez à droite.
  Ensuite, tournez à gauche.
  Enfin, allez tout droit.
2 Le centre sportif, s'il vous plaît?
  D'abord, allez tout droit.
  Ensuite, tournez à droite.
  Enfin, tournez à gauche.
3 Le supermarché, s'il vous plaît?
  D'abord, tournez à gauche.
  Ensuite, tournez à droite.
  Enfin, allez tout droit.

Lisez!

Total marks for reading: 20.

Activity 1 (AT3.2; L5.1)
Mark out of 10.

Answers
1 d, f   2 b, g   3 c, h   4 e, i   5 j, a

Activity 2 (AT3.2–3; L5.1)
Mark out of 10.

Answers
1 Where is the swimming pool please?
  First of all, go straight on…
  then turn left.
  Finally turn right.
  Thank you!
2 What time is it?
  It's half past nine.
  Where are you going?
  I'm going to the baker's.
  I'm going to the sports centre.

Écrivez!

Total marks for writing: 20.

Activity 1 (AT4.1–2; L5.2, L5.3, O5.2)
Mark out of 10 (2 marks per sentence).

Answers
1 J'aime les bonbons.
2 J'aime les pommes.
3 Je n'aime pas les frites.
4 Je n'aime pas les carottes.
5 J'aime les gâteaux.

Activity 2 (AT4.2–3; L5.2, L5.3)
Mark out of 10 (2 marks per sentence).

Answers
1 Il est neuf heures. Je vais au marché.
2 Il est dix heures. Je vais au supermarché.
3 Il est onze heures. Je vais à la boulangerie.
4 Il est deux heures. Je vais à la piscine.
5 Il est trois heures. Je vais au jardin public.

Rigolo 2 — Unit 5: En vacances

National criteria

KS2 Framework objectives

O5.1	Prepare and practise a simple conversation, re-using familiar vocabulary and structures in new contexts
O5.2	Understand and express simple opinions
O5.3	Listen attentively and understand more complex phrases and sentences
O5.4	Prepare a short presentation on a familiar topic
L5.1	Re-read frequently a variety of short texts
L5.2	Make simple sentences and short texts
L5.3	Write words, phrases and short sentences, using a reference source
IU5.1	Look at further aspects of their everyday lives from the perspective of someone from another country
IU5.2	Recognise similarities and differences between places

QCA Scheme of Work

Unit 7 On y va
Unit 20 Notre monde
Unit 22 Ici et là

National Curriculum attainment levels

AT1.2–3, AT2.2–3, AT3.2–3, AT4.2–3

Language ladder levels

Listening: Breakthrough, Grades 2–3
Reading: Breakthrough, Grades 2–3
Speaking: Breakthrough, Grades 2–3
Writing: Breakthrough, Grades 2–3

5–14 guideline strands   Levels A–C

Listening
Listening for information and instructions   A, B, C
Listening and reacting to others   A, B, C

Speaking
Speaking to convey information   A, B, C
Speaking and interacting with others   A, B, C
Speaking about experiences, feelings and opinions   A, B, C

Reading
Reading for information and instructions   A, B, C
Reading aloud   A, B, C

Writing
Writing to exchange information and ideas   A, B, C
Writing to establish and maintain personal contact   A, B, C
Writing imaginatively to entertain   A, B, C

Unit objectives

- Ask and say where you're going on holiday
- Express opinions about holidays
- Talk about what you're going to do on holiday
- Talk about holiday plans

Key language

- *Où vas-tu en vacances? Je vais à la campagne. Je vais à la montagne. Je vais au bord de la mer. Je vais au camping. Je vais au parc d'attractions.*
- *J'aime ça, Je n'aime pas ça. J'adore ça. Je déteste ça.*
- *Qu'est-ce que tu vas faire en vacances? Je vais faire du bateau. Je vais faire du ski. Je vais nager. Je vais faire du sport. Je vais faire du vélo. Je vais voir mes grands-parents. Je vais faire les manèges.*
- Consolidation of all the above

Grammar and skills

- Use *au/à la/à l'/à* correctly with places
- Recognise patterns and apply knowledge of rules
- Express opinions
- Say what you're going to do using *Je vais* + infinitive
- Apply grammatical knowledge to make sentences

Unit outcomes

Most children will be able to:
- Name holiday destinations
- Express opinions about different holidays
- Say what they're going to do

Some children will also be able to:
- Use *au/à la/à l'/à* correctly
- Recognise patterns and apply knowledge of rules
- Apply rules to talk about future plans
- Make longer sentences about holiday plans

Unit 5 — Lesson 1

Lesson summary

Context
Asking and saying where you're going on holiday

National criteria
KS2 Framework: **O5.1, O5.2, O5.3, L5.1, L5.2, L5.3, IU5.2**
Attainment levels: **AT1.2–3, AT2.2, AT3.2–3, AT4.2–3**
Language ladder levels:
 Listening: **Grades 2–3**; Speaking: **Grade 2**;
 Reading: **Grades 2–3**; Writing: **Grades 2–3**

Cross-curricular links
Geography, literacy

Key vocabulary
à la campagne, à la montagne, au bord de la mer, au camping, au parc d'attractions

Language structures and outcomes
Revise à [+ towns]: Paris, Bordeaux, Nice, Grenoble, Strasbourg
Où vas-tu en vacances? Je vais au/à la/à l'…

---

1. Starter activity: Où vas-tu?
5–10 mins — AT1.2 O5.1, AT2.2 IU5.2, AT3.2

Materials
CD-ROM, whiteboard, map of France (for support activity).

Description
A quick revision of à + place names using the *Rigolo 1* presentation (Unit 10, Lesson 1).

Delivery
- Ask pupils if they can remember how to ask and answer questions about where someone is going. Write any suggestions on the board, or just ask pupils to remember the ideas. Refer back to these answers when you begin the activity.
- Pupils come to the board to tap on the different place names. Encourage the class to repeat both the question and the answer. Continue until all place names have been selected.
- Remind pupils that *à* is used with towns/cities to mean 'to' or 'in'.

Extension
Ask more confident pupils to come to the front of the class, in pairs. Each pair then predicts the dialogue they will hear for a chosen destination and taps on that town/city to check their version was correct.

Support
If pupils need further help with the structures, repeat the activity, or provide additional practice by displaying a map of France and selecting additional towns/cities (perhaps based on well-known football teams!).

---

2. Animated story: Les vacances (1)
10 mins — AT1.3 O5.2, AT3.3 O5.3, IU5.2 L5.1

Materials
CD-ROM, whiteboard, Unit 5 Flashcards (Holiday destinations).

Description
Watch and listen to this interactive story presenting the language for Lessons 1 and 2. You can pause and rewind the story at any point, or record your own version too.

Delivery
- Display the flashcards and write the names of the characters (Didier, Polly, Bof) on the board.
- Ask pupils to watch the animation and to note where each character will be spending their holidays.
- Play the story through, then invite pupils to the board to match the characters with the holiday destinations.
- Replay the animation so that pupils can check their answers.
- Pupils are not expected to remember how to say the destinations in French at this stage; detailed practice will follow.

Support
If pupils find there is too much information to remember, pause the animation after each destination has been mentioned and ask pupils to match the character/card.

---

3. Presentation: Où vas-tu en vacances?
5–10 mins — AT1.2 O5.1, AT2.2 O5.3, AT3.2

Materials
CD-ROM, whiteboard.

Description
Tap on the map icons to hear the characters say where they are going on holiday. Use the additional features to practise sound/spelling links, word classes and spelling, or to record your own version of each word.

Delivery
- When the place on the map is tapped, a character pops up and replies to Jake's question about where they're going on holiday. The whole class listens to the dialogue and repeats.
- Continue for all five destinations and repeat if further practice is required.
- Draw pupils' attention to the use of *à la* and *au*. Check if they can remember from Unit 4 what the rules/patterns are, i.e. *au* for masculine words, *à la* for feminine words and *à l'* for words beginning with a vowel or 'h'. You may want to point out the two different possibilities in pronunciation when saying *Je vais au/à la…* . Some people make a liaison between the 's' of *Je vais* when it's followed by a vowel, and some don't.

Refer to the Introduction for notes on the *Record*, *Spell*, *Sound* and *Word* features.

---

4. Oracy activity: Je vais à la campagne
5–10 mins — AT1.2 O5.3, AT2.2

Materials
CD-ROM, whiteboard, possibly Unit 5 Flashcards (Holiday destinations) for support activity.

Description
Tap on *Allez*. Listen to Bof as he says where he's going on holiday, then drag and drop him into the correct place.

Delivery
- We hear Bof being asked where he is going on holiday, followed by his reply. The pupil drags Bof to the correct place on the map.
- Continue for all five places and repeat if further practice is required.

Support
Encourage less confident pupils to use the *Encore* button as much as necessary. You could also display the flashcards during the activity as additional prompts.

Worksheet 1: *Parlez!* may be used from this point onwards.

Knowledge about language

Recognising patterns in simple sentences and applying knowledge of rules when building sentences

- At some point in this lesson ask pupils what they notice about the key sentences, i.e. some of them use *à la* and some use *au*.
- Check that pupils are aware of the reasons each is used, i.e. the concept of masculine and feminine words in French.
- Look again at the places mentioned in Unit 4 and revisit which places were masculine and which were feminine. Encourage pupils to remember this when writing their own sentences i.e. in Activities 5 and 6, and in the worksheets.
- If necessary, colour-code words and phrases to show visually which are talking about masculine and which are talking about feminine places.

5 Literacy activity: Au bord de la mer
5–10 mins   AT3.2 L5.1 L5.2

Materials
Unit 5 Flashcards (Holiday destinations), map of France for extension activity.

Description
Pupils play a game matching place flashcards to sentences.

Delivery
- In advance, write in the left-hand column on the board: *Je vais…* In the right-hand column write:
à la campagne / à la montagne / au bord de la mer / au camping / au parc d'attractions.
- Ask five volunteers to come to the front. Give each of them a flashcard that they don't show anyone. Ask them one by one: *Où vas-tu en vacances?* The pupil draws a line from *Je vais* to the correct end of sentence (as above), then hold up the flashcard.
- Ask the class to confirm if it is correct. Then do an oral ask-and-answer activity with the class, using the flashcards as prompts.

Extension
Recycle previously covered French place names using the map of France. Invite two pupils to the front: Pupil 1 asks *Où vas-tu en vacances?* Pupil 2 points to a place on the map and replies *Je vais à [Paris].*

Worksheet 2: *Grammaire* may be used from this point onwards.

6 Plenary activity: Au parc d'attractions
5–10 mins   AT1.2 O5.1 AT2.2

Materials
Unit 5 Flashcards (Holiday destinations), possibly Unit 4 Flashcards (Places in the town).

Description
A game of charades to revise the vocabulary and structures covered in this lesson.

Delivery
- If necessary, use the flashcards to elicit and review quickly the sentences *Je vais au/à la /à l'…*
- Ask for a pupil volunteer. Give them a flashcard but don't show it to anyone else.
- Encourage the class to chorus *Où vas-tu en vacances?* and the pupil must act out the answer. Pupils guess what the pupil should answer using *Je vais au/à la/à l'…* [+ place].

Worksheet 1: Parlez!
5–10 mins   AT1.2 O5.1 AT2.2

Description
An information-gap activity where pupils ask and answer questions about holiday destinations. It may be used at any point after Activity 4.

Delivery
- Model the first exchange with a confident pupil at the front of the class (you hold Part A; the pupil holds Part B of the sheet).
- Hand out copies of Part A to half the class, and Part B to the others. Pupils work in pairs (A and B) to complete the thought bubbles with the correct destinations.

Answers
Polly:	Je vais au bord de la mer.
Mme Moulin:	Je vais au camping.
Gustave:	Je vais au parc d'attractions.
Olivier:	Je vais à la campagne.
Nathalie:	Je vais à la montagne.
Bof:	Je vais à Paris.

Worksheet 2: Grammaire
10 mins   AT3.2 L5.2 AT4.2–3 L5.3

Description
This worksheet provides further practice in using *au/à la/à l'/à* in sentences. It may be used at any point after Activity 5.

Delivery
- If necessary, model the rules on the board with some places from Unit 4. If you have not already done so, re-visit the concept of masculine and feminine nouns in French and remind pupils that *à* on its own is always used with towns.

Answers
1 à la h	3 au c	5 à la b	7 à l' f
2 à a	4 au g	6 au d	8 au e

Unit 5 — Lesson 2

Lesson summary

Context
Expressing opinions about holidays

National criteria
KS2 Framework: **O5.1, O5.2, O5.3, L5.1, L5.2, L5.3, IU5.2**
Attainment levels: **AT1.2–3, AT2.2–3, AT3.2–3, AT4.2–3**
Language ladder levels:
   Listening: **Grades 2–3**; Speaking: **Grades 2–3**;
   Reading: **Grades 2–3**; Writing: **Grades 2–3**

Cross-curricular links
Literacy, PSHE (Feelings and opinions), geography

Language structures and outcomes
Revised: *J'aime/Je n'aime pas ça.*
J'adore/Je déteste ça.

---

1. Starter: J'aime ça! — 5 mins — AT1.2 O5.1 / AT2.2

Materials
Unit 2 Flashcards (Likes/dislikes) plus additional flashcards, depending on topic selected (see below).

Description
Pupils revise expressing likes/dislikes.

Delivery
- Choose an area for revision (e.g. food, colours, animals, school subjects) and prepare the relevant flashcards.
- Revise expressing likes and dislikes using *J'aime/Je n'aime pas* flashcards.
- Hold up the revision topic cards and ask pupils to say what they like or dislike.

Extension
You could build up to a chain activity where one pupil starts and says one sentence, a second pupil repeats the sentence and adds another, then each subsequent pupil repeats all the previous sentences and adds another. Challenge pupils to see how many sentences they can manage.

2. Animated story: Les vacances (1) — 5–10 mins — AT1.3 O5.2 / AT3.3 O5.3 / L5.1 / IU5.2

Materials
CD-ROM, whiteboard, Unit 2 Flashcards (Likes/dislikes), Unit 5 Flashcards (Holiday destinations).

Description
Watch and listen again to this interactive story presenting the language for Lessons 1 and 2. You can pause and rewind the story at any point, or record your own version too.

Delivery
- Watch the animated story again, this time to focus on the expressions of likes and dislikes.
- Play the story through as far as Didier saying *Je vais au bord de la mer. J'adore ça*. Pause the film, hold up the seaside flashcard, and ask a pupil to select the 'like' or 'dislike' flashcard to represent how Didier feels about the seaside.
- Continue the film, pausing just after each expression of likes and dislikes to use the flashcards as above. Encourage pupils to repeat the expressions.

3. Presentation: Je déteste ça! — 5–10 mins — AT1.2–3 O5.1 / AT2.2–3 O5.2 / AT3.2–3 O5.3 / L5.1

Materials
CD-ROM, whiteboard, Units 2 and 5 Flashcards (Holiday destinations and Likes/dislikes) for extension and support activities.

Description
Tap on the map icons to hear that place being presented and whether the character likes/dislikes it. Use the additional features to practise word classes, or to record your own version of each word.

Delivery
- Each character tells us where they're going and how they feel about their holiday destination. Pupils listen and repeat.
- Continue for all five destinations and repeat if further practice is required. You may want to point out the two different possibilities in pronunciation when saying *Je vais au/ à la...* . Some people make a liaison between the 's' of *Je vais* when it's followed by a vowel, and some don't.

Refer to the Introduction for notes on the *Record* and *Word* features.

Extension
Invite more confident pupils to stand with their backs to the board. After listening to the presentation without looking at the screen, they select the relevant flashcards to illustrate what has just been said.

Support
- You may wish to spend more time explaining the differences between *aime/aime pas* and *adore/déteste* (the former being much milder than the latter).
- Hold up the flashcards in turn and really exaggerate feeling positive or negative as you and the pupils say the words.

4. Oracy activity: Je n'aime pas ça — 10 mins — AT1.2–3 O5.1 / AT2.2–3 O5.2

Materials
Units 2 and 5 Flashcards (Holiday destinations and Likes/dislikes).

Description
Pupils use the flashcards to make sentences expressing opinions about holiday.

Delivery
- Select two groups of pupils (five in one and four in the other). Give pupils in the first group the holiday destinations flashcards, and pupils in the second group the likes/dislikes cards.
- Each group stands in a circle and pupils pass round the cards until a designated pupil shouts *Stop/Arrêtez*.
- At this point, the pupil calls out the names of two pupils, one from each group. Each named pupil holds up their card to say, for example, *Je vais à la montagne* followed by *J'aime ça*.

5. Literacy activity: J'adore ça!
10 mins — AT3.2 L5.2, AT4.2–3

Materials
CD-ROM, whiteboard.

Description
Drag the words into the machine to form a sentence about holiday likes/dislikes. Tap on *Fini* when you have completed each answer, and the machine will illustrate the sentence.

Delivery
- When the pupil is happy with their text they tap on *Fini*.
- Continue until as many variations as possible have been completed.

Extension
- Divide the class into groups and give a piece of blank paper to each group.
- Allow a maximum of two minutes for the groups to compile as many different sentence combinations as possible from the phrases on the board. The winning team is the one with the most correct sentences!

Support
This activity can be done as a whole-class activity: the class suggests what the sentence should be, and discusses their choices if necessary, before the pupil taps on *Fini*.

Worksheets 3: *Écrivez!* and 4: *Lisez!* may be used from this point onwards.

6. Plenary activity: Tu aimes ça?
5–10 mins — AT1.2–3 O5.1, AT2.2–3

Materials
A selection of flashcards from previous topics, e.g. food (Unit 3), colours (**Rigolo 1** Unit 2), animals (**Rigolo 1** Unit 4), school subjects (Unit 2).

Description
Plenary activity to give further practice in expressing opinions.

Delivery
- Distribute a few flashcards to each table/group.
- Pupils take it in turn to hold up a flashcard and express their opinion about that item.
- Move around the group to listen and help where required.

Extension
More confident pupils could link sentences using *et* ('and') or *mais* ('but') to make this activity more challenging.

Worksheet 3: Écrivez!
10 mins — AT4.2–3 L5.2 L5.3

Description
This worksheet provides further writing practice in holiday destinations and opinions. It may be used at any point after Activity 5.

Answers
1. Où vas-tu? Je vais au parc d'attractions. J'aime ça.
2. Où vas-tu? Je vais à la montagne. Je déteste ça.
3. Où vas-tu? Je vais au bord de la mer. J'adore ça.
4. Où vas-tu? Je vais au camping. Je n'aime pas ça.

Worksheet 4: Lisez!
10 mins — AT3.2 L5.1

Description
This worksheet provides further reading practice in holiday destination and opinions. It may be used at any point after Activity 5.

Unit 5 — Lesson 3

Lesson summary

Context
Talking about what you're going to do on holiday.

National criteria
KS2 Framework: **O5.1, O5.2, O5.3, L5.1, L5.2, L5.3, IU5.2**
Attainment levels: **AT1.2–3, AT2.2–3, AT3.2–3, AT4.2–3**
Language ladder levels:
  Listening: **Grades 2–3**; Speaking: **Grades 2–3**;
  Reading: **Grades 2–3**; Writing: **Grades 2–3**

Cross-curricular links
Geography, food technology

Key vocabulary
Je vais faire du bateau. Je vais faire du ski. Je vais nager. Je vais faire du sport. Je vais faire du vélo. Je vais voir mes grands-parents. Je vais faire les manèges.

Language structures and outcomes
Je vais + infinitive expressions

---

1. Starter activity: Je déteste les pommes
⏱ 5 mins — AT1.2–3 O5.1 AT2.2–3

Materials
Units 2 and 5 Flashcards (Likes/dislikes) plus other topic flashcards, e.g. Unit 3 Flashcards (Food).

Description
A class activity with flashcards to revise *J'aime/Je n'aime pas* and *J'adore/Je déteste* with known food items or other word families.

Delivery
- Hold up the opinions flashcards to elicit and practise *J'aime/Je n'aime pas* and *J'adore/Je déteste*.

- Hold up another flashcard with a food or other item and ask a pupil *Tu aimes [les pommes]?* Pupils give their opinion of that item.

- Repeat with further cards/items.

---

2. Animated story: Les vacances (2)
⏱ 10 mins — AT1.3 O5.2, AT3.3 O5.3, L5.1, IU5.2

Materials
CD-ROM, whiteboard, Unit 5 Flashcards (Holiday activities).

Description
Watch and listen to this interactive story presenting the language for Lessons 3 and 4. You can pause and rewind the story at any point, or record your own version too.

Delivery
- Display the flashcards randomly on the board.

- Ask pupils to watch the animation and to note the order in which the various activities are mentioned. They don't need to know or remember the French words for the activities at this stage.

- Play the story through, then ask a few pupils to come to the board and arrange the cards in the order in which the activities are mentioned.

- Play the story through one more time to check/discuss answers.

Support
Pause the video after each activity is mentioned and place the relevant flashcard in order on the board.

---

3. Presentation: Qu'est-ce que tu vas faire?
⏱ 10 mins — AT1.2 O5.1, AT2.2 O5.3, AT3.2

Materials
CD-ROM, whiteboard, possibly Unit 5 Flashcards (Holiday activities).

Description
Tap on the characters to hear what they are going to do on holiday. Use the additional features to practise sound/spelling links and word classes, or to record your own version of each word.

Delivery
- We hear the question *Qu'est-ce que tu vas faire en vacances?* The characters tell us their plans and an appropriate illustration of each activity appears on screen.

- Encourage pupils to repeat both the question and the answer each time, with correct pronunciation.

- Continue for all seven characters and activities, and repeat if further practice is required.

- Ask pupils if they can see a pattern common to all these sentences (*Je vais* + verb). Explain that this is how you say what you're going to do, i.e. talk about future plans.

Refer to the Introduction for notes on the *Record*, *Sound* and *Word* features.

Extension
More confident pupils could take turns to stand at the front with their backs to the board. When the characters say what they are going to do, the pupils must hold up the appropriate flashcards.

Support
Using the flashcards, repeat each part of the presentation to give additional practice. If necessary, split each expression into two parts and practise each part separately before combining the two.

---

4. Oracy activity: Je vais faire du bateau
⏱ 10 mins — AT1.2 O5.1, AT2.2–3 O5.3

Materials
CD-ROM, whiteboard, Unit 5 Flashcards (Holiday destinations) and (Holiday activities) for the support activity.

Description
Tap on *Allez*. Look at the pictures of three different activities and listen to the question. Choose the picture which matches the question and say the correct answer out loud. Then check your answer.

Delivery

- Pupils select the most appropriate activity for the holiday destination asked about and predict the character's answer. Warn them they have to listen really carefully for the destination mentioned in the question. They say the answer out loud before tapping on the audio check button to hear the correct answer.

- Tap on the tick button if their answer is correct or the cross if not.

- Repeat for all six dialogues, and repeat if required.

- This is a good opportunity to focus on pronunciation and compare pupils' pronunciation with that of the characters/Virtual Teacher.

Extension
Pupil can make up their own-mini-dialogues after doing the activity, using the visuals on the whiteboard.

Support
Use the flashcards if further help is required. After each question, display the relevant destination flashcard. Hold up the three activity cards for that question and help pupils say all three sentences before they make their final choice and tap on the screen.

Worksheet 5: *Parlez!* may be used from this point onwards.

Language learning strategies

Applying grammatical knowledge to make sentences

- Explain that the structure *Je vais* + infinitive is used to talk about future plans.

- Brainstorm with the class to find as many verbs as you can, then work together to form sentences about what you're going to do.

- If pupils understand the structure, it will then be easier for them to form their own sentences (as in Activities 5 and 6 and in the worksheets) and to apply this knowledge.

- To practise forming sentences give pupils a starter sentence in which they must change just one word each time, e.g. *Je vais écouter la radio* ➔ *Je vais écouter mes CD*.

5. Literacy activity: Je vais faire du vélo
10 mins — AT3.2 L5.1 / AT4.2 L5.2

Materials
Unit 5 Flashcards (Holiday activities).

Description
Pupils make sentences using *Je vais* + verb/activity.

Delivery
- Hold up the cards one by one to elicit the target sentences.
- Stick a picture flashcard on the board and ask pupils to come to the board and write out the sentence in full.
- You could make this into a team game: ask pupils from alternate teams to write the sentence and award one point for each correct answer.

Extension
Encourage more confident pupils to use other verb phrases already met, e.g. *écouter la radio/jouer au football*.

Support
Use both the text and picture flashcards. Leave all the text cards displayed on the board so less confident pupils can use them as prompts when writing out the sentences.

Worksheet 6: *Grammaire* may be used from this point onwards.

6. Plenary activity: Je vais nager et...
5–10 mins — AT1.2–3 O5.1 / AT2.2–3

Materials
Unit 5 Flashcards (Holiday destinations).

Description
Pupils make cumulative sentences about what they're going to do on holiday.

Delivery
- Quickly revise the activities using the flashcard prompts. Line the picture flashcards up on the board.

- Remind pupils of the words met in Unit 4: *d'abord* ('first of all'), *ensuite* ('then') and *enfin* ('finally').

- Demonstrate how the game works by giving three sample sentences based on the first three cards, e.g. *D'abord, je vais faire du ski. Ensuite, je vais faire les manèges. Enfin, je vais nager*.

- One pupil starts the story with the first sentence. A second pupil continues the story by repeating the first sentence and adding a second sentence. The third pupil repeats the first two sentences before adding a third. Then start a new series of three sentences.

- Repeat if time allows.

Worksheet 5: Parlez!
10 mins — AT2.2 O5.1

Description
This provides further speaking practice of using *Je vais...* to talk about future plans. It may be used at any point after Activity 4.

Delivery
- Pupils write out sentences using the target structure *Je vais* [+ verb]. They can then play a game of pairs with a partner.

- Give a sheet to each pupil; pupils then cut up their own set of cards. You may wish to ask them to stick their worksheet onto a piece of card beforehand, otherwise the cards produced may be too flimsy for the game.

Worksheet 6: Grammaire
10 mins — AT4.2–3 L5.2 L5.3

Description
This provides further practice in using *Je vais...* to talk about future plans. It may be used at any point after Activity 5.

Answers
1
1. Je vais faire du bateau.
2. Je vais faire du sport.
3. Je vais faire du ski.
4. Je vais faire du vélo.
5. Je vais nager.
6. Je vais faire les manèges.
7. Je vais voir mes grands-parents.

Unit 5 (Lesson 4)

Lesson summary

Context
Talking about holiday plans (consolidation).

National criteria:
KS2 Framework: O5.1, O5.2, O5.3, O5.4, L5.1, L5.2, L5.3, IU5.1, IU5.2
Attainment levels: AT1.2–3, AT2.2–3, AT3.2–3, AT4.2–3
Language ladder levels:
   Listening: **Grades 2–3**; Speaking: **Grades 2–3**;
   Reading: **Grades 2–3**; Writing: **Grades 2–3**

Cross-curricular links
Geography, literacy

Language structures and outcomes
Revision: *Je vais* [+ holiday destinations]
Je vais [+ verb/activity]
J'adore ça, etc.

---

1. Starter activity: *C'est où en France?* — 5–10 mins — AT1.2–3 O5.1 / AT2.2–3 O5.3

Materials
Map of France, Unit 5 Flashcards (Holiday destinations and activities).

Description
Pupils identify the different regions of France (e.g. mountain regions, beaches) and talk about the various activities we can do in these places.

Delivery
- Hold up the holiday destinations picture cards and ask pupils to identify where these places might be found in France.
- Invite pupils to stick the cards on the map.
- Do the same with the activity cards: ask where pupils think they could do these activities.

NB: there are, of course, multiple possible answers so you may wish to focus mainly on towns/places you have already covered to avoid the discussion becoming too wide!

2. Animated story: *Les vacances (2)* — 5–10 mins — AT1.3 O5.2 / AT3.3 O5.3 / L5.1 / IU5.2

Materials
CD-ROM, whiteboard.

Description
Watch and listen again to this interactive story presenting the language for Lessons 3 and 4. You can pause and rewind the story at any point, or record your own version, too.

Delivery
- Watch the animation again, this time to focus on the opinions expressed by the characters.
- Play through both parts of the animated story for this unit.
- Pause the story after each opinion and ask pupils to repeat what they have just heard, indicating with a 'thumbs up' or a 'thumbs down' gesture whether the opinion is positive or negative.

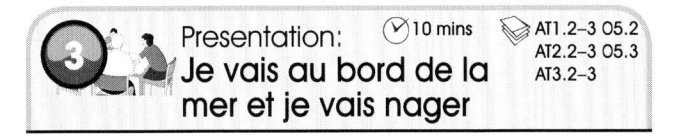

3. Presentation: *Je vais au bord de la mer et je vais nager* — 10 mins — AT1.2–3 O5.2 / AT2.2–3 O5.3 / AT3.2–3

Materials
Unit 5 Flashcards (Holiday destinations and activities).

Description
A teacher-led presentation of holiday plans and opinions.

Delivery
- Display the place flashcards in a row on the board and display the activity cards underneath.
- Select a card from each row and model sentences using *Je vais à* [+ place] and *Je vais* [+ verb], joining them up with *et*, e.g. *Je vais au bord de la mer et je vais nager*. Pupils listen and repeat.
- Continue making sentence pairs until you have used all the cards.

Extension
If pupils are coping well at this stage, you may wish to introduce other places and activities covered in previous units.

Support
Use the text flashcards to give further prompts to less confident pupils.

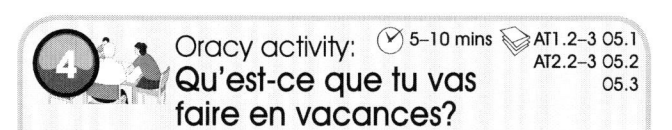

4. Oracy activity: *Qu'est-ce que tu vas faire en vacances?* — 5–10 mins — AT1.2–3 O5.1 / AT2.2–3 O5.2 / O5.3

Materials
Unit 5 Flashcards (Holiday destinations and activities).

Description
A class activity practising compound sentences about holiday plans.

Delivery
- Display the cards on the board. Model the activity with a pupil at the front: ask the pupil *Qu'est-ce que tu vas faire en vacances?* Then ask them to select two cards, then to say where they are going and what they are going to do.
- Repeat a few times with different pupils.
- Hand out a selection flashcards to each table. Pupils continue the role-play in pairs whilst you move around the class and monitor the activity.
- Worksheet 7: *Lisez!* may be used from this point onwards.

Extension
More confident pupils could add an additional sentence to express their opinion about their holiday, e.g. *J'adore ça, J'aime ça*, etc.

Unit 5: Lesson 4

5. Literacy activity: Je vais au camping. J'aime ça
⏱ 10 mins — AT3.3 L5.2, AT4.3

Materials
CD-ROM, whiteboard.

Description
Tap on *Allez*. Look at the symbols in each character's speech bubble. Read the text options at the bottom of the screen and drag the text into the correct order to match the symbols.

Delivery
- This activity provides practice in forming longer sentences. Pupils drag the relevant text into the correct order and press *Fini* when they have finished. The character will read out the complete statement if it is correct. If the statement is wrong, a 'life' will be lost and pupils can try again.

- The game ends when all six compound sentences/ statements have been completed, or if all three 'lives' are lost. Pupils are invited to start another game if they wish.

- Worksheet 8: *Écrivez!* may be used from this point onwards.

Extension
Encourage pupils to make their own longer sentences from flashcard prompts, and to use language from previous units.

Support
You could do the activity as a whole class. Alternatively, as a team activity, two or three pupils at a time could go to the board and make the sentence.

6. Plenary activity: Le jeu des vacances
⏱ 10 mins — AT1.2–3 O5.1, AT2.2–3

Materials
Draughts boards, counters and dice, sets of Unit 5 Flashcards (Holiday destinations and activities).

Description
Board game to give pupils further practice in making sentences about holiday plans.

Delivery
- Give out a set of the above materials to each table/group.

- Each group divides their flashcards into two piles: 'dark' (destinations) and 'light' (activities).

- Move the counters around the board according to the roll of the dice (say the numbers in French). When their counter lands on a square, pupils must say a sentence from the corresponding flashcard pile.

- If they say it correctly they stay on that square. If it's not correct, they go back to where they were.

Extension
Include places and activities from previous units.

Worksheet 7: Lisez!
⏱ 10 mins — AT3.3 O5.1, AT4.2–3 L5.1, L5.3

Description
This worksheet provides practice in reading longer texts. It may be used at any point after Activity 4.

Answers
Bof: j (seaside) h swimming e (boat) b (*j'adore*)
Polly: i (theme park) f (rollercoaster) c (*j'aime*)
Gustave: a (mountains) g (skiing) d (*je déteste*)

Worksheet 8: Écrivez!
⏱ 10 mins — AT2.3 L5.1, AT3.3 L5.2, AT4.3 L5.3

Description
This worksheet provides practice in writing about travel plans. It may be used at any point after Activity 5.

Answers
1. Je vais à Nice.
2. Je vais au bord de la mer et je vais nager.
3. Ensuite, je vais à Strasbourg.
4. Je vais à la campagne et je vais faire du vélo.
5. Ensuite, je vais à Grenoble.
6. Je vais à la montagne et je vais faire du ski.
7. Ensuite, je vais à Paris.
8. Je vais faire les manèges et je vais voir mes grands-parents.

Intercultural understanding

- The project on French theme parks gives an opportunity to compare them with theme parks pupils have visited in their own country. Use their internet research to discuss similarities/differences between French theme parks and those in the UK. What sort of rides do they have? What sort of eating places are there? What languages are spoken? What facilities are there for disabled people? What rides are there for younger children?

- Also encourage pupils to download/send for theme park brochures, to encourage them to read some authentic texts and then to use a dictionary to find out some key words.

Project work: Un parc d'attractions en France
⏱ 1–2 hours — AT2.2–3 O5.2, AT3.2–3 O5.4, AT4.2–3 L5.1, L5.2 L5.3, IU5.1 IU5.2

Description
Pupils find out about theme parks in France and prepare a short presentation.

Materials
Internet access and printer if possible, card and paper to display the pictures and text in the classroom.

Delivery
- In small groups, pupils research a theme park in France, e.g. Parc Astérix, Disneyland Paris, Parc du Futuroscope.

- Ask each group to find out where the park is and what sort of rides/activities there are. How much does it cost? Would they like to go there? Why? Why not?

- Each group compiles a basic display with some key information in French, e.g. location, activities, the group's opinion about the park. Pupils then present the information to the rest of the class.

Rigolo 2 — Unit 6: Chez moi

National criteria

KS2 Framework objectives

O5.1 Prepare and practise a simple conversation, re-using familiar vocabulary and structures in new contexts
O5.2 Understand and express simple opinions
O5.3 Listen attentively and understand more complex phrases and sentences
O5.4 Prepare a short presentation on a familiar topic
L5.1 Re-read frequently a variety of short texts
L5.2 Make simple sentences and short texts
L5.3 Write words, phrases and short sentences, using a reference source
IU5.2 Recognise similarities and differences between places
IU5.3 Compare symbols, objects or products which represent their own culture with those of another country

QCA Scheme of Work

Unit 16 Scène de plage
Unit 18 Les planètes

National Curriculum attainment levels

AT1.1–3, AT2.1–3, AT3.1–3, AT4.1–3

Language ladder levels

Listening: Breakthrough, Grades 1–3
Reading: Breakthrough, Grades 1–3
Speaking: Breakthrough, Grades 1–3
Writing: Breakthrough, Grades 1–3

5–14 guideline strands   Levels A–C

Listening
Listening for information and instructions   A, B, C
Listening and reacting to others   A, B, C

Speaking
Speaking to convey information   A, B, C, D
Speaking and interacting with others   A, B, C, D
Speaking about experiences, feelings and opinions   A, B, C

Speaking
Reading for information and instructions   A, B, C
Reading aloud   A, B, C

Writing
Writing to exchange information and ideas   A, B, C, D
Writing to establish and maintain personal contact   A, B
Writing imaginatively to entertain   A, B, C

Unit objectives

- Name rooms in the house
- Describe rooms in the house
- Say what people do at home
- Say what people do and where

Key language

- *Chez moi, il y a une salle de bains/une cuisine/une salle à manger/des WC/un salon/un balcon/un jardin/deux chambres*
- *C'est grand/petit/vert/blanc/bleu/jaune/rose/rouge*
  C'est petit et rouge
- *Qu'est-ce qu'il/elle fait? Il/Elle mange [un sandwich]/ regarde la télé/écoute de la musique/lit [un livre]/joue avec l'ordinateur/joue au tennis...*
- Activities as above + *dans le salon/les WC*, etc.

Grammar and skills

- Use *il y a* [+ indefinite article]
- Prepare a short presentation
- Use *c'est* [+ adjective]
- Join sentences with *et*
- Practise new language with a friend
- Use 3rd person verbs
- Manipulate language by changing an element in a sentence
- Use and understand both the definite and indefinite articles
- Make longer sentences

Unit outcomes

Most children will be able to:

- Name places in a home
- Give simple descriptions using *c'est* [+ adjective]
- List some activities using *il* and *elle*

Some children will also be able to:

- Use definite and indefinite articles correctly
- Join sentences with *et*
- Adapt sentences by changing elements
- Make longer sentences

Rigolo 2 Teacher's Notes © Nelson Thornes Ltd 2008

Unit 6 — Lesson 1

Lesson summary

Context
Rooms (places) in the house

National criteria
KS2 Framework: **O5.1, O5.2, O5.3, L5.1, L5.3, IU5.2, IU5.3**
Attainment levels: **AT1.1–3, AT2.1–2, AT3.1–3, AT4.1–2**
Language ladder levels:
  Listening: **Grades 1–3**; Speaking: **Grades 1–2**;
  Reading: **Grades 1–3**; Writing: **Grades 1–2**

Cross-curricular links
ICT (designing ideal house), geography (buildings in town), numeracy

Key vocabulary
une salle de bains, une cuisine, une salle à manger, des WC, un salon, un balcon, un jardin, une chambre, deux/trois/quatre chambres

Language structures and outcomes
Chez moi, il y a...

---

1. Starter activity: Un, deux, trois (5 mins) — AT1.1 O5.1, AT2.1, AT3.1

Materials
CD-ROM, whiteboard.

Description
A quick revision of low numbers, using a presentation from *Rigolo 1* (Unit 1, Lesson 5).

Delivery
Go through the above activity, or play another quick number game to refresh pupils' memory of low numbers.

Intercultural understanding

- Use the videos in this unit to look at similarities and differences between homes in France and in the UK. Ask pupils to look at the details of the rooms in the video and the accommodation features, and to note anything that looks different. Point out that many families live in flats in France whereas relatively few families do so in the UK. Encourage pupils to look at details of windows, doors, furniture, décor, colours, etc.

- The project at the end of the unit offers pupils the opportunity to do further research on the internet about French homes and to present their findings. If you have any French contacts, ask them to send you pictures and magazine pages showing houses, flats and rooms in the house so that you can use them throughout the unit.

2. Video story: Venez chez moi (1) (10 mins) — AT1.2–3 O5.2, AT3.2–3 O5.3, L5.1, IU5.2 IU5.3

Materials
CD-ROM, whiteboard.

Description
Watch and listen to this video story presenting the language for Lessons 1 and 2. You can pause and rewind the story at any point.

Delivery
Explain that the context is going to be rooms in the house, and that pupils will have a guided tour of Thomas's home. Ask pupils to listen and see how many different rooms are mentioned. Can they pick out any French words for the rooms? Ask them to look at the rooms in this French home and note anything which interests them.

Support
- Remind pupils not to worry about understanding everything that is said in the video at this stage, and that they will cover all the language in more detail throughout this lesson.

- You may wish to replay the video line by line at the end of the lesson, before letting pupils view it all the way through again.

3. Presentation: Qu'est-ce qu'il y a? (10 mins) — AT1.2 O5.1, AT2.2 O5.3, AT3.2

Materials
CD-ROM, whiteboard.

Description
Tap on the windows to hear the words for the different places in the château, with *il y a*. Use the additional features to practise sound/spelling links, word classes and spelling, or to record your own version of each word.

Delivery
- The whole class listens to the presentation of each room and repeats.

- Continue for all eight places and repeat if further practice is required.

Refer to the Introduction for notes on the *Record*, *Spell*, *Sound* and *Word* features.

Support
Use Unit 6 Flashcards (Rooms/places in the home) for further practice of the rooms.

4. Oracy activity: Il y a un salon (5–10 mins) — AT1.1–2 O5.3, AT2.1–2

Materials
CD-ROM, whiteboard, possibly Unit 6 Flashcards (Rooms/places in the home).

Description
Tap on *Allez*. Listen to the audio and tap on the correct picture for each place in the home.

---

56 — Rigolo 2 Teacher's Notes © Nelson Thornes Ltd 2008

Delivery

- We hear a place in the château being introduced, and the pupil taps on the relevant picture.

- The picture will become animated and the Virtual Teacher will congratulate the pupil if the selection is correct. Otherwise, the pupil will be invited to try again.

- Tap on *Allez* to go on to the next question.

- Continue for all eight places and repeat if further practice is needed.

- The last two items mention two different places so make sure the pupil taps both places.

Extension
Make this into a competitive game for more confident pupils: invite two pupils up to the board at a time; when they hear the audio prompt they race to be the first to tap on the correct picture.

Support
Encourage less confident pupils to use the *Encore* button as much as necessary. You could also display the picture and text flashcards during the activity as additional prompts.

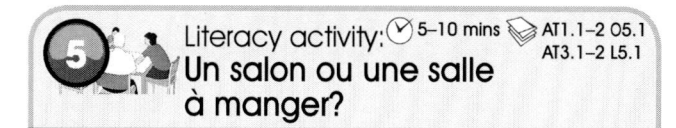

5. Literacy activity: Un salon ou une salle à manger? (5–10 mins, AT1.1–2 O5.1, AT3.1–2 L5.1)

Materials
Unit 6 Flashcards (Rooms/places in the home).

Description
Pupils play a game matching words to pictures flashcards.

Delivery
- Display the places flashcards on the board: captions on one side and pictures on the other.

- Call out one of the places, holding the relevant card, and ask a pupil to come to the board and select the corresponding word card.

- Repeat for all eight places.

- You could make this into a team game by dividing the class into two teams: invite pupils from alternate teams to match the cards and award one point for each correct pair.

Extension
More confident pupils could play this game in small groups: give out to each group/table a set of small symbols representing each room, with separate captions. On your signal, groups race to be the first to match up the set of words and pictures.

Worksheets 1: *Lisez!* and 2: *Écrivez!* may be used from this point onwards.

6. Plenary activity: Les maisons en France et en Grande-Bretagne (5–10 mins, AT1.2–3 O5.3, AT3.2–3 L5.1, IU5.2, IU5.3)

Materials
CD-ROM, whiteboard, possibly Unit 6 Flashcards (Rooms/places in the home).

Description
Discussion of differences and similarities between homes in France and the UK.

Delivery
- Show Part 1 of the *Venez chez moi* video again (see Activity 2 above), but this time concentrate on differences between the home they see in France and what they might see in the UK.

- Before showing the film again, ask pupils how many live in a house and how many in a flat. Explain that most French people living in towns (not just major cities) live in flats.

- Play the video, pausing several times to enable pupils to comment on any differences they notice. Possible differences could include the entrance to the flats, the flooring, the décor, the windows, separate toilet, style and size of kitchen.

- Re-play the whole video without stopping for pupils to enjoy.

Worksheet 1: Lisez! (5–10 mins, AT3.2 L5.1)

Description
This provides further reading practice of places in the home. It may be used at any point after Activity 5.

Answers
1   1 b   2 c   3 a

2   Plan can be set out in various different ways but must show: living room, kitchen, dining room, two bathrooms, four bedrooms, two balconies and a garage.

Worksheet 2: Écrivez! (10 mins, AT4.1–2 L5.3)

Description
This provides further writing practice of places in the home. It may be used at any point after Activity 5.

Delivery
If time allows, invite pupils to make a short oral presentation of the home they have drawn in Activity 2.

Unit 6 — Lesson 2

Lesson summary

Context
Descriptions of rooms (colour and size)

National criteria
KS2 Framework: **O5.1, O5.2, O5.3, O5.4, L5.1, L5.2, L5.3, IU5.2, IU5.3**
Attainment levels: **AT1.1–3, AT2.1–3, AT3.2–3, AT4.2–3**
Language ladder levels:
  Listening: **Grades 1–3**; Speaking: **Grades 1–3**;
  Reading: **Grades 2–3**; Writing: **Grades 2–3**

Cross-curricular links
Geography

Key vocabulary
C'est grand/petit/vert/blanc/bleu/jaune/rose/rouge
C'est petit et rouge

Language structures and outcomes
C'est [+ adjective]. Use of *et*

---

1. Starter activity: C'est quelle couleur? (5 mins) — AT1.1–2 O5.1, AT2.1–2 O5.3

Materials
Rigolo 1 Unit 2 Flashcards (Colours).

Description
Quick oral revision of colour adjectives using *Rigolo 1* flashcards.

Delivery
- Hold up the flashcards and elicit the colours.
- Ask pupils to come to the front and say to each one, e.g. *Trouve-moi quelque chose de la couleur [bleu]*. Pupils then point to something in the classroom of that colour.

2. Video story: Venez chez moi (1) (5–10 mins) — AT1.2–3 O5.2, AT3.2–3 O5.3, L5.1, IU5.2, IU5.3

Materials
CD-ROM, whiteboard, Unit 6 Flashcards (Rooms/places in the home), *Rigolo 1* Unit 2 Flashcards (Colours) and Unit 4 Flashcards (*grand/petit*).

Description
Watch and listen again to this video story presenting the language for Lessons 1 and 2. You can pause and rewind the story at any point.

Delivery
- Re-play the video presenting the places in the home, this time to focus on the room descriptions.
- Using the flashcards (see above), quickly revise the places in the home.
- Stick all the flashcards on the board: the rooms on one side, the adjectives on the other.
- Play the video through until just after the first room description. Pause it and ask a pupil to come to the board to draw a line between that room and any adjectives used to describe it.
- Continue for all the rooms.
- Play the film through one more time, without pausing.

3. Presentation: C'est comment? (5–10 mins) — AT1.2 O5.1, AT2.2 O5.2, AT3.2

Materials
CD-ROM, whiteboard, flashcards (see Activity 2 above) for support activity.

Description
Tap on the rooms to hear a description of each. Use the additional features to practise sound/spelling links and word classes, or to record your own version of each word.

Delivery
- This presents simple descriptions with *c'est* (avoiding agreement of adjectives). Draw attention to *et* and its meaning.
- We hear M. Chanson describing the room. Mme Chanson then repeats his description and adds an additional description.
- Pupils repeat both descriptions.
- Continue for all six rooms and repeat if further practice is required.

Refer to the Introduction for notes on the *Record, Sound* and *Word* features.

Extension
Encourage pupils to join sentences with *et* in future lessons.

Support
In order to check and reinforce comprehension, ask pupils to hold up the relevant flashcards after each room description.

4. Oracy activity: C'est grand et vert (10 mins) — AT1.2 O5.2, AT2.2 O5.3

Materials
Unit 6 Flashcards (Rooms/places in home), magazine pictures of rooms in the home for the extension activity.

Description
Pupils use the target language to describe the places depicted on the flashcards.

Delivery
- Model the activity by holding up a card and describing the picture, e.g. *C'est grand/petit. C'est [rose]*.
- Hand out a set of magazine pictures of rooms to each group. The pictures are placed face down in the middle. Pupils take turns to turn over a card and describe that room.

Extension
Ask more confident pupils to make up longer descriptions, e.g. *Il y a un salon. C'est grand et jaune.*

📄 Worksheet 3: *Parlez!* may be used from this point onwards

5 — Literacy activity: C'est petit et jaune
⏱ 10 mins 📚 AT3.2 L5.2 / AT4.2

Materials
CD-ROM, whiteboard.

Description
Tap on *Allez*. Look at the room and the symbols in each. Read the text options at the bottom of the screen. Drag the text into the correct order.

Delivery
- This activity gives pupils practice in forming sentences with two adjectives using *et*.
- Pupils drag the text into the correct order to make a sentence which describes the room.
- Tap on *Fini* to see if the sentence is correct.
- The room becomes animated if the answer is right.
- One of three 'lives' is lost for each incorrect answer. If three 'lives' are lost pupils are invited to start a new game.
- Continue until all six rooms have been covered, and repeat if necessary.

Support
If pupils are not confident about sentence-building this activity can be done as a whole-class activity: the class suggests what the sentence should be (and discusses their choices if necessary) before the pupil taps on *Fini*.

📄 Worksheet 4: *Grammaire* may be used from this point onwards.

6 — Plenary activity: C'est petit et bleu
⏱ 5–10 mins 📚 AT1.2 O5.1 / AT2.1–2 O5.3

Materials
Unit 6 Flashcards (Rooms/places in the home), additional pictures of rooms in the home for the Extension activity.

Description
Pupils identify the room being described by the teacher.

Delivery
- Divide the class into two teams. Display the flashcards on the board.
- Call out a description of one of the rooms, e.g. *C'est petit et jaune.*
- The first team to shout out the correct room in French wins a point.
- Continue for all the rooms.

Extension
If you have additional large pictures of rooms in the home, display these on the board to make the game more challenging for confident groups.

Support
Invite a representative from each team to stand by the board (choose different pupils for each 'round'). The first pupil to touch the correct picture wins a point for their team.

Worksheet 3: Parlez!
⏱ 10 mins 📚 AT1.2–3 O5.1 / AT2.2–3 O5.2 / O5.3

Description
This worksheet provides further speaking practice in descriptions of rooms. It may be used at any point after Activity 4.

Delivery
This is an information gap activity, in pairs: hand out sheet A to half the class and sheet B to the other half. Pupils must not show their sheet to their partner!

Answers

pink and green bedroom	small yellow dining room	blue and green living room
blue and yellow bathroom	large red bedroom	pink and white kitchen

Language learning strategies

Practise new language with a friend or someone out of the classroom

- Use Activities 2 and 3 from Worksheet 4: *Grammaire* to encourage pupils to practise their new language with a friend. Before they give their presentation in Activity 3 to the rest of the class, encourage them to practise it with their partner or someone at home. They should ask the person listening how it comes across and ask for constructive criticism, e.g. Is my speech clear? Can you hear every word? Is my accent good? Do I speak with expression?

- Encourage pupils to take their French out of the classroom whenever they can, e.g. adapting/performing a song for someone, practising a conversation for homework, asking a parent to listen to a presentation. It will help pupils learn the language and remember the words and phrases.

Worksheet 4: Grammaire
⏱ 10–15 mins 📚 AT2.2–3 O5.4 / AT3.2–3 L5.1 / AT4.2–3 L5.3

Description
This worksheet provides further writing practice in descriptions of rooms. It may be used at any point after Activity 5.

Unit 6 (Lesson 3)

Lesson summary

Context
Saying what people do at home

National criteria
KS2 Framework: O5.1, O5.3, L5.1, L5.2, L5.3, IU5.2, IU5.3
Attainment levels: AT1.2–3, AT2.2–3, AT3.2–3, AT4.2–3
Language ladder levels:
  Listening: **Grades 2–3**; Speaking: **Grades 2–3**;
  Reading: **Grades 2–3**; Writing: **Grades 2–3**

Cross-curricular links
Geography, literacy, drama

Language structures and outcomes
Qu'est-ce qu'il/elle fait? Il/Elle mange [un sandwich]/ regarde la télé/écoute de la musique/lit [un livre]/joue avec l'ordinateur/joue au tennis

---

1 Starter activity: Je regarde la télé
5–10 mins — AT1.2 O5.1, AT2.2

Materials
Rigolo 1 Unit 8 Flashcards (Leisure activities) and Unit 11 Flashcards (Party activities).

Description
Quick revision of verbs covered in *Rigolo 1* using flashcards.

Delivery
- Hold up the flashcards one by one to elicit the various verbs.
- Remind pupils about the difference between *je danse* and *on danse*; make sure they understand the pronouns *je* ('I') and *on* ('we').
- Stick the cards on the board. Divide the class into two teams and invite two pupils (one from each team) to the front. Call out an action; pupils race to be the first to touch the correct card. Continue with different pupils until you have covered all the verbs on the cards.

2 Video story: Venez chez moi (2)
10 mins — AT1.3 O5.3, AT3.3 L5.1, IU5.2, IU5.3

Materials
CD-ROM, whiteboard, Unit 6 Flashcards (Activities in the home).

Description
Watch and listen to this video story presenting the language for Lessons 3 and 4. You can pause and rewind the story at any point.

Delivery
- Watch the second part of the video story, which presents the various activities taking place in different parts of the home.
- Ask pupils to watch the video and to note which activities are mentioned.
- Play the video through and elicit pupils' answers.
- Ask pupils to look out for any similarities they notice between French homes and British ones.

Support
- Pause the video during the first viewing after each action is mentioned. Ask pupils to identify the relevant flashcard on the board and circle it.

3 Presentation: Qu'est-ce qu'il fait?
10 mins — AT1.2 O5.1, AT2.2 O5.3, AT3.2

Materials
CD-ROM, whiteboard, Unit 6 Flashcards (Activities in the home) for Extension and Support activities.

Description
Tap on a character to hear what they are doing. Use the additional features to practise sound/spelling links and word classes, or to record your own version of each word.

Delivery
- We hear what the characters are doing using the *il/elle* (3rd person form).
- The whole class repeats each answer, copying the gestures where appropriate.
- Draw pupils' attention to the meaning and distinct pronunciation of the pronouns *il* ('he') and *elle* ('she').
- Continue for all six characters and repeat if further practice is required.

Refer to the Introduction for notes on the *Record*, *Sound* and *Word* features.

Extension
- More confident pupils could take turns to stand at the front with their backs to the board. When they hear what the characters are doing, they hold up the appropriate flashcards.
- Encourage early application of the patterns in these verb structures so pupils can produce alternative sentences e.g. *Il mange une pizza*.

Support
Stick all the relevant verb flashcards (words and pictures) on the board. After each presentation, ask pupils to come and hold up the relevant flashcards, then ask the whole class to repeat the sentence.

4 Oracy activity: Il regarde la télé
10 mins — AT1.2 O5.1, AT2.2–3

Materials
CD-ROM, whiteboard, Unit 6 Flashcards (Activities in the home) for Support activity.

Description
Tap on *Allez*. Look at the highlighted character. Listen to the question and say the answer out loud. Then check your answer.

Delivery
- Pupils say out loud what each character is doing e.g. *Il lit… Il lit un livre*. Tap on the audio check button to compare the answer. Focus pupils on accurate pronunciation of the answers and correct usage of *il* and *elle*.
- Repeat for all six characters and repeat if required.
- By dividing the class into two groups you could make this into a team game, awarding a point for each correct answer.

Support
If further reinforcement is required, ask pupils to come and hold up the relevant flashcards after each dialogue and ask the whole class to repeat both sentences each time.

Worksheet 5: *Grammaire* may be used from this point onwards.

Knowledge about language

Manipulate language by changing an element in a sentence

- It is important, even at primary level, that pupils do not learn the language as static phrases. They need to realise that language is flexible and they can use patterns and change elements within a sentence to say different things. In this way, they can take more control of their language learning by working out how to say things rather than simply learning set phrases.

- Once they understand the structure, they can re-use known language in different situations: the verb phrases in this lesson are particularly useful in this respect. In Activity 5 (see below) pupils are encouraged to change just one element: the pronoun, the verb or the noun. Do a few examples on the board to demonstrate this, e.g. *Elle lit un livre* could change to *Il lit un livre, Elle lit un magazine* or *Elle lit une lettre*, etc.

5. Literacy activity: Il regarde un DVD
10 mins — AT3.3 L5.2, AT4.3 L5.3

Materials
Unit 6 Flashcards (Activities in the home – pictures and text).

Description
Pupils use key structures to create new sentences.

Delivery
- Display the flashcard captions on the board. Focus on one sentence, e.g. *Elle mange un sandwich*. Illustrate how you can change an element to mean something very different without changing the pattern, e.g. *Il mange une pizza*.
- Encourage pupils to make further suggestions. Accept even bizarre sentences as long as they are correct, e.g. *Il mange un ordinateur*.
- You could make this into a team game: allow up to five minutes for teams to create as many new sentences as possible using the models on the board, and any words covered in this and other lessons. Check through the answers at the end: the team with the most correct sentences wins.

Extension
Encourage pupils to write up 10 sentences of their own.

Support
Provide some alternative words on the board for pupils.

Worksheet 6: *Lisez!* may be used from this point onwards

6. Plenary activity: Les charades
5 mins — AT2.2 O5.1, AT3.2 L5.1

Materials
Unit 6 Flashcards (Activities in the home).

Description
A game of charades to revise the verbs and pronouns covered in this lesson.

Delivery
- Ask for a volunteer to come to the front. Show them a flashcard depicting an activity that they must mime.
- The rest of the class must correctly describe what the pupil is doing, including using the correct pronoun.
- When the correct answer has been called out, another volunteer comes to the front to mime the next action. Continue for all five activities.

Worksheet 5: Grammaire
10 mins — AT4.2–3 L5.2 L5.3

Description
This worksheet provides further practice in 3rd person verbs. It may be used at any point after Activity 4.

Answers
1
1. Qu'est-ce qu'il fait?
2. Qu'est-ce qu'elle fait?
3. Qu'est-ce qu'il fait?
4. Qu'est-ce qu'elle fait?
5. Qu'est-ce qu'il fait?
6. Qu'est-ce qu'elle fait?

2
1. Il regarde la télé.
2. Elle lit un livre.
3. Il joue avec l'ordinateur.
4. Elle mange une pizza.
5. Il écoute de la musique.
6. Elle mange un sandwich.

Worksheet 6: Lisez!
10 mins — AT3.2–3 L5.1

Description
This worksheet provides further practice in 3rd person verbs. It may be used at any point after Activity 5.

Delivery
Pupils read sentences, including some unknown words, and match them to the correct pictures. This provides good practice in working out the meaning of some unknown words from the context and visual clues.

Answers
1
| 1h | 3i | 5b | 7a | 9f |
| 2j | 4g | 6d | 8c | 10e |

2
1. un magazine
2. un concert
3. avec
4. un journal
5. (un père noël en) chocolat
6. un œuf de Pâques
7. un ballon

3 Pictures need to show:
1. female eating an apple
2. male listening to a CD
3. female playing with Jake
4. male looking at Bof

Unit 6 — Lesson 4

Lesson summary

Context
Saying what people do and where

National criteria
KS2 Framework: **O5.1, O5.2, O5.3, O5.4, L5.1, L5.2, L5.3, IU5.2, IU5.3**
Attainment levels: **AT1.2–3, AT2.2–3, AT3.2–3, AT4.2–3**
Language ladder levels:
  Listening: **Grades 2–3**; Speaking: **Grades 2–3**;
  Reading: **Grades 2–3**; Writing: **Grades 2–3**

Cross-curricular links
ICT (construct model or plan of ideal dwelling), geography, design, literacy, music

Language structures and outcomes
Qu'est-ce qu'il/elle fait? Il/Elle mange [un sandwich]/ regarde la télé/écoute de la musique/lit [un livre]/joue avec l'ordinateur/joue au tennis...
... dans [le salon]

Knowledge about language

Apply knowledge of rules when building sentences
- This lesson is a good place to establish the relationship between and revise the meaning of *le/la/les* and *un/une/des* (see Activity 1 below for details).

- Many pupils need to be reminded of the meaning and usage of these words. Draw up a table (see below) on the whiteboard and colour code according to masculine and feminine articles.

- Make a version of the table to display on the wall as a reference and reminder. By this stage you would like pupils to be able to start manipulating language, so if they have learned, e.g. *une cuisine*, they can say, *Je mange une pizza dans la cuisine*.

	masculine	feminine	plural
'the'	le (or l')	la (or l')	les
'a' or 'some'	un	une	des

1. Starter activity: *Un salon – le salon* ⏱ 5–10 mins AT1.2 O5.1 / AT2.2

Materials
Unit 6 Flashcards (Rooms/places in the home).

Description
Pupils learn the connection between *un* and *le*, and *une* and *la*.

Delivery
- Hold up a flashcard and ask *Qu'est-ce que c'est?* to elicit, e.g. *C'est un salon*. Continue in the same way with all the cards.

- Go back to the first card and say, e.g. *C'est **un** salon. Je regarde la télé dans **le** salon*.

- Write up the sentence on the board and circle *un* and *le*.

- Do another example with, e.g. *la cuisine* to illustrate the feminine equivalent.

- Ask pupils to tell you what rules/patterns they can see, and check that they understand which one means 'a' and which means 'the'.

2. Video story: *Venez chez moi (2)* ⏱ 5–10 mins AT1.3 O5.3 / AT3.3 L5.1 / IU5.2 / IU5.3

Description
Watch and listen again to this video story presenting the language for Lessons 3 and 4. You can pause and rewind the story at any point.

Delivery
- Re-play the video, this time to focus on the use of articles in the dialogue.

- Ask pupils to watch the video and listen out in particular for which words have *un/le* and which have *une/la*.

- Write answers on the board and play the story through one more time for pupils to double-check their answers.

Extension
Ask more confident pupils to include sentences about what each character is doing and where.

Support
Write the key nouns (without articles) on the board before viewing so that pupils can concentrate on listening for the articles.

3. Presentation: *Dans le salon* ⏱ 10–15 mins AT1.3 O5.1 / AT2.3 O5.3 / AT3.3

Materials
CD-ROM, whiteboard, possibly Unit 6 Flashcards (Rooms/places in the home and Activities in the home) for the Support and Extension activities.

Description
Tap on the windows to hear what the characters are doing and where. Use the additional features to practise sound/spelling links and word classes, or to record your own version of each word.

Delivery
- The aim of this lesson is to adapt known language in order to produce and understand longer sentences.

- We hear the question, *Qu'est-ce qu'il/elle fait?* and answers about what each character is doing and where they are. Pupils listen and repeat, copying any gestures to reinforce the language.

- Continue for all six places and repeat if necessary.

Refer to the Introduction for notes on the *Record*, *Sound* and *Word* features.

Unit 6: Lesson 4

Extension
Use the flashcards to practise putting different together combinations of rooms and activities.

Support
Break the longer sentences into two halves if necessary and give further practice with the flashcards.

4. Literacy activity: Qu'est-ce qu'elle fait, Polly?
10 mins — AT3.2–3 L5.2

Materials
CD-ROM, whiteboard; for pre-activity, character flashcards from **Rigolo 1** (Unit 1: Polly, Jake, Bof, Nathalie, Didier, M. Mills, Mme Moulin; Unit 4: Mme Chanson; Unit 7: Olivier, Nathalie, Marine, Bernard; Unit 8: M. Mills; Unit 11: Mme Mills) and **Rigolo 2** (Unit 1: Gustave); plus Unit 6 Flashcards (Rooms/places in the home and Activities in the home).

Description
Tap on *Allez*. Read the description. Look at the symbol options on the left of the screen. Drag the three correct symbols to the blank boxes at the bottom of the screen to match the description.

Delivery
- As a pre-activity, use the flashcards and the presentation screen to practise activities + locations. Ask, e.g. *Qu'est-ce qu'elle fait, Polly?* Build up to the full answer: *Elle regarde… un DVD… dans le salon.*
- Pupils drag three symbols into the correct order to match the description, starting with a male/female symbol according to whether they hear *il* or *elle*, and press *Fini* when they have finished.
- The character will read out the sentence if it is correct.
- Continue for all six sentences.

Extension
After doing the interactive activity, more confident pupils could make their own sentences and the rest of class suggests symbols from the whiteboard to match them.

Worksheet 7: *Parlez!* may be used from this point onwards.

5. Song: Qu'est-ce qu'il fait, Jake?
10–15 mins (to include worksheet) — AT1.3 O5.1, AT2.3 O5.2, AT3.3 O5.3 L5.1

Materials
CD-ROM, whiteboard.

Description
Watch and listen to the interactive karaoke song practising activities and places. Choose either *Practice* or *Sing* mode: *Practice* to go through the song line by line; *Sing* to sing it all the way through. Switch the music and words on or off as you prefer, or try recording your own version.

Delivery
- Write the names 'Polly' and 'Jake' on the board and display Unit 6 Flashcards (Rooms/places in the house) underneath. Ask pupils to listen to/watch the song and to note which character is where.
- Play the song through without stopping (in *Sing* mode) and go through the answers. Remove the surplus flashcards from the board. Ask if pupils can remember what Jake and Polly were doing in each room.
- Go through the song line by line in *Practice* mode, checking comprehension and adding actions where appropriate.
- Go through the song again in *Sing* mode; this time each group sings the verses sung by 'their' character.
- Encourage pupils to memorise the song and to practise and perform it, either for another teacher or for other classes in assembly time.

Extension
- More confident pupils could invent another verse, following the pattern of the previous verses, and perform it for the rest of the class.
- You could also provide a gapped version of the text or a version where the lines are in the wrong order. Cut out the lines on individual pieces of paper, then pupils re-order them correctly as they listen.

Support
Stick the relevant activities and rooms flashcards, in chronological order, on the board as you go through the song in *Practice* mode, to provide additional support if required.

Worksheet 8: *Écrivez!* may be used from this point onwards.

6. Plenary activity: Qu'est-ce qu'elle fait?
5–10 mins — AT3.3 L5.2, AT4.3 L5.3

Materials
Unit 6 Flashcards (Rooms/places in the home and Activities in the home).

Description
A mime game using flashcards as prompts.

Delivery
- Divide the flashcards into two piles: places and activities. Turn the activity cards face down.
- Ask a volunteer to come to the front and select a place card, which they stick on the board. The pupil then takes an activity card without showing it to anyone, and must mime that activity to the class.
- The first pupil to say the correct compound sentence, e.g. *Elle joue avec l'ordinateur dans les WC*, has the next turn, and so on.

Extension
Encourage more confident classes to include other activities that have been covered in this unit, not just those on the flashcards.

Worksheet 7: Parlez!
10 mins — AT3.2–3 O5.1, AT2.2–3 L5.1

Description
This provides further speaking practice in the language of the unit. It may be used at any point after Activity 4.

Delivery
- if you are going to play the pairs game, you may wish to stick the worksheet onto card first. Allow a few minutes for them to cut up the cards and match the captions to the pictures. Go through the answers together.

Worksheet 8: Écrivez!
10 mins — AT4.2–3 L5.2 L5.3

Description
This provides further practice in building compound sentences. It may be used at any point after Activity 5.

Answers
1. 1 Elle mange un sandwich dans la chambre.
   2 Il joue avec l'ordinateur dans le salon.
   3 Elle lit un magazine dans le jardin.

Unit 6 — Extra!

Project work: Chez moi

1–2 hours
AT2.2–3 O5.4
AT3.2–3 L5.1
AT4.2–3 L5.2
         L5.3
IU5.2   IU5.3

Description
Pupils plan and construct a model/layout of their ideal house, or research French homes and make comparisons with homes in Britain.

Materials
Internet access and printer if possible, French and British homes and interiors magazines, card and paper for the displays.

Delivery
- Divide the class into small groups. If feasible, give pupils a choice of projects. Otherwise, choose the best project for the whole class and go through it with them.

- Pupils can research French homes on the internet and download pictures to include in the display or presentation.

- Encourage them to compare British and French homes and show the differences in a display.

- In their display, pupils label the places around the home they have learned in this unit.

- Each group delivers a short presentation on their findings.

Sound/spelling activity: Les sons 'ou' et 'u'

10 mins AT1.1
         AT2.1
         AT3.1

Description
Practice mode: Listen and practise pronouncing the 'ou' sound and the 'u' sound on their own and then in words that have been covered in **Rigolo** so far.

Activity mode: Listen to the words as they are read out. If they contain the 'ou' sound, tap on the red button, and if they contain the 'u' sound, tap on the green button. Listen carefully and choose your answer before the time runs out!

Delivery
- This sound/spelling activity focuses specifically on the 'ou' and 'u' sounds.

- There are two parts to the activity: the first (*Practice*) allows pupils to familiarise themselves with the two sounds and to compare their pronunciation with the Virtual Teacher model. The second part (*Activity*) is an exercise where pupils have to listen out for the sounds within a list of French words that they have encountered so far in **Rigolo**.

- Select *Practice* mode and tap on *Next* to start this part. Then tap on *Allez*. The Virtual Teacher will say the 'ou' sound, first on its own and then as part of several words that have been met in **Rigolo**. For each of these, get the class to repeat the words chorally several times, checking the model each time using the *Encore* button. You can also use the *Record* feature here to compare a pupil's pronunciation more closely with the model. Then tap on *Next sound* to follow suit with the 'u' sound, for which you will hear the sound on its own and then with other nouns covered in **Rigolo**.

- Once you have finished this part, tap on *Activity* to test pupils' recognition of both sounds. Tap on *Allez* to start. Pupils will hear 12 words read out. For each word they must work out whether they can hear the 'ou' sound or the 'u' sound.

They'll have to listen carefully and tap on the right button before the time runs out! Tap on *Encore* to hear the word again.

- Pupils score a point when they correctly identify the sound within the word.

- Repeat the activity if pupils need further practice.

Assessment for Units 5-6

Écoutez!

Play each audio 2–3 times, or more if necessary. Pause during each activity as required.

Total marks for listening: 20.

Activity 1 (AT1.1–2; O5.3)
Mark out of 5.

Answers
2 f   3 d   4 c   5 b   6 e

Activity 2 (AT1.2; O5.3)
Mark out of 5.

Answers
b blanc   c grand   d jaune   e rose   f petit

1 Il y a une salle à manger. C'est bleu.
2 Il y a une salle de bains. C'est petit.
3 Il y a une cuisine. C'est jaune.
4 Il y a un jardin. C'est grand.
5 Il y a un salon. C'est blanc.
6 Il y a une chambre. C'est rose.

Activity 3 (AT1.2–3; O5.3)
Mark out of 10.

Answers
1 b, h   2 d, i   3 c, g   4 e, j   5 a, f

1 – Où vas-tu en vacances?
  – Je vais à la montagne.
  – Et qu'est-ce que tu vas faire?
  – Je vais faire du ski.
2 – Où vas-tu en vacances?
  – Je vais au camping.
  – Et qu'est-ce que tu vas faire?
  – Je vais faire du sport.
3 – Où vas-tu en vacances?
  – Je vais au bord de la mer.
  – Et qu'est-ce que tu vas faire?
  – Je vais nager.
4 – Où vas-tu en vacances?
  – Je vais voir mes grands-parents.
  – Et qu'est-ce que tu vas faire?
  – Je vais faire du bateau.
5 – Où vas-tu en vacances?
  – Je vais à la campagne.
  – Et qu'est-ce que tu vas faire?
  – Je vais faire du vélo.

Parlez!

Pupils can work in pairs for the speaking tasks. If it is not possible to assess each pair, then assess a few pairs for each assessment block and mark the rest of the class based on the spoken work they do in class.

Total marks for speaking: 10.

Activity 1 (AT2.2–3; O5.1, O5.2)
Mark out of 5 (one per sentence).

Answers
(*any 5 – pupils add own adjectives*)
Il y a une cuisine. C'est…
Il y a trois chambres. C'est…
Il y a une salle de bains. C'est…
Il y a des WC. C'est…
Il y a une salle à manger. C'est…
Il y a un jardin. C'est…
Il y a un balcon. C'est…
Il y a un garage. C'est…

Activity 2 (AT2.3; O5.1, O5.2)
Mark out of 5 (two for the first two answers and one for the third).

Answers
(*sample*)
A: Où vas-tu en vacances?
B: Je vais <u>à la montagne/au bord de la mer</u>.
A: Et qu'est-ce que tu vas faire?
B: Je vais <u>faire du vélo/nager</u>.
A: Tu aimes ça?
B: Oui, <u>j'aime ça/Non, je n'aime pas ça/Non, je déteste ça</u>.

Lisez!

Total marks for reading: 20.

Activity 1 (AT3.2; L5.1)
Mark out of 10 (one for each true/false answer and one for saying whether each is a girl or a boy).

Answers
a ✗ (G)   b ✓ (G)   c ✗ (B)   d ✗ (B)   e ✓ (G)

Activity 2 (AT3.2–3; L5.1, O5.2)
Mark out of 10.

Answers
1 Luc
2 Sarah
3 Rachid
4 Sarah
5 Luc
6 Rachid
7 Luc
8 Rachid
9 Sarah
10 Rachid

Écrivez!

Total marks for writing: 20.

Activity 1 (AT4.2; L5.2, L5.3)
Mark out of 10 (two per sentence).

Answers
b Il lit un livre.
c Elle écoute de la musique.
d Elle regarde la télé.
e Il joue au tennis.
f Il mange un sandwich.

Activity 2 (AT4.2–3; L5.2, L5.3, O5.2)
Mark out of 10 (three per note and one for general accuracy).

Answers
a Je vais faire du vélo. Je n'aime pas ça.
b Je vais faire du ski. J'adore ça.
c Je vais voir mes grands-parents. J'aime ça.

Rigolo 2 Unit 7: Le week-end

National criteria

KS2 Framework objectives

O6.1	Understand the main points and simple opinions in a spoken story, song or passage
O6.2	Perform to an audience
O6.3	Understand longer and more complex phrases or sentences
O6.4	Use spoken language confidently to initiate and sustain conversations and to tell stories
L6.1	Read and understand the main points and some detail from a short written passage
L6.2	Identify different text types and read short, authentic texts for enjoyment or information
L6.3	Match sound to sentences and paragraphs
L6.4	Write sentences on a range of topics using a model
IU6.1	Compare attitudes towards aspects of everyday life
IU6.2	Recognise and understand some of the differences between people

QCA Scheme of Work

Unit 16	Scene de plage
Unit 20	Notre monde
Unit 22	Ici et là

National Curriculum attainment levels

AT1.2–4, AT2.2–4, AT3.2–4, AT4.2–4

Language ladder levels

Listening:	Breakthrough, Grades 2–4
Reading:	Breakthrough, Grades 2–4
Speaking:	Breakthrough, Grades 2–4
Writing:	Breakthrough, Grades 2–4

5–14 guideline strands — Levels A–D

Listening
Listening for information and instructions	A, B, C, D
Listening and reacting to others	A, B, C, D

Speaking
Speaking to convey information	A, B, C, D
Speaking and interacting with others	A, B, C, D
Speaking about experiences, feelings and opinions	A, B, C

Reading
Reading for information and instructions	A, B, C, D
Reading aloud	A, B, C, D

Writing
Writing to exchange information and ideas	A, B, C, D
Writing to establish and maintain personal contact	A, B, C, D
Writing imaginatively to entertain	A, B, C

Unit objectives

- Ask and talk about regular activities
- Say what you don't do
- Ask and say what other people do
- Talk about what you like/dislike doing

Key language

- *Qu'est-ce que tu fais [le mercredi/le samedi]?*
  Le lundi… j'écoute de la musique, je joue (au basket), je mange [du gâteau], je regarde [la télé], je bois [du chocolat chaud], je fais du vélo, je fais du roller
  Tu fais… ? joues… ? regardes… ?
- *Je n'écoute pas… Je ne regarde pas… Je ne joue pas …*
  Je ne bois pas de… Je ne mange pas de… Je ne fais pas de… (+ activities from Lesson 1 + negatives)
- *Qu'est-ce qu'il/elle fait le week-end? … le lundi matin/ après-midi/soir?*
  Le lundi matin, il/elle… fait [du sport/du vélo], écoute [la radio/des CD], mange [un sandwich], boit [du jus d'orange], regarde (la télé), joue [au tennis/au foot]
- *Est-ce que tu aimes faire/écouter/jouer/regarder… ?*
  J'aime, Je n'aime pas, J'adore, Je déteste… faire du vélo, écouter des CD/la radio, regarder la télé, jouer au football/tennis, faire du sport

Grammar and skills

- Use several verbs in 1st person
- Use negatives
- Use verbs in 3rd person
- Using *j'aime/je n'aime pas,* etc. with an infinitive
- Recognise patterns in French
- Build longer sentences
- Adapt sentences to say different things
- Listen for clues
- Plan and prepare a task and evaluate others

Unit outcomes

Most children will be able to:

- Say what they do using the 1st person
- Say what they don't do using set phrases
- Say what other people do using *il/elle*
- Say what they like/dislike doing

Some children will also be able to:

- Adapt language to say different things
- Build longer sentences
- Apply negatives to most phrases
- Use verbs with different pronouns

Unit 7 — Lesson 1

Lesson summary

Context
Asking and talking about regular activities

National criteria
KS2 Framework: O6.1, O6.3, O6.4, L6.1, L6.4, IU6.1, IU6.2
Attainment levels: AT1.2–4, AT2.2–4, AT3.2–4, AT4.3
Language ladder levels:
  Listening: **Grades 2–4**; Speaking: **Grades 2–4**;
  Reading: **Grades 2–4**; Writing: **Grade 3**

Key vocabulary
Days of the week (revised)

Language structures and outcomes
Qu'est-ce que tu fais (le mercredi/le samedi)?
Le lundi… j'écoute de la musique, je joue (au basket), je mange (du gâteau), je regarde (la télé), je bois (du chocolat chaud), je fais du vélo, je fais du roller
Tu fais… ? joues… ? regardes… ?

Knowledge about language

Recognising patterns; using knowledge of words, text and structure to build simple spoken and written passages

- The aim of this unit is to revise various language and structures met so far in *Rigolo* and to extend and build on them. The revised language includes days of the week; using verbs in the first person; negatives; using verbs in the 3rd person. Throughout the unit, encourage your pupils to build on the structures they are learning in order to say new sentences e.g. *Je mange un gâteau* can easily be adapted to say what other things they eat using previously learned vocabulary e.g. *Je mange une glace/je mange un sandwich*, etc.
- Also encourage pupils to recognise patterns throughout the unit, e.g. verbs in the *je* form and *il/elle* forms have an 'e' ending whereas verbs in the *tu* form have an '-es' ending.

Description
Watch and listen to this interactive story presenting the language for Lessons 1 and 2. You can pause and rewind the story at any point, or record your own version too.

Delivery
- Display the flashcards on the board and ask pupils to note which activities are mentioned in the animation.
- Freeze the opening screen showing Polly and Mme Chanson on the telephone. Ask pupils to predict what they are discussing.
- Play the story through, so that pupils can check if any predictions were correct and can confirm which of the flashcard activities were mentioned. Accept answers in English and French at this stage as pupils will focus on the activity language during this lesson.
- Summarise the story and key words together, then replay the animation through one more time.

Support
- Pause the animation each time an activity is mentioned and point to the relevant flashcard during the first viewing.

1. Starter activity: Les jours et les activités (5–10 mins) — AT1.2 O6.3 AT2.2

Materials
Flashcards depicting activities (*Rigolo 1*, Units 8 & 11; *Rigolo 2*, Unit 6); French calendar and/or days of the week flashcards, if possible.

Description
A quick revision of days and activities.

Delivery
- Say and write which day it is. Quickly revise the days of the week if necessary.
- Model a couple of sentences combining activities with days, using the flashcards as prompts, e.g. *Le samedi, je joue au football*.
- Use flashcards to revise quickly/reactivate the verbs *regarder, écouter, jouer, manger, boire*, with as many complements to these words as the pupils can think of. You could write them on the board as they brainstorm them (so far pupils have used verbs with *je/il/elle/on*).

2. Animated story: Le samedi soir (1) (10 mins) — AT1.3–4 O6.1, AT3.3–4 O6.3, L6.1 L6.3, IU6.1

Materials
CD-ROM, whiteboard; Unit 7 Flashcards (Activities with *je*).

3. Presentation: Qu'est-ce que tu fais le lundi? (5–10 mins) — AT1.2 O6.3, AT2.2, AT3.2

Materials
CD-ROM, whiteboard; Unit 7 Flashcards (Activities with *je*).

Description
Tap on the frames to hear characters talk about what activities they do on particular days of the week. Use the additional features to practise sound/spelling links and word classes, or to record your own version of each expression.

Delivery
- Most of these structures have been covered in previous *Rigolo* units so pupils may be familiar with them.
- We first hear the question, *Qu'est-ce que tu fais le [lundi]*, then see a character doing an activity and hear their reply to the question.
- The whole class listens to the dialogue and repeats.
- Continue for all seven days and repeat if further practice is required.
- You may wish to point out that French speakers say *le lundi* (singular) as opposed to 'on Mondays' (plural) in English. Refer to the Introduction for notes on the *Record*, *Sound* and *Word* features.

Extension
- Encourage more confident pupils to extend their sentences where possible, e.g. using the verbs with different sentence endings (*je regarde* [*un match*], etc.).
- Encourage pupils also to combine as many verbs and nouns as possible, e.g. *Il* [*mange*] [*une pizza*].

Support
Use Unit 7 Flashcards for further oral practice of the structures.

4. Oracy activity: 5–10 mins AT1.2–3 AT2.2–3 O6.4
Le lundi, je joue au basket

Materials
CD-ROM, whiteboard; Unit 7 Flashcards (Activities with *je*) for support activities.

Description
Tap on *Allez*. Look at the images of three different activities on different days. Listen to the question and say the correct answer out loud.

Delivery
- We hear Bof asking *Qu'est-ce que tu fais [le mardi]?* and see three activities taking place. Pupils listen carefully to pick out the day of the week in Bof's question.
- Pupils look and find the picture with the correct day of the week, as in Bof's question. They say the correct answer aloud and tap on the audio check button in the correct picture. If the answer is correct, tap on the tick button and the character will confirm the answer. In the case of an incorrect answer, tap on the cross: a 'life' is lost and pupils are invited to try again. Remember to encourage pupils to give full answers, e.g. *Le mardi, je regarde la télé.*
- Continue for all six questions and repeat if further practice is needed.

Support
- Encourage less confident pupils to use the *Encore* button as much as necessary.
- You could also invite three pupils to the front: one selects the relevant 'day' flashcard, another the relevant 'activity' flashcard, and a third pupil says the answer aloud and taps on the correct picture.

Worksheet 1 *Lisez!* can be used from this point onwards.

5. Literacy activity: 5–10 mins AT3.2–3 L6.4
Le mercredi, je fais du vélo

Materials
Unit 7 Flashcards; blank card for making own flashcards with days of the week listed.

Description
Pupils use flashcard prompts to make sentences about activities they do on certain days.

Delivery
In advance, write the following table on the board:

Le	lundi mardi mercredi jeudi vendredi samedi dimanche	je regarde j'écoute je joue je fais je mange je bois	la télé. mes DVD. la radio. mes CD. au football. au basket. au tennis. du sport. du vélo. une pizza. du gâteau. un sandwich. de la limonade. du chocolat chaud. du jus de pomme.

- Ask three volunteers to make up a sentence, each pupil selecting the beginning/middle/end from the choices on the board. Do a quick poll by asking pupils to raise their hands if that sentence is true for them.
- Continue until all pupils have participated in sentence-building. Remember to highlight the flexibility of the language – it is possible to say many different things by combining a relatively small selection of phrases in different ways.

Extension
- You could add to the lists on the board by brainstorming ideas with the class.
- Ask more confident pupils to produce their own set of flashcards. Set them a timed activity to make as many different sentences as possible from the cards.

Support
Reduce the number of options on the board and gradually build up the lists as suggested above once pupils have gained more confidence.

Worksheet 2 *Écrivez!* may be used from this point onwards.

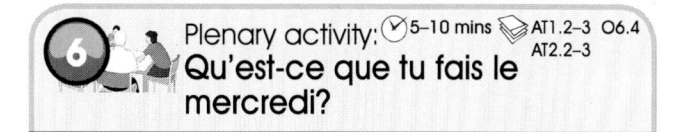

6. Plenary activity: 5–10 mins AT1.2–3 AT2.2–3 O6.4
Qu'est-ce que tu fais le mercredi?

Materials
Flashcards Unit 7 (Activities with *je*); 'days of the week' captions; possibly microphone prop for interviewer.

Description
Pupils interview each other about their weekly activities.

Delivery
- Stick the flashcards on the board as prompts, or leave the sentence prompts from the previous activity on the board.
- Model the interview by asking two (confident) volunteer pupils out to the front. Ask each one a question, e.g. *Qu'est-ce que tu fais [le dimanche]?* in the style of a TV interviewer. Pupils can give true or made-up answers.
- Invite another group of three volunteers to do another interview at the front.
- Continue the activity in small groups around the class.
- Pupils may wish to assume the identity of a celebrity to add a bit of fun and imagination to the interviews.

Worksheet 1: Lisez! 10 mins AT1.2 AT2.2–3 AT3.2 O6.4

Description
A board game to give further practice in reading and speaking about activities in the first person. It may be used at any point after Activity 4.

Worksheet 2: Écrivez! 10 mins AT2.3–4 AT4.3 O6.2 O6.4 L6.4

Description
This worksheet provides further practice of writing sentences about weekly activities. It may be used at any point after Activity 5.

Delivery
If necessary, model answers to the first question orally before pupils begin writing their answers. Show pupils how they can form sentences by selecting items from each column.

Unit 7 (Lesson 2)

Lesson summary

Context
Saying what you don't do

National criteria
KS2 Framework: O6.1, O6.2, O6.3, O6.4, L6.1, L6.2, L6.3, L6.4, IU6.1
Attainment Levels: AT1.2–4, AT2.2–4; AT3.2–4, AT4.2–3
Language Ladder Levels:
   Listening: **Grades 2–4**; Speaking: **Grades 2–4**;
   Reading: **Grades 2–4**; Writing: **Grades 2–3**

Cross-curricular Links
Literacy

Key vocabulary
Expressions from Lesson 1

Language structures and outcomes
Je n'écoute pas... Je ne regarde pas... Je ne joue pas ... Je ne bois pas de... Je ne mange pas de... Je ne fais pas de... (activities from Lesson 1 + negatives)

1. Starter activity: Je fais du vélo
⏱ 5 mins — AT1.2 O6.4, AT2.2

Materials
Unit 7 Flashcards (Activities using *je*).

Description
A flashcard game revising activities covered in the last lesson.

Delivery
● Hold up four of the flashcards and elicit the sentences, with days of the week if possible. Stick the cards face down onto the board.
● Say one of the activities e.g. *Je joue au tennis*. Ask a pupil to guess which card depicts this activity. They turn their chosen card over and say the activity shown on that card. Chorally repeat the sentence before adding a new card and inviting a new volunteer to the front.

2. Animated story: Le samedi soir (1)
⏱ 5–10 mins — AT1.3–4 O6.1, AT3.3–4 O6.3, L6.1 L6.3 IU6.1

Materials
CD-ROM, whiteboard; Unit 7 Flashcards (Activities with *je*).

Description
Watch and listen again to this interactive story presenting the language for Lessons 1 and 2. You can pause and rewind the story at any point, or record your own version too.

Delivery
● Pupils listen again to the animated story, this time to focus on Bof's negative sentences.
● Pause the animation after each time Bof speaks and ask pupils to repeat what he said.
● Play the story through one more time without stopping.

Support
Revise negative sentences previously covered (e.g. *je n'aime pas...*) before asking pupils to view the animation.

Language learning strategies

Using language known in one context or topic in another context or topic
Make sure pupils are aware that they're seeing again vocabulary and expressions they've met earlier in *Rigolo* and using them in a different context i.e. days of the week and verbs with *je*. Also, they met negatives in Unit 2 with school subjects and now they're meeting them with everyday activities. It's important that pupils realise that language is transferable to other topic areas and can be combined with new language to say different things – see in particular the plenary activity, where pupils adapt the language they have been learning to make new sentences.

3. Presentation: Je ne fais pas de vélo
⏱ 5–10 mins — AT1.3 O6.3, AT2.2–3 O6.4, AT3.3

Materials
CD-ROM, whiteboard.

Description
Tap on each of the doors in turn. The doors will open and we hear a question and two possible responses. Use the additional features to record your own version of each expression.

Delivery
● The two characters are asked questions about their activities on a given day. One gives an affirmative reply, and when you tap on *Continuez*, the other gives a negative reply.
● Pupils listen and repeat.
● Continue for all seven days and repeat if further practice is required.
Refer to the Introducion for notes on the *Record* feature.

Extension
Ask pupils to compare the negative sentences and the positive ones. Which words are added when a sentence is negative? Write up some negative sentences on the board so that pupils can see the pattern. Where do the *ne* and *pas* go in the sentences? (Around the verb.) Make sure that pupils understand the pattern of negative sentences. For some pupils, point out that after a negative, *un*, *une* or *des* become *de*. Show the examples in the presentation.

Support
Use the KS2 Framework suggestions for teaching parts of speech when repeating sentences, e.g. two hands on head for a noun, one hand on head for a pronoun, etc.

4. Oracy activity: Tu joues au basket le mardi?
⏱ 10 mins — AT1.2–3 O6.3, AT2.2–3 O6.4

Materials
CD-ROM, whiteboard; two cards depicting a '+' and a '-' to indicate affirmative and negative sentences.

Description
Pupils respond to questions from Activity 3 (see above) then play the scene to check their answers.

Delivery
● Invite two pupils to the front of the class. Give each pupil a '+' or '-' card. Ask them a question from Activity 3. Each must reply with an affirmative or negative sentence, according to their card.
● Pupils tap on the relevant door to check their answer. Repeat with different pairs of pupils.

Unit 7: Lesson 2

- The questions are: *Tu joues au basket le lundi? Tu écoutes de la musique le mardi? Tu fais du vélo le mercredi? Tu manges du gâteau le jeudi? Tu bois du chocolat chaud le vendredi? Tu regardes la télé le samedi? Tu fais du roller le dimanche?*

Extension
Challenge pupils to make new questions with other days and activities.

Worksheet 3 *Parlez!* can be used from this point onwards.

5 Literacy activity: 10 mins AT3.3 L6.4 AT4.3
Je ne joue pas au basket

Materials
CD-ROM, whiteboard; selection of Unit 7 Flashcards (Activities) and possibly previous units (for Extension activity).

Description
Tap on *Allez*. Look at the pictures. Drag the text into the correct order to match each picture.

Delivery
- Pupils must build a sentence which best describes each picture. This is done by dragging the five words into the correct position.
- When the pupil is happy with their text they tap on *Fini*.
- Correct answers are rewarded with an appropriate animation, otherwise a 'life' is lost and pupils are invited to try again.
- Continue until all six sentences have been completed and repeat if further practice is required.

Extension
Using various activity flashcards, brainstorm other negative sentences and ask pupils to write them on the board.

Support
This can be done as a whole-class activity. First, remind pupils where *ne* and *pas* should be positioned. The class then suggests what the sentence should be – discuss their choices if necessary – before the pupil taps on *Fini*.

Worksheet 4 *Grammaire* may be used from this point onwards.

6 Plenary activity: 5–10 mins AT2.2–4 O6.2 O6.4
Je ne regarde pas la télé L6.1

Materials
CD-ROM, whiteboard; Unit 7 Flashcards (Activities with *je*), plus other activity flashcards for Extension activity.

Description
Pupils have further practice of making negative sentences about regular/routine activities.

Delivery
- Look at the animated story again, focusing in particular on the exchanges where Polly and Bof make contrasting sentences.
- Play the story until just after Bof says *Moi, je ne joue pas au basket*.
- Invite three pupils to the front to re-enact the scene (as Mme Chanson, Polly, and Bof – you may wish to substitute Jake for Polly to give more scope for boys' roles).
- Repeat for each exchange, inviting three new pupils to the front each time.

Extension
More confident pupils could invent their own dialogues based on those in the story, using different activities. Display various activity flashcards on the board as prompts.

Worksheet 3: Parlez!
10 mins AT2.2–3 O6.4 AT3.2–3 L6.2

Description
This worksheet provides further practice in activities in the 1st person including negatives. It may be used at any point after Activity 5.

Answers
Picture A
Mme Chanson: Je ne joue pas au basket
Nathalie: Je ne mange pas de gâteau
Mme Moulin: Je n'écoute pas de musique
Picture B
Olivier: Je ne fais pas de vélo
M. Mills: Je ne bois pas de chocolat chaud
Chi Chi: Je ne regarde pas la télé.

Worksheet 4: Grammaire!
10 mins AT4.2–3 L6.4

Description
This worksheet provides further practice in negatives. It may be used at any point after Activity 5.

Answers
1 1 d 2 a 3 g 4 e 5 f 6 b 7 c

2 1 Je ne fais pas de vélo.
   2 Je mange de la glace.
   3 Je ne joue pas au tennis.
   4 Je regarde la télé.
   5 Je n'écoute pas la radio.
   6 Je bois du chocolat chaud.
   7 Je ne regarde pas mes DVD.

Unit 7 — Lesson 3

Lesson summary

Context
Asking and saying what other people do

National criteria
KS2 Framework: **O6.1, O6.3, O6.4, L6.1, L6.2, L6.3, L6.4, IU6.1**
Attainment levels: **AT1.2–4, AT2.2–4; AT3.2–4, AT4.3–4**
Language Ladder Levels:
  Listening: **Grades 2–4**; Speaking: **Grades 2–4**;
  Reading: **Grades 2–4**; Writing: **Grades 3–4**

Cross-curricular links
Literacy

Key vocabulary
Le week-end, lundi matin, mardi soir, samedi après-midi

Language structures and outcomes
Qu'est-ce qu'il/elle fait le week-end? … le lundi matin/après-midi/soir?
Le lundi matin, il/elle… fait (du sport/du vélo), écoute (la radio/des CD), mange (un sandwich), boit (du jus d'orange), regarde (la télé), joue (au tennis/au foot)

---

1. Starter activity: Les activités
5–10 mins — AT1.2 O6.3, AT2.2 O6.4

Materials
Activity Flashcards (*Rigolo 2*, Units 6 and Unit 7; *Rigolo 1*, Unit 8); days of the week captions for Extension activity.

Description
A flashcard class activity to revise activity verbs using *je*, *il*, and *elle*.

Delivery
- Write *je*, *il*, and *elle* on the board. Make sure pupils know what all three words mean.
- Hold up a flashcard, point to a pronoun, and ask the class to make an appropriate sentence e.g. *Je regarde la télé*.
- Do a few sentences chorally, then divide the class into two teams and award a point each time a team makes a correct sentence.

Extension
Display days of the week captions to encourage more confident pupils to make longer sentences e.g. *Le lundi, je regarde la télé*.

---

2. Animated story: Le samedi soir (2)
10 mins — AT1.3–4 O6.1, AT3.3–4 O6.3, L6.1 L6.3 IU6.1

Materials
CD-ROM, whiteboard; Unit 7 Flashcards (Activities with *il/elle*).

Description
Watch and listen to this interactive story presenting the language for Lessons 3 and 4. You can pause and rewind the story at any point, or record your own version too.

Delivery
- Write the names of Jake, Polly, Nathalie, Olivier on the board.
- Display the flashcards randomly on the board.
- Ask pupils to watch the animation and to note who does which activity according to Nathalie and Olivier's conversation.
- Play the story through. Ask a few pupils to come to the board and stick the cards under the name of the relevant character.
- Play the story through one more time to check and discuss answers.

Support
For less confident pupils, pause the video after each activity is mentioned and place the relevant flashcard under the correct name on the board.

Language learning strategies

Listening for clues to meaning
Use the listening texts and the animated story in this lesson to remind pupils to look for clues to meaning. Remind them when they hear French spoken, they will not understand everything but will pick up clues in a variety of ways: listening out for words they know; listening to tone of voice; looking for clues to meaning in the animated story pictures. Pupils also sometimes have to listen for detail, e.g. in this unit they have to differentiate between *il* and *elle* to find out who is doing a particular activity.

---

3. Presentation: Il fait du vélo
10 mins — AT1.3 O6.3, AT2.2–3, AT3.3

Materials
CD-ROM, whiteboard; possibly days of the week captions and cards to symbolise morning/afternoon/evening; Unit 7 Flashcards (Activities) for Support and Extension activities.

Description
Tap on each door to see the activity and to hear the question and the response. Use the additional features to practise sound/spelling links and word classes, or to record your own version of each phrase.

Delivery
- This presents activities in 3rd person and introduces specific times of day. We hear Gustave asking Olivier what each character does on various mornings/afternoons/evenings of the week. Olivier replies and the door opens to show the character doing an activity.
- Encourage pupils to repeat both the question and the answer each time.
- Continue for all seven activities and repeat if further practice is required.

Refer to the Introduction for notes on the *Record*, *Sound* and *Word* features.

Extension
More confident pupils could take turns to stand at the front with their backs to the board. When Olivier says what the characters do, the pupils hold up the appropriate flashcards.

Support
- Repeat each part of the presentation using the flashcards.
- If necessary, draw pupils' attention to the use of *il* and *elle*. Hold up the flashcards showing male and female characters and ask, *Il ou elle?* to ensure pupils can differentiate between them.

4 Oracy activity: 10 mins AT1.3 O6.3
Elle joue au football

Materials
CD-ROM, whiteboard; Unit 7 Flashcards (Activities) for Support activity.

Description
Tap on *Allez*. Listen to the conversation and tap on the correct picture.

Delivery
- Pupils hear a conversation about the activities of each character. There are three images depicting different activities. Pupils don't have to understand everything. The language is heard in conversations, to enable pupils to become accustomed to picking out main points from longer exchanges. They need to listen out in particular for *il* (he) and *elle* (she).
- Pupils select the picture which best corresponds to the conversation.
- Continue for all eight dialogues and repeat if required.

Extension
Ask pupils if they can pick out any opinions mentioned in the conversations.

Support
- Use the flashcards if further help is required. After each dialogue, hold up flashcards representing the three options. Together, say a sentence to describe each option.
- Write *il* and *elle* on the board. Point to the words, then say them out loud to check pupils have heard the correct pronoun.

Worksheet 5 *Grammaire* may be used from this point onwards.

5 Literacy activity: 10 mins AT3.3 L6.4
Il regarde un film

Materials
Pre-prepared word cards (see below).

Description
Pupils make sentences using word cards.

Delivery
- Prepare word cards on A4 card for the following words (you may add more words if you wish):

il, elle, regarde, joue, écoute, fait, la télé, des DVD, au football, au tennis, au basket, des CD, de la musique, la radio, du sport, du vélo, du roller, le lundi matin, le vendredi soir, le week-end, le dimanche après-midi

- Stick the cards on the board and invite pupils to select a few cards at a time to make sentences.
- You could make this into a team game: ask pupils from alternate teams to make a sentence and award a point for each correct answer.

Extension
Prepare smaller sets of word cards for each group, and see which group can produce the most sentences in five minutes.

Worksheet 6 *Lisez!* may be used from this point onwards.

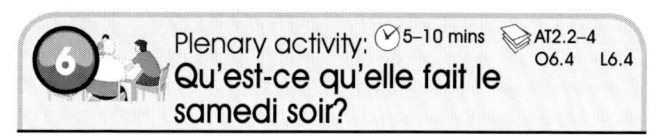

6 Plenary activity: 5–10 mins AT2.2–4 O6.4 L6.4
Qu'est-ce qu'elle fait le samedi soir?

Materials
Rigolo character flashcards; Unit 7 Flashcards (Activities) to illustrate suggestions; pictures of celebrities cut out of magazines.

Description
Pupils make sentences about what activities various characters do each day.

Delivery
- Hold up a flashcard of a ***Rigolo*** character and ask *Qu'est-ce qu'il/elle fait [le matin/l'après-midi/le soir]?*
- Encourage pupils to build up a series of sentences, e.g. *Le matin, il/elle… L'après-midi il/elle… Le soir il/elle…*
- Repeat for other characters, or use magazine pictures of celebrities (especially footballers or pop stars) popular with pupils. Encourage pupils to use their imagination and make humorous suggestions, to give as much scope as possible to their sentence-building skills.
- Ask pupils to write out one sentence each for a display.

Extension
Each table could prepare a profile display for a character or celebrity, including a picture and a description of routine.

Worksheet 5: Grammaire 10 mins AT3.2–3 L6.1 L6.2

Description
This worksheet provides practice in using singular pronouns with verbs. It may be used at any point after Activity 4. (First ensure pupils that are clear about the meaning of all the singular pronouns.)

Answers
1 **1** tu, je **2** il, elle **3** elle **4** il, il
2 **1** Olivier **2** Jake **3** Mme Moulin **4** Nathalie **5** Marine

Worksheet 6: Lisez! 10 mins AT3.3–4 AT4.3–4 L6.1 L6.2 L6.4

Description
This provides practice in reading and writing a longer text using 3rd person. It may be used at any point after Activity 5.

Answers
1 **1** faux **2** vrai **3** faux **4** faux **5** vrai **6** faux **7** vrai **8** vrai **9** faux

Unit 7 — Lesson 4

Lesson summary

Context
Talking about what you like/dislike doing

National criteria
KS2 Framework: O6.1, O6.2, O6.3, O6.4, L6.1, L6.3, L6.4, IU6.1, IU6.2,
Attainment levels: AT1.2–4, AT2. 2–4; AT3. 2–4, AT4. 3–4
Language ladder levels:
   Listening: **Grades 2–4**; Speaking: **Grades 2–4**;
   Reading: **Grades 2–4**; Writing: **Grades 3–4**

Cross-curricular links
Numeracy; Art and design; ICT (project work)

Language structures and outcomes
J'aime, Je n'aime pas, J'adore, Je déteste… faire du vélo, écouter des CD/la radio, regarder la télé, jouer au football/tennis, faire du sport
Est-ce que tu aimes faire/écouter/jouer/regarder… ?

---

1. Starter activity: *J'adore les pommes* — 5–10 mins — AT1.2 O6.4 / AT2.2

Materials
Unit 2 (*J'aime, Je n'aime pas*), Unit 5 (*J'adore, Je déteste*), Unit 3 (Food), Unit 7 (Activities) Flashcards.

Description
Pupils revise saying what they like/dislike with nouns.

Delivery
- Display the food/activity flashcards on the board.
- Quickly revise the four like/dislike expressions using the flashcards.
- Invite pupils to the front of the class and hand them a like/dislike card. Ask them to make a sentence by combining *J'aime, Je n'aime pas, J'adore, Je déteste* with a food or activity illustrated on the board e.g. *Je déteste le football*.
- Repeat with different pupils until each like/dislike card has been used a couple of times.

Support
Focus simply on the food items at this point and leave the activities until later in the lesson.

---

2. Animated story: *Le samedi soir (2)* — 5–10 mins — AT1.3–4 O6.1 / AT3.3–4 O6.3 / L6.1 L6.3 IU6.1

Materials
CD-ROM, whiteboard; Unit 5 Flashcards (*J'aime, Je n'aime pas*), Unit 7 Flashcards (Activities).

Description
Watch and listen again to this interactive story presenting the language for Lessons 3 and 4. You can pause and rewind the story at any point, or record your own version too.

Delivery
- Focus this time on the opinions expressed by the characters.
- On the board write the names 'Nathalie' and 'Olivier'. Make two wide columns and stick a *J'aime* and a *Je n'aime pas* flashcard at the top of each. Display the other flashcards randomly on the board.
- Ask pupils to take notice of which activities each character likes or dislikes.
- Play the story through and invite pupils to come to the board and stick the flashcards in the correct place in the grid.
- Watch the story a second time if necessary to check answers.

Support
- Pause the film after each expression of like or dislike and invite pupils to come and position the flashcards on the board as you go along.
- Play the story right through again without pausing.

---

3. Presentation: *J'aime faire du sport* — 10 mins — AT1.2–3 O6.3 / AT2.2–3 / AT3.2–3

Materials
CD-ROM, whiteboard.

Description
Tap on the activity symbols to hear a question and then the answer about how Madame Moulin feels about that activity. Use the additional features to practise sound/spelling links and word classes, or to record your own version of each word.

Delivery
- This presentation uses *J'aime/Je n'aime pas*, etc. with an infinitive rather than with a noun as previously. When pupils tap on an activity symbol, we hear Madame Moulin answering interview questions about that particular activity.
- Pupils listen and repeat, using gestures to reinforce the language.
- Continue for all seven questions and repeat if necessary.

Refer to the Introduction for notes on the *Record*, *Sound* and *Word* features.

Extension
Ask pupils if they can see a pattern in the language used here ([*J'aime*] + infinitive). They may notice that *J'aime*, etc. is often followed by a verb ending in *-er*. You could mention that this is the 'infinitive' or 'title' of the verb and that many French verbs, though not all, do end in *-er*. Pupils can begin to experiment using *J'aime*, etc. with other verbs they have met in this unit.

Support
Use flashcards to illustrate further Madame Moulin's answers.

---

4. Oracy activity: *Tu aimes jouer au tennis?* — 5–10 mins — AT2.2–3 O6.4

Materials
Unit 7 Flashcards (Activities).

Description
A whole-class activity to practise *J'aime, Je n'aime pas, J'adore, Je déteste* + verb.

Delivery
- Model the question/answer with a pupil as follows: hold up a flashcard and ask *Tu aimes [jouer au tennis]*? The pupil then replies using *J'aime/Je n'aime pas/J'adore/Je déteste [jouer au tennis]*.
- Hold up other flashcards and ask pupils around the class whether they like the illustrated activity.

Extension
You could hold up two flashcards at a time to encourage pupils to make longer sentences linked by *et*. As a further challenge ask pupils to make sentences about things they like and don't like using *mais* (e.g. *J'aime jouer au tennis mais je n'aime pas jouer au football*).

Support
If pupils are struggling with longer sentences, accept shorter replies, e.g. *J'aime ça. Je n'aime pas ça*, etc.

5. Literacy activity: Je déteste jouer au tennis
⏱ 10 mins AT3.2 L6.4

Materials
CD-ROM, whiteboard.

Description
Look at the icons then select and drag the correct words together to form a sentence. Tap on *Fini* when you have completed each answer, and see the sentence illustrated.

Delivery
- Using the jumbled up text on the screen, pupils look at the icons for clues and build a short sentence to match the illustration.
- Pupils tap on *Fini* when they have finished their sentence. The character will read out the sentence if it is correct. If the sentence is wrong, the machine breaks down and pupils can try again.
- Continue for all eight sentences.

Support
For less confident pupils you may wish to do the activity as a whole class. Alternatively, two or three pupils at a time could go to the board and make the sentence as a team activity.

📄 Worksheets 7 *Écrivez!* and 8 *Parlez!* may be used from this point onwards.

6. Plenary activity: Qu'est-ce que tu aimes faire?
⏱ 10–20 mins AT2.2–3 O6.4

Materials
Results of Worksheet 8 *Parlez!* survey; blank paper/card or access to computers to print off the results display.

Description
Pupils present the results of the survey from Worksheet 8 *Parlez!*

Delivery
- Ask pupils to call out the results of their surveys and note results on the board.
- Each group then writes out an illustrated results chart or produces one on the computer.
- Display the findings around the classroom.

Extension
Extend the survey to include other verbs and activities.

Worksheet 7: Écrivez!
⏱ 10 mins AT4.3 L6.4

Description
This provides further practice of writing sentences about likes / dislikes. It may be used at any point after Activity 5.

Answers
1 J'aime jouer au football.
2 Je n'aime pas regarder mes DVD.
3 Je déteste regarder la télé.
4 J'adore faire du sport.
5 Je déteste écouter la radio.

Worksheet 8: Parlez!
⏱ 10 mins AT2.3–4 O6.2 O6.4

Description
This worksheet provides further speaking practice of expressing likes/dislikes. It may be used at any point after Activity 5.

Language learning strategies

Planning and preparing; applying a range of linguistic knowledge to create simple written production; evaluating work
The project work provides opportunities for pupils to experience the above strategies. Encourage pupils to plan and prepare their project carefully in their group. Decide in advance who is doing what and what needs to be done to carry out the task successfully.
- Encourage pupils also to use their language knowledge to create the presentation. They can draw not only on language from this unit but also on language learned previously.
- Finally, encourage pupils to evaluate each other's work. They should find positive points about everyone's presentation and if they have negative comments, they should make suggestions on how it could be improved.

Project work: Une semaine typique
⏱ 1–2 hours AT2.3–4 O6.2 AT4.3–4 O6.4 L6.4 IU6.1 IU6.2

Description
Pupils present a typical profile of the activities of a British pupil and compare, if possible, with a French-speaking pupil of similar age.

Materials
Internet access and printer if possible; card and paper to display the pictures and text in the classroom or access to PowerPoint; emails or letters from French-speaking pupils if available.

Delivery
- Ask each group to decide on what activities a British pupil might do in a typical week. They then produce an illustrated list to display, on paper or using PowerPoint (or similar presentation software). Pupils present their information in the 1st or 3rd person.
- If the necessary information is available, half the class could decide on a typical week's activities for a French-speaking pupil and produce a display in the same way.
- Each group then presents their profile to the rest of the class.
- The rest of the class evaluate and comment on each presentation.

Rigolo 2 — Unit 8: Les vêtements

National criteria

KS2 Framework objectives

O6.1	Understand the main points and simple opinions in a spoken story, song or passage
O6.2	Perform to an audience
O6.3	Understand longer and more complex phrases or sentences
O6.4	Use spoken language confidently to initiate and sustain conversations and to tell stories
L6.1	Read and understand the main points and some detail from a short written passage
L6.2	Identify different text types and read short, authentic texts for enjoyment or information
L6.3	Match sound to sentences and paragraphs
L6.4	Write sentences on a range of topics using a model
IU6.1	Compare attitudes towards aspects of everyday life
IU6.2	Recognise and understand some of the differences between people
IU6.3	Present information about an aspect of culture

QCA Scheme of Work

Unit 18	Les planètes
Unit 19	Notre école
Unit 22	Ici et là

National Curriculum attainment levels

AT1.1–4, AT2.1–4, AT3.1–4, AT4.2–4

Language ladder levels

Listening:	Breakthrough, Grades 1–4
Reading:	Breakthrough, Grades 1–4
Speaking:	Breakthrough, Grades 1–4
Writing:	Breakthrough, Grades 2–4

5–14 guideline strands — Levels A–D

Listening
Listening for information and instructions	A, B, C, D
Listening and reacting to others	A, B, C, D

Speaking
Speaking to convey information	A, B, C, D
Speaking and interacting with others	A, B, C, D
Speaking about experiences, feelings and opinions	A, B, C, D

Reading
Reading for information and instructions	A, B, C, D
Reading aloud	A, B, C, D

Writing
Writing to exchange information and ideas	A, B, C, D
Writing to establish and maintain personal contact	A, B, C, D
Writing imaginatively to entertain	A, B, C, D

Unit objectives

- Ask and say what clothes you'd like
- Give opinions about clothes
- Say what clothes you wear
- Ask and talk about prices (including 60–80)

Key language

- Qu'est-ce que tu veux? Tu veux… ? Je voudrais un t-shirt, un pantalon, un chapeau, une veste, une jupe, une chemise, des chaussures, des lunettes de soleil + et
- C'est comment? C'est moche, beau, trop grand, trop petit, trop cher… et/mais…
- Je porte… un pantalon, un chapeau, un t-shirt, une veste, une chemise, une jupe, des chaussures, des lunettes de soleil…
  rose, orange, marron, rouge(s), jaune(s), vert(e)(s), bleu(e)(s), noir(e)(s) , blanc(s), blanche(s)
- C'est combien? Ça coûte [soixante-douze] euros
  Numbers 60 to 80

Grammar and skills

- Using *des* with plural words
- Giving opinions using *c'est*…
- Using *et* and *mais* to make longer sentences
- Agreement of adjectives
- Practising new language with a friend
- Techniques for memorising language

Unit outcomes

Most children will be able to:
- Say what clothes they'd like
- Give opinion about clothes
- Say what clothes they're wearing
- Use numbers 60 to 80

Some children will also be able to:
- Use *et* and *mais* to make longer sentences
- Understand and use agreement of adjectives
- Understand and use *des* with plural words

Unit 8 Lesson 1

Lesson summary

Context
Asking and saying what clothes you'd like

National Criteria
KS2 Framework: **O6.1, O6.2, O6.3, O6.4, L6.1, L6.4, IU6.1, IU6.2**
Attainment levels: **AT1.1–4, AT2.1–3; AT3.1–4, AT4.2–3**
Language ladder levels:
   Listening: **Grades 1–4**; Speaking: **Grades 1–3**; Reading: **Grades 1–4**; Writing: **Grades 2–3**

Cross-cirricular links
Textiles

Key vocabulary
un t-shirt, un pantalon, un chapeau, une veste, une jupe, une chemise, des chaussures, des lunettes de soleil

Language structures and outcomes
Qu'est-ce que tu veux? Tu veux… ? Je voudrais… (un t-shirt, etc.) + et

---

1. Starter activity: Les vêtements ⏱ 5 mins AT1.1 / AT2.1 / AT3.1 O6.3

Materials
Rigolo 1 CD-ROM, whiteboard.

Description
A quick revision of clothes items from *Rigolo 1* (Unit 12, Lesson 3, Presentation).

Delivery
Show again the *Rigolo 1* presentation from Unit 12 to refresh pupils' memory about clothes items.

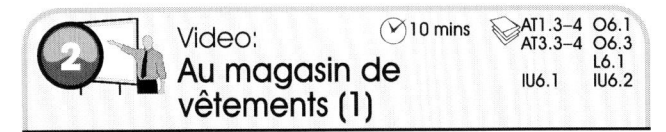

---

2. Video: Au magasin de vêtements (1) ⏱ 10 mins AT1.3–4 / AT3.3–4 / IU6.1 O6.1 / O6.3 / L6.1 / IU6.2

Materials
CD-ROM, Whiteboard; Unit 8 Flashcards (Clothes).

Description
Watch and listen to this video story presenting the language for Lessons 1 and 2. You can pause and rewind the story at any point.

Delivery
● Display the clothes flashcards on the board. Ask pupils to note the order in which each item of clothing is mentioned.
● Play the video through.
● Ask pupils to come to the board and arrange the flashcards in order of appearance.
● Replay the video without stopping. Check whether their list of cards is in the correct order.

Support
Pause the video after each item of clothing is mentioned. Ask pupils to come to the board and place the cards in the correct order.

Intercultural understanding

Use the video to ask pupils to look carefully at the types of clothes and shops featured. Are the clothes the same as those they buy in their own country? What differences can they see? What is the currency they use? Take the opportunity to note that these French children are buying clothes for school as there is no school uniform in France. Discuss with the class differences between this and their own situation.

---

3. Presentation: Quel vêtement? ⏱ 10 mins AT1.1–2 / AT2.1–2 / AT3.1–2 O6.1 / O6.4

Materials
CD-ROM, whiteboard; Unit 8 Flashcards (Clothes).

Description
Tap on the clothes to hear them presented. Use the additional features to practise sound/spelling links, word classes and spelling, or to record your own version of each word.

Delivery
● Invite pupils to the front to tap on an item of clothing. The class listens to the presentation of each item and repeats. They can repeat just the item or the full sentence including *je voudrais* ('I would like').
● Continue in this way for all eight items and repeat if further practice is required.

Refer to the Introduction for notes on the *Record, Sound, Spell* and *Word* features.

Extension
Remind pupils that *des* ('some') is used as a plural article when referring to objects in a general way, whereas *les* is used to refer to specific objects and means 'the'. *Un* and *une* become *des* in the plural. *Le, la* and *l'* become *les* in the plural. If useful, draw a table on the board to show the patterns.

Support
Use the flashcards to do further oral practice of the items of clothing.

---

4. Oracy activity: Qu'est-ce que tu veux? ⏱ 5–10 mins AT1.3 O6.3

Materials
CD-ROM, whiteboard; Unit 8 Flashcards (Clothes).

Description
Tap on *Allez*. Listen and tap on the correct picture for each piece of clothing mentioned in the dialogues.

Delivery
● We hear one or two items of clothing being mentioned. The pupil at the front taps on the relevant picture(s).
● The picture(s) will become highlighted if the selection is correct. Otherwise, the pupil will be invited to try again.
● Continue for all eight dialogues and repeat if further practice is needed.

Extension
Ask pupil if they can pick out any additional information from the dialogues.

Support
- Encourage less confident pupils to use the *Encore* button as necessary. Remind them that they don't need to understand everything that is said, just the key words.
- Display the picture and text flashcards during the activity as additional prompts.

📄 Worksheet 1 *Parlez!* may be used from this point onwards.

5. Literacy activity: Le jeu des étiquettes
⏱ 5–10 mins 📚 AT3.1–2 L6.4

Materials
Items of clothing; pre-prepared labels for clothing items, or blank paper for pupils to make their own labels.

Description
Pupils play a game matching words to real items of clothing.

Delivery
- Bring in a bag of clothing (see the list of Key vocabulary for this lesson) and spread out the items on a table at the front of the class.
- Hand out your labels, or give each group a piece of paper. Dictate an item of clothing for them to write out.
- Ask each group to match their label to the correct item.

Extension
Develop work on plural articles and nouns by bringing in multiple items and organising plural labels accordingly.

Support
Put labels on the board in advance, for pupils' reference.

📄 Worksheet 2 *Lisez!* may be used from this point onwards.

6. Plenary activity: Je voudrais une jupe
⏱ 10 mins 📚 AT1.2 O6.3

Materials
Items of clothing (see previous activity) or two sets of Unit 8 Flashcards (Clothes) if real clothes not available.

Description
Further listening practice in identifying the correct items of clothing.

Delivery
- Bring in a bag of clothing, including multiple items where possible (see the Key vocabulary for this lesson) and share the items between two tables at the front of the class.
- Divide the class into two teams and ask two representatives from each team to come to the front.
- Call out *Je voudrais [un pantalon] et [deux chapeaux]*. The first team to hold up the requested items wins a point for each item.
- Invite two more representatives from each team to the front and repeat, requesting different items.
- Continue until all items have been covered at least once.

Extension
Include some additional information, e.g. *Je voudrais un chapeau bleu* or *Il fait beau. Je voudrais des lunettes de soleil*.

Support
Request one item at a time until pupils become more confident.

Worksheet 1: Parlez!
⏱ 10 mins 📚 AT2.2–3 O6.2 O6.4

Description
This worksheet provides further speaking practice in items of clothing. It may be used at any point after Activity 4.

Answers
(*any order acceptable*)
Je voudrais…
Partner A:
1 un pantalon et un chapeau
3 des chaussures et une chemise
5 une veste et des lunettes de soleil
7 un t-shirt et une jupe
Partner B:
2 une veste et une jupe
4 un t-shirt et des lunettes de soleil
6 une chemise et un pantalon
8 un chapeau et des chaussures

Worksheet 2: Lisez!
⏱ 10 mins 📚 AT3.2 L6.1 AT4.2–3 L6.4

Description
This worksheet provides further reading and writing practice in items of clothing. It may be used at any point after Activity 5.

Answers
a 5 b 3 c 6 d 4 e 2 f 1

Unit 8 — Lesson 2

Lesson summary

Context
Giving opinions about clothes

National Criteria
KS2 Framework: **O6.1, O6.2, O6.3, O6.4, L6.1, L6.4, IU6.1, IU6.2**
Attainment Levels: **AT1.2–4, AT2.2–4; AT3.2–4, AT4.2–4**
Language Ladder Levels:
   Listening: **Grades 2–4**; Speaking: **Grades 2–4**;
   Reading: **Grades 2–4**; Writing: **Grades 2–4**

Cross-curricular links
Drama (fashion show)

Key vocabulary
C'est... moche, beau, trop grand, trop petit, trop cher

Language structures and outcomes
C'est comment? C'est [moche] et/mais...

---

1. Starter activity: C'est comment? — 5 mins
AT1.2 O6.3
AT2.2 O6.4
AT3.2

Materials
CD-ROM (Unit 6, Lesson 2 Presentation), whiteboard.

Description
Quick revision of colour and size descriptions.

Delivery
- Re-show the presentation from Unit 6 Lesson 2 to revise describing colour and size using *C'est...*
- We hear M. Chanson describing the room. Mme Chanson then repeats his description and adds an additional description.
- Pupils repeat both descriptions.
- Continue for all six rooms.

2. Video story: Au magasin de vêtements (1) — 5–10 mins
AT1.3–4 O6.1
AT3.3–4 O6.3
           L6.1
IU6.1   IU6.2

Materials
CD-ROM, whiteboard.

Description
Watch and listen again to this video story presenting the language for Lessons 1 and 2. You can pause and rewind the story at any point.

Delivery
- Tell pupils that this time they must listen out for any opinions/descriptions of the clothes featured.
- Play the video and ask for pupils' answers. Accept answers in English or French at this stage. Note their suggestions on the board.
- Play the video through again, pausing to check pupils' suggestions.

Extension
Ask pupils to note also the reasons for the purchases (e.g. Thomas needs a shirt and trousers to visit his grandparents).

Support
Pause the video after each description/opinion on the first viewing.

3. Presentation: C'est beau mais c'est trop grand — 5–10 mins
AT1.2–3 O6.3
AT2.2–3 O6.4
AT3.2–3

Materials
CD-ROM, whiteboard.

Description
Tap on Olivier to hear the question and answer. Use the additional features to practise sound/spelling links and word classes, or to record your own version of each question and answer exchange.

Delivery
- Pupils listen to and repeat Olivier's question, then do the same for Didier's answer.
- Continue for all seven t-shirts and repeat if further practice is required.
- The last two build up to saying two opinion using *et* and *mais*. Go over the meaning of these conjunctions of necessary.

Refer to the Introduction for notes on the *Record, Sound* and *Word* features.

4. Oracy activity: C'est trop cher! — 10 mins
AT1.2–3 O6.3
AT2.2–3 O6.4

Materials
CD-ROM (whiteboard)

Description
Pupils practise describing and giving opinions on clothes using the previous whiteboard activity (see Activity 3 above).

Delivery
- Turn off the sound on the Presentation from Activity 3 and invite two pupils to reproduce the dialogue.
- Turn on the sound to check their answers.
- Repeat with different pupils for the other seven t-shirts.

Extension
Ask more confident pupils to make up longer descriptions, e.g. by adding colours to the descriptions.

Unit 8: Lesson 2

5. Literacy activity: C'est beau mais...
⏱ 10 mins　AT3.2–3　L6.4

Materials
CD-ROM, whiteboard.

Description
Tap on *Allez*. Look at the pictures of Gustave wearing different jackets and drag the text into the correct order.

Delivery
- Pupils make a sentence which describes Gustave's jacket (all sentences use *et* or *mais*), then on *Fini* to see if the sentence is correct.
- The scene becomes animated if the answer is right. One of three 'lives' is lost for each incorrect answer. If three 'lives' are lost pupils are invited to start a new game.
- Continue until all six jackets have been covered, and repeat if necessary.

Extension
Hold up items from your clothes bag and ask pupils to make similar sentences about them.

Support
If pupils are not confident about sentence-building, this activity can be done as a whole-class activity. The class suggests what the sentence should be (and discusses their choices if necessary) before the pupil taps on *Fini*.

Worksheets 3 *Grammaire* and 4 *Écrivez* may be used from this point onwards.

6. Plenary activity: C'est moche!
⏱ 10 mins　AT2.2–3　O6.4

Materials
Bag of clothes (see the Key vocabulary for this lesson) of different sizes and styles, some with a visible price tag (in euros) attached.

Description
Pupils give their opinions on clothes being modelled on the 'catwalk'.

Delivery
- Ask for a few volunteer pupils to dress up in the clothes. The 'models' do a quick walk round the room so all pupils get a good look.
- The models stand at the front, one by one, and the audience volunteers opinions/descriptions on each item of clothing e.g. *C'est trop grand*.
- Continue for all the clothes.

Extension
Encourage pupils to make longer sentences linked by *et* or *mais*, e.g. *C'est beau mais c'est trop cher*.

Worksheet 3: Grammaire
⏱ 10 mins　AT3.2　L6.1
AT4.2–3　L6.4

Description
This worksheet provides further practice in forming sentences using *c'est* with *et* and *mais*. It may be used at any point after Activity 5.

Answers
1.
   a C'est trop petit.
   b C'est trop grand.
   c C'est moche.
   d C'est trop cher.
   e C'est beau.
   f C'est trop petit.

Language learning strategies

Practise new language with a friend and outside the classroom

Where possible, encourage pupils to work in pairs or small groups to practise new language. The dialogues in Worksheet 4 give a good opportunity for pupils to practise their dialogues with a friend. Encourage them to listen carefully to each other and to correct pronunciation where necessary. You could also encourage more confident pupils to perform their dialogues for the rest of the class. It also helps language learning if they can memorise their dialogues; this will help them recall short phrases in future lessons.

Worksheet 4: Écrivez!
⏱ 10–15 mins　AT2.3–4　O6.2
AT3.3–4　L6.1
AT4.3–4　L6.4

Description
This worksheet provides practice in reading, writing and taking part in longer dialogues. It may be used at any point after Activity 5.

Answers
1.
   - Salut!
   - **Salut! Où vas-tu?**
   - Je **vais** au magasin de vêtements.
   - **Qu'est-ce que tu veux?**
   - Je **voudrais** un pantalon.
   - **Un pantalon? C'est pour l'école ?**
   - Oui.
   - **Voilà un beau pantalon!**
   - Je vais essayer.
   - **Ça va?**
   - Ah **non**, ça ne va pas.
   - **C'est comment?**
   - C'est **trop** petit.
   - **Ah zut!**

2.
   - Salut!
   - **Salut! Où vas-tu?**
   - Je vais au magasin de vêtements.
   - **Qu'est-ce que tu veux?**
   - Je voudrais un chapeau.
   - **Un chapeau? C'est pour les vacances?**
   - Oui. Je vais au bord de la mer.
   - **On va regarder? Voilà un chapeau!**
   - Je vais essayer
   - **C'est comment?**
   - C'est beau, mais c'est trop cher.
   - **Ah, zut!**

Unit 8 — Lesson 3

Lesson summary

Context
Saying what clothes you wear

National Criteria
KS2 Framework: O6.1, O6.2, O6.3, O6.4, L6.1, L6.2, L6.3, L6.4, IU6.1, IU6.2
Attainment Levels: AT1.2–4, AT2.2–3; AT3.2–4, AT4.3–4
Language Ladder Levels:
  Listening: **Grades 2–4**; Speaking: **Grades 2–3**;
  Reading: **Grades 2–4**; Writing: **Grades 3–4**

Cross-curricular links
Literacy, music, numeracy

Key vocabulary
Je porte… un pantalon, un chapeau, un t-shirt, une veste, une chemise, une jupe, des chaussures, des lunettes de soleil…
rose, orange, marron, rouge(s), jaune(s), vert(e)(s), bleu(e)(s), noir(e)(s), blanc(s), blanche(s)

Language structures and outcomes
Je porte [un pantalon] [noir]. Je porte [une veste] [noire].

---

1. Starter activity: 5 mins — Les vêtements et les couleurs
AT1.2–3 O6.3
AT2.2–3 O6.4
AT3.2–3

Materials
CD-ROM (*Rigolo 1*, Unit 12, Lesson 4 Presentation), whiteboard.

Description
Quick revision of clothes and colours.

Delivery
- Re-show the presentation from *Rigolo 1*, Unit 12 Lesson 4 to revise clothes and colours.
- Pupils tap on the pots of paint and the clothes, and listen/repeat.

Extension
Highlight the agreement of adjectives and focus pupils' attention on the pronunciation and spelling of *vert/verte*, etc.

Knowledge about language

Noticing and matching agreements
For more confident pupils, this unit gives the opportunity to focus on agreement of adjectives. Put some clothing items + colours on the board and ask pupils to note the pattern, e.g. *un pantalon noir; une veste noire; des chaussures noires*.
- If you wish, you can explain the rule that adjectives which describe masculine nouns stay the same; those which describe feminine nouns add an '*e*' (unless the adjective already ends in an '*e*'); those which describe masculine plural nouns add an '*s*'; and those which describe feminine plural nouns add '*-es*'.
- Use Worksheet 5 *Grammaire* to do some specific practice but first give plenty of examples on the board. Draw attention to these patterns as they occur throughout the lesson. NB: exceptions to the pattern are *marron*, which never changes, and *blanc/blanche*.

2. Video story: 10 mins — Au magasin de vêtements (2)
AT1.3–4 O6.1 IU6.1
AT3.3–4 O6.3 IU6.2
         L6.1

Materials
CD-ROM, whiteboard; *Rigolo 1* Unit 2 Flashcards (Colours).

Description
Watch and listen to this video story presenting the language for Lessons 3 and 4. You can pause and rewind the story at any point.

Delivery
- Pupils watch the video story and note which colours are mentioned.
- Elicit pupils' answers. Stick the relevant colour flashcards on the board.
- Play the video story through once more, pausing after each colour to check it is on the board.
- Draw pupils' attention to the agreement of colours e.g. *blanc/blanches*.

Support
For less confident pupils, pause the video during the first viewing after each colour is mentioned. Stick the flashcards on the board as you go along.

3. Presentation: 10 mins — Qu'est-ce que tu portes?
AT1.2–3 O6.3
AT2.2–3 O6.4
AT3.2–3

Materials
CD-ROM, whiteboard.

Description
Tap on a garment to hear the question and answer. Use the additional features to practise sound/spelling links and word classes, or to record your own version of each question and answer exchange.

Delivery
- We hear the question *Qu'est-ce que tu portes?* then see Polly wearing the item and saying what it is (*Je porte une jupe bleue*).
- The whole class repeats the question and the answer.
- Again, draw pupils' attention to the agreement of colours/nouns.
- Point out that in French the colours come after the noun.
- Continue for all eight items and repeat if further practice is required.

Refer to the Introduction for notes on the *Record*, *Sound* and *Word* features.

Extension
Ask pupils to look carefully at the spellings of the colours and to tell you whether the noun is feminine, masculine or plural.

4. Oracy activity: Je porte une chemise rouge
10 mins — AT1.2–3 O6.3, AT2.2–3 O6.4

Materials
CD-ROM, whiteboard.

Description
Tap on *Allez*. Answer the question about what each character is wearing.

Delivery
- When pupils hear the question, they say aloud what the character is wearing e.g. *Je porte une jupe rouge, un t-shirt bleu et des chaussures blanches*. Tap on the audio check button to compare. Focus pupils on accurate pronunciation of the answers.
- Repeat for all six characters and repeat if required.
- By dividing the class into two groups you could make this into a team game, awarding a point for each correct answer.

Extension
Highlight the intonation in these longer sentences, rising at a comma and falling at a full-stop.

Worksheet 5 *Grammaire* may be used from this point onwards.

5. Literacy activity: Le jeu des couleurs
10–15 mins — AT3.3 L6.4

Materials
Items of clothing (see Lesson 1 notes), blank card or pre-prepared labels (see below).

Description
Pupils label items of clothing, incorporating agreement of colour adjectives.

Delivery
- Re-use clothing labels from Lesson 1, or make a new set.
- Write out separate colour labels in all possible variations (i.e. singular masculine, singular feminine, plural masculine, plural feminine).
- Hold up one item of clothing at a time and invite pupils to come up and select the appropriate labels (i.e. clothing plus colour).
- Continue with other items, sometimes holding up multiple items to practise plurals.
- If time allows pupils can dress up and describe what they're wearing.

Extension
Divide the class into teams. Silently, stick a description on the board. The first team to read and select correctly the item of clothing wins a point.

Support
First introduce the masculine/feminine agreement of the colours. When pupils are confident with this you can add the plurals.

Worksheet 6 *Écrivez!* may be used from this point onwards.

6. Plenary activity: Coco le Clown
10 mins — AT1.3 O6.1, AT2.3 O6.2, AT3.3 O6.3, L6.1 L6.2 L6.3

Materials
CD-ROM (*Rigolo 1*, Unit 12 Lesson 4 Song), whiteboard; cut-up printouts of lyrics (one per group).

Description
Song to revise clothes and colours.

Delivery
- Re-play the song from Rigolo 1, Unit 12 Lesson 4, which contain clothes and colours.
- Hand out the cut-up lyrics (one set for each group of pupils) and ask pupils to re-arrange the lyrics in the correct order.
- Play the song one more time for pupils to check/modify their answers.

Extension
Print off the full lyrics and blank out some of the words so that pupils must fill in the gaps. Remember to turn off the text when you play the song!

Worksheet 5: Grammaire
10 mins — AT3.3 L6.4, AT4.3

Description
This worksheet provides further practice in agreement of adjectives. It may be used at any point after Activity 4.

Answers
1

masc. sing.	fem. sing.	masc. plural	fem. plural
jaune	jaune	jaunes	jaunes

masc. sing.	fem. sing.	masc. plural	fem. plural
bleu	bleue	bleus	bleues
noir	noire	noirs	noires

2
1. Je voudrais un chapeau **noir**.
2. Je porte un pantalon **rouge**.
3. Jake porte des chaussures **vertes**.
4. Je voudrais une jupe **bleue**.
5. Je voudrais des lunettes de soleil **jaunes**.
6. Tu veux des chemises **blanches**?

3
1. une jupe bleue
2. des chaussures noires
3. une veste verte
4. des lunettes de soleil rouges
5. une chemise jaune

Worksheet 6: Écrivez!
10 mins — AT3.4 L6.1, AT4.3–4 L6.2, L6.4

Description
This worksheet provides further practice in agreement of adjectives. It may be used at any point after Activity 5.

Answers
1. Le samedi à neuf heures, je vais à l'école. Je porte *une jupe bleue* et une **chemise blanche**. À trois heures, je vais au centre sportif. Je porte un **pantalon bleu**, un **t-shirt rouge** et des **chaussures blanches**.
Le dimanche à deux heures, je vais chez Polly. On écoute de la musique, on danse et on chante dans le salon. Je porte une **jupe verte**, une **veste noire**, et des **lunettes de soleil jaunes**.

Unit 8 — Lesson 4

Lesson summary

Context
Asking and talking about prices (including numbers 60-80).

National Criteria
KS2 Framework: O6.1, O6.2, O6.3, O6.4, L6.1, L6.2, L6.3, L6.4, IU6.1, IU6.2
Attainment Levels: AT1.1–4, AT2.1–4; AT3.1–4, AT4.2–4
Language Ladder Levels:
  Listening: **Grades 1–4**; Speaking: **Grades 1–4**;
  Reading: **Grades 1–4**; Writing: **Grades 2–4**

Cross-curricular links
Numeracy; ICT – Project work, Art and design, Music

Key vocabulary
Numbers 60 to 80

Language structures and outcomes
C'est combien?
Ça coûte [soixante-douze] euros.

---

1. Starter activity: Les nombres (1–60)
5–10 mins — AT1.1–2, AT2.1–2, O6.4

Materials
Possibly *Rigolo 1* CD-ROM (any of the number activities from Units 2 or 6) or pre-prepared number flashcards.

Description
Pupils revise numbers 1 – 60.

Delivery
- Do any of the above-mentioned activities, or play your own favourite number game to quickly revise numbers 1 to 60.
- You could also play *Buzz-Bof*: Each pupil says a number in sequence, but when someone comes to a number with 7 in it (or a multiple of 7), they must say 'Bof' instead of the number. Failure to remember this means the pupil is out of the game! Continue until there is just one winner.

2. Video story: Au magasin de vêtements (2)
5–10 mins — AT1.3–4, AT3.3–4, O6.1, O6.3, L6.1, IU6.1, IU6.2

Materials
CD-ROM, whiteboard.

Description
Watch and listen again to this video story presenting the language for Lessons 3 and 4. You can pause and rewind the story at any point.

Delivery
- Ask pupils to watch the video and listen out in particular for the prices.
- Write their answers on the board and play the film through one more time for pupils to double-check their answers.

Extension
Ask more confident pupils if they can also listen out for the question (*C'est combien?*) *and* tell you how the prices were given (*Ça coûte [20] Euros*).

Support
Write four prices on the board, including the two correct prices, from which pupils choose their answers.

3. Presentation: Les nombres 60–80
10–15 mins — AT1.1–2, AT2.1–2, AT3.1–2, O6.3, O6.4

Materials
CD-ROM, whiteboard.

Description
Tap on a number to hear it presented, or listen to a group of numbers presented in sequence. Use the additional features to practise spelling and sound/spelling links, or to record your own version of each word.

Delivery
- After tapping on a number, pupils can then tap on *Comptez!* to hear a continuous presentation of the numbers. Ask pupils to listen and join in if/where they can.
- Invite pupils to tap on the same numbers individually, giving time for the class to listen and repeat.
- Approach the second group of numbers (71 to 80) in the same way.
- Repeat as necessary.
- Once the numbers have been practised as numbers you can practise them as prices. Prepare for this and further oral activities by starting at 60 and counting around the class. Gradually add conditions, e.g. missing out numbers that include a '7'.
- Then use real garments or Unit 8 Flashcards, with a number chart or prepared prices. Ask *C'est combien?* Show a number + euros. Elicit the answer *Ça coûte… euros*.
- Ask who knows how much a euro is worth (generally between 60p and 70p).
- Build up to shop dialogues, e.g.
A: *Bonjour.*
B: *Bonjour. Qu'est-ce que tu veux?*
A: *Je voudrais [une jupe bleue], s'il vous plaît.*
B: *Voici [une jupe bleue].*
A: *Mmm. C'est beau. C'est combien?*
B: *Soixante-dix euros.*
A: *Ah non, c'est trop cher. Au revoir!*
B: *Au revoir!*

Refer to the Introduction for notes on the *Record*, *Spell* and *Sound* features.

Extension
- Encourage children to establish and discuss how these composite numbers are made up. Elicit the fact that counting in scores is a relic of counting on fingers and toes.
- If pupils can cope, you may wish to cover numbers up to 100.

Support
Consolidate the new numbers with further number games in class.

4. Song: Je voudrais un pantalon bleu
15 mins — AT1.3–4, AT2.3–4, AT3.3–4, O6.1, O6.2, O6.3, L6.1, L6.2, L6.3

Materials
CD-ROM, whiteboard.

Description
Watch and listen to the interactive karaoke song about buying clothes. Choose either *Practice* or *Sing* mode: *Practice* to go through the song line by line; *Sing* to sing it all the way through. Switch the music and words on or off as you prefer, or try recording your own version.

Delivery
- Write the names of the three featured characters on the board (Jake, Didier and Polly).
- Ask pupils to listen for the item of clothing each character wants to buy, and any other information they hear about the item (e.g. price, what the problem is).
- Play the song through once in *Sing* mode and elicit pupils' answers. Note the answers on the board.
- Go through the song in *Practice* mode, checking general comprehension and verifying the information on the board.
- Play the song through once more in *Sing* mode for pupils to sing along. If time allows, divide the class into groups and make this final stage into a Karaoke competition.
- Pupils could perform the song at an assembly in front of fellow pupils/parents.

Extension
Pupils could use the song as a model and write/sing their own verses. Divide the class into three groups and assign a verse to each group. Each group must then reconstruct their verse and perform it to the class.

Support
Give pupil the lines of the song jumbled up. They cut up the lines and reconstruct them as they listen.

Worksheet 7 *Parlez!* may be used from this point onwards.

Language learning strategies

Comparing and reflecting on techniques for memorising language
- Discuss ways of memorising language with pupils. Brainstorm ideas on this topic by asking, e.g.
- Do they prefer to use the 'look/cover/write' technique they used in younger years for English words?
- Is it better with French words if they also say the words out loud, or perhaps learn the words with a partner and work together orally rather than writing them down?
- How do they best learn phrases rather than words?
- Does rhythmic repetition help them learn?
- Try learning a verse of the song by heart or even the whole song. It's often easier to memorise phrases when set to music. Try to do this as a class and evaluate afterwards. Did it work better than just learning set phrases without music? Reflect on this from time to time and pool ideas for other techniques from the whole class.

5 Literacy activity: 10–15 mins — AT3.2 L6.1
Loto des nombres

Materials
CD-ROM, whiteboard.

Description
Play bingo in teams, using completed cards, filling your own cards in on screen, or using a printed grid. Then mark off the word on your card if you see the number appear on-screen. The first player or team with all their numbers marked off wins.

Delivery
- Divide the class into two teams. Select the required type of bingo cards (one for Team A, one for Team B.)
- Tap on *Allez* to hear a number, in the form of a price in euros. Pupils tap on the numbers in their grid each time a relevant number is called.
- The game ends with one team completing their card. Play again to give further practice if required.

Worksheet 8 *Lisez!* may be used from this point onwards

6 Plenary activity: 10 mins — AT1.2–3 O6.3 / AT2.2–3 O6.4
Le Juste Prix

Materials
Bag of clothing items or Unit 8 Flashcards (Clothes); pre-prepared list of clothes and prices in euros (only seen by teacher!).

Description
A game based on the TV show 'The Price is Right' to give further practice in using higher numbers.

Delivery
- Divide the class into two teams and display the clothes at the front of the class.
- Hold up an item of clothing and ask *C'est combien?* Each team guesses the price in euros. The team with the answer closest to the correct price wins a point.
- Hand the item or card to the team and continue until all items have been done.

Support
Play a simpler number game before this one, to revise numbers.

Worksheet 7: Parlez! — 10 mins AT2.3–4 O6.2 O6.4

Description
This worksheet provides practice in shop conversations. It may be used any point after Activity 4.

Worksheet 8: Lisez! — 10 mins AT3.4 L6.1 L6.2

Description
This worksheet provides more extended reading practice. It may be used at any point after Activity 5.

Answers
1. 1 (*any four*): une jupe, une chemise, une veste, mon chapeau, mes lunettes de soleil
   2. histoire-géo, anglais, français, maths
   3. (*any four*): à l'école, à la montagne, à la piscine, au centre sportif, au café, au parc d'attractions
   4. j'aime ça, c'est super, j'aime Polly, elle est sympa.

2. 1 A black skirt, a red shirt and a white jacket.
   2. She plays tennis after school.
   3. She's going to the mountains (to ski)
   4. Lessons cost 20€ an hour. She thinks that's expensive.
   5. Thursdays at 5.00.
   6. She goes to the café, has an orange juice and a sandwich.
   7. She wears her hat and sunglasses because it's hot.
   8. She goes to the amusement park at 1.00. She'll go on the rides.
   9. She sees Polly at 3.00. She thinks Polly's nice.
   10. They dance, sing, listen to CDs and watch TV.

Unit 8 **Extra!**

Project work: L'uniforme scolaire
⏱ 1 hour 📄 AT3.3–4 L6.2 / AT4.2–4 L6.4 / IU6.1 IU6.2 / IU6.3

Description
Pupils prepare a labelled display/PowerPoint presentation on their school uniform.

Materials
Photos of a school uniform or real items of clothing (borrowed from Lost Property?), blank display card/labels; if possible, access to a PC (ideally with internet access) and printer.

Delivery
- Divide the class into small groups. Pupils prepare a display/PowerPoint presentation in which they label their uniform and take turns to present it to the rest of the class. Encourage more confident pupils to speak in sentences or to prepare short paragraphs rather than just labels.

- If you are in contact with a French school, pupils could email one of the displays and ask the French pupils to send one on their own typical school clothes. This would make for an interesting cultural comparison, and pupils could discuss the pros and cons of having a uniform.

Sound/spelling activity: Les sons 'an', 'en', 'in', 'on' et 'un'
⏱ 10–15 mins 📄 AT1.1 AT2.1

Description:
Practice mode:
Listen and practise pronouncing nasal sounds on their own and then in words that have been covered in *Rigolo* so far.

Activity mode:
Listen to the words and phrases and count how many nasal sounds you hear in each, then tap on the correct number on the screen.

Delivery
- This sound/spelling activity focuses specifically on the different nasal sounds.

- Select *Practice* and tap on *Next* to start this part. Then tap on *Allez*. The Virtual Teacher will say the nasal sounds as part of words that have been met in *Rigolo*. For each of these, get the class to repeat the words chorally several times, checking the model each time using the *Encore* button. You can also use the *Record* feature here to compare a pupil's pronunciation more closely with the model.

- Once you have finished this part, tap on *Activity* to move on to test pupils' recognition of these sounds. Tap on *Allez*. Pupils will hear 12 phrases read out. For each phrase they must work out how many nasal sounds they hear. They tap on the correct number button on screen, between 0 (if they don't hear it at all) and 4.

- To show pupils how the activity works, tap on *Example* and *Encore* to hear the phrase again. You can ask the whole class to vote on how many times they hear the sound and ask individual pupils to come forward to select the right number.

- When they have selected the right number, you will see the phrase appear on screen and the nasal sound will be highlighted at the appropriate stage of the audio. Tap on *Encore* if you want to hear the phrase again and review answers.

- Repeat the activity if pupils need further practice.

Extension
Ask pupils to listen to the video or song again and ask them to raise their hand whenever they hear one of these nasal sounds.

Support
Divide the class into groups and allocate a sound to each group. They must try to find as many words as possible with 'their' sound during the next lesson. Swap sounds/groups each week so everyone covers each sound.

Assessment for Units 7–8

Écoutez!

Play each audio 2–3 times, or more if necessary. Pause during each activity as required.

Total marks for listening: 20.

Activity 1a, 1b (AT1.2; O6.3)
Mark out of 10.

Answers
2b (m) 3 c (f) 4f (f) 5e (m) 6a (m)

> Example:
> 1 – Qu'est-ce qu'il fait le lundi?
>   – Le lundi matin, il joue au tennis.
> 2 – Qu'est-ce qu'il fait le mardi?
>   – Le mardi après-midi, il fait du vélo.
> 3 – Qu'est-ce qu'elle fait le mercredi?
>   – Le mercredi soir, elle regarde un film.
> 4 – Qu'est-ce qu'elle fait le jeudi?
>   – Le jeudi après-midi, elle joue au football.
> 5 – Qu'est-ce qu'il fait le vendredi?
>   – Le vendredi après-midi, il fait du roller.
> 6 – Qu'est-ce qu'il fait le samedi?
>   – Le samedi matin, il écoute la radio.

Activity 2 (AT1.3; O6.3)
Mark out of 10.

Answers

	object	colour	comment
1	(t-shirt)	red	(✓)
2	trousers	black	✗
3	sun-glasses	blue	✗
4	hat	green	✓

Unit 8: Extra!

> **1**
> – Qu'est-ce que tu veux?
> – Je voudrais *un t-shirt*.
> – Quelle couleur?
> – Un t-shirt rouge.
> – Voilà un t-shirt rouge.
> – *Oui, c'est beau!*
>
> **2**
> – Qu'est-ce que tu veux?
> – Je voudrais un pantalon.
> – Quelle couleur?
> – Un pantalon noir.
> – Voilà un pantalon noir.
> – Oh non, c'est trop grand
>
> **3**
> – Qu'est-ce que tu veux?
> – Je voudrais des lunettes de soleil.
> – Quelle couleur?
> – Des lunettes de soleil bleues.
> – Voilà des lunette de soleil bleues.
> – Non, c'est moche!
>
> **4**
> – Qu'est-ce que tu veux?
> – Je voudrais un chapeau.
> – Quelle couleur?
> – Un chapeau vert.
> – Voilà un chapeau vert.
> – Oui, c'est beau!

Parlez!

Pupils can work in pairs for the speaking tasks. If it is not possible to assess each pair, then assess a few pairs for each assessment block and mark the rest of the class based on the spoken work they do in class.

Total marks for speaking: 10.

Activity 1/2 (AT2.2; O6.4)
5 marks.

Answers
a: Je porte un pantalon [noir], des chaussures [bleues], un t-shirt [blanc], une veste [rouge] et un chapeau [vert].
b: Je porte une jupe [rouge], une chemise [bleue], des chaussures [noires], des lunettes de soleil [blanches] et un chapeau [jaune].

Activity 3 (AT2.3; O6.4)
5 marks (1 mark per answer).

Lisez!

Total marks for reading: 20.

Activity 1 (AT3.2; L6.1)
Mark out of 5.

Answers
a sunglasses 70€
b shoes 78€
c jacket 68€
d t-shirt 80€
(e *trousers 65€*)
f skirt 74€

Activity 2 (AT3.3–4; L6.1)
Mark out of 5.

Answers
correct sentences = 1, 3, 6, 8, 9

Écrivez!

Total marks for writing: 20.

Activity 1a (AT4.2; L6.4)
Mark out of 5.

Answers
a *le t-shirt*
b *les chaussures*
c *le chapeau*
d *les lunettes de soleil*
e *le pantalon*
f *la veste*

Activity 1b (AT4.2, L6.4)
Mark out of 5.

Answers
a *C'est trop petit!*
b *C'est trop grand!*
c *C'est beau!*
d *C'est moche!*
e *C'est trop cher!*
f *C'est moche!*

Activity 2 (AT4.3–4, L6.4)
Mark out of 10 (2 per sentence).

Rigolo 2 — Unit 9: Ma journée

National criteria

KS2 Framework objectives

O6.1	Understand the main points and simple opinions in a spoken story, song or passage
O6.2	Perform to an audience
O6.3	Understand longer and more complex phrases or sentences
O6.4	Use spoken language confidently to initiate and sustain conversations and to tell stories
L6.1	Read and understand the main points and some detail from a short written passage
L6.2	Identify different text types and read short, authentic texts for enjoyment or information
L6.3	Match sound to sentences and paragraphs
L6.4	Write sentences on a range of topics using a model
IU6.1	Compare attitudes towards aspects of everyday life
IU6.2	Recognise and understand some of the differences between people
IU6.3	Present information about an aspect of culture

QCA Scheme of Work

Unit 10	Vive le sport!
Unit 19	Notre école
Unit 15	En route pour l'école

National Curriculum attainment levels

AT1.2–4, AT2.2–4, AT3.2–4, AT4.2–4

Language ladder levels

Listening:	Breakthrough, Grades 2–4
Reading:	Breakthrough, Grades 2–4
Speaking:	Breakthrough, Grades 2–4
Writing:	Breakthrough, Grades 2–4

5–14 guideline strands — Levels A–D

Listening
Listening for information and instructions	A, B, C, D
Listening and reacting to others	A, B, C, D

Speaking
Speaking to convey information	A, B, C, D
Speaking and interacting with others	A, B, C, D
Speaking about experiences, feelings and opinions	A, B, C, D

Reading
Reading for information and instructions	A, B, C, D
Reading aloud	A, B, C, D

Writing
Writing to exchange information and ideas	A, B, C, D
Writing to establish and maintain personal contact	A, B, C, D
Writing imaginatively to entertain	A, B, C, D

Unit objectives

- Ask and talk about daily routine
- Talk about times of daily routine
- Ask and talk about breakfast
- Talk about details of a typical day

Key language

- *Je me lève, Je prends mon petit déjeuner, Je vais à l'école, Je prends mon déjeuner, Je quitte l'école, Je prends mon dîner, Je me couche*
- Daily routine phrases (Lesson 1) + *à… une heure, deux heures (moins) cinq, dix, vingt, vingt-cinq*
- *Qu'est-ce que tu prends au petit déjeuner? Je prends… un chocolat chaud, un café, un jus de pomme, un croissant, un pain au chocolat, des céréales, une tartine*
- *normalement, d'abord, ensuite, enfin, après l'école* + language from Lesson 3

Grammar and skills

- Use 1st person present tense including some reflexives
- Make longer sentences with times
- Use *et* to join sentences together
- Use adverbs and time expressions to make longer paragraphs
- Formulate questions
- Cope with longer reading texts
- Reflect and share ideas about language learning

Unit outcomes

Most children will be able to:
- Talk about their daily routine
- Say what time they do things
- Say what they have for breakfast
- Use *et* to join sentences together

Some children will also be able to:
- Formulate questions
- Write longer paragraphs using adverbs and time expressions
- Cope with longer reading texts

Unit 9 (Lesson 1)

Lesson summary

Context
Asking and talking about daily routine

National criteria
KS2 Framework: O6.1, O6.3, O6.4, L6.1, L6.3, L6.4, IU6.1, IU6.2
Attainment levels: AT1.2–4, AT2.2, AT3.2–4, AT4.2–3
Language ladder levels:
  Listening: **Grades 2–4**; Speaking: **Grade 2**;
  Reading: **Grades 2–4**; Writing: **Grades 2–3**

Cross-curricular links
Citizenship

Language structures and outcomes
Je me lève, Je prends mon petit déjeuner, Je vais à l'école, Je prends mon déjeuner, Je quitte l'école, Je prends mon dîner, Je me couche

---

1. Starter activity: La routine en Grande-Bretagne et en France
5–10 mins — IU6.1 IU6.2

Materials
Unit 9 Flashcards (Routine activities).

Description
A quick discussion/comparison of daily routines for pupils in Britain and in France.

Delivery
- Ask pupils to describe their daily weekday routine, including timings in English. Display the relevant flashcards on the board as the activities are mentioned.
- Ask the class if they know or can guess whether French pupils' routines are similar or different. (Remember, French school days usually start earlier and finish later, but have a longer lunch break. Also, French schools sometimes operate on Saturday mornings but are closed for a day or half a day on Wednesdays.)

2. Animated story: La routine (1)
10 mins — AT1.3–4, AT3.3–4, O6.1, O6.3, L6.1, L6.3, IU6.1, IU6.2

Materials
CD-ROM, whiteboard; Unit 9 Flashcards (Routine activities).

Description
Watch and listen to this interactive story presenting the language for Lessons 1 and 2. You can pause and rewind the story at any point, or record your own version too.

Delivery
- Display the flashcards on the board and ask pupils to note whether all activities are mentioned in the animation.
- Freeze the opening screen showing Monsieur and Madame Mills preparing to leave. Ask pupils to predict what they are doing, and what will happen during their absence.
- Play the story through, so that pupils can check if any predictions were correct and confirm which of the flashcard activities were mentioned. Accept answers in English and French at this stage as pupils will focus on activities language during this lesson.
- Summarise the story and key words together, then re-play the animation through one more time.

Support
Pause the animation each time an activity is mentioned and point to the relevant flashcard during the first viewing.

3. Presentation: Je vais à l'école
5–10 mins — AT1.2, AT2.2, AT3.2, O6.3

Materials
CD-ROM, whiteboard.

Description
Tap on each picture in turn to hear each action presented. Use the additional features to practise sound/spelling links and word classes, or to record your own version of each word.

Delivery
- The whole class listens to Olivier and repeats each sentence, miming the actions to reinforce learning.
- Continue for all seven actions and repeat if further practice is required.
- You may wish to point out that some French verbs have *me* in front of them. This indicates that we are doing the action to ourselves, i.e. getting (myself) up, washing (myself), putting myself to bed, etc.

Refer to the Introduction for notes on the *Record, Sound* and *Word* features.

Extension
Use the flashcards to provide further oral practice of the new expressions.

Support
Call out the actions one at a time and ask pupils to go to the board and tap on the relevant picture.

4. Oracy activity: Je me lève
5–10 mins — AT1.2, AT2.2, O6.4

Materials
CD-ROM, whiteboard.

Description
Tap on *Allez*. Imagine you are Olivier and describe what you are doing.

Delivery
- Pupils say aloud what Olivier is doing each time (using *Je…*). Tap on the audio check button to compare their answer with the correct one.
- Pupils tap on the tick button if their answer is correct. Otherwise, they tap on the cross and try again.
- Continue for all seven scenes and repeat if further practice is needed.

Support
Make this into a team activity so that less confident pupils can work together on the answer before saying it out loud.

📄 Worksheet 1 *Lisez!* may be used from this point onwards.

5. Literacy activity: 5–10 mins AT3.2 L6.3
Je prends mon petit déjeuner

Materials
Unit 9 Flashcards (Routine activities: pictures and captions).

Description
Pupils match flashcard captions and pictures.

Delivery
- Display the picture flashcards on the board. Place the captions in a pile.
- Invite two pupils to the front. One pupil selects a caption, holds it up and reads it out. The second pupil must identify the correct picture on the board.
- Repeat with different pupils and captions until you've covered all actions at least once.

Extension
Ask the first pupil to read out the caption without showing it, to make the activity more challenging. As a follow-up you could hold up a picture and get pupils to write down the phrases from memory.

Support
Start the activity with just three pictures + captions, and gradually increase the number of flashcards as pupils gain confidence.

📄 Worksheet 2 *Écrivez!* may be used from this point onwards.

6. Plenary activity: 5–10 mins AT1.2 O6.4
Je prends mon déjeuner

Materials
Unit 9 Flashcards (Routine activities).

Description
Flashcard game to reinforce language from the lesson.

Delivery
- Divide the class into two teams. Stick the picture flashcards, face-down, on the board.
- Say one of the routine activities out loud and invite the teams, in turn, to guess where the matching picture card is.
- Each time a team correctly identifies a card they score a point.

Worksheet 1: Lisez! 10–15 mins AT2.2 O6.4 AT3.2

Description
A mini-flashcard game to reinforce reading about routine activities. It may be used at any point after Activity 4.

Worksheet 2: Écrivez! 10 mins AT4.2–3 L6.4

Description
This worksheet provides further writing practice in daily routine phrases. It may be used at any point after Activity 5.

Answers
1.
   a. Je vais à l'école.
   b. Je me couche.
   c. Je prends mon petit déjeuner.
   d. Je quitte l'école.
   e. Je me lève.
   f. Je prends mon dîner.
   g. Je prends mon déjeuner.

2. 1 d 2 b 3 a 4 g 5 e 6 f 7 c

Unit 9 — Lesson 2

Lesson summary

Context
Talking about times of daily routines

National criteria
KS2 Framework: O6.1, O6.3, O6.4, L6.1, L6.3, L6.4, IU6.1, IU6.2
Attainment levels: AT1.2–4, AT2.2–4, AT3.2–4, AT4.3
Language Ladder Levels:
 Listening: **Grades 2–4**; Speaking: **Grades 2–4**;
 Reading: **Grades 2–4**; Writing: **Grade 3**

Cross-curricular links
Numeracy

Language structures and outcomes
Daily routine phrases from Lesson 1
More complex time phrases: à *une heure, deux heures (moins) cinq, dix, vingt, vingt-cinq*

---

1. Starter activity: 5 mins — *Il est trois heures et quart*
AT1.2, AT2.2, O6.4

Materials
CD ROM, whiteboard; teaching clock.

Description
A warm-up activity revising the time using the Presentation from Unit 2 Lesson 3.

Delivery
Watch and listen again to the Unit 2 Presentation to revise times.

Support
Use the teaching clock to check that pupils remember the patterns used in time-telling (on the hour, quarter to/past, and half-past).

2. Animated story: 5–10 mins — *La routine (1)*
AT1.3–4, AT3.3–4, L6.1, L6.3, O6.1, O6.3, IU6.1, IU6.2

Materials
CD-ROM, teaching clock.

Description
Watch and listen again to this interactive story presenting the language for Lessons 1 and 2. You can pause and rewind the story at any point, or record your own version too.

Delivery
- Ask pupils to listen carefully to the times of Polly's activities.
- Discuss any similarities/differences in between Polly's daily schedule and that of the pupils in your class.

Support
Pause the story after each time is mentioned and illustrate (or ask pupils to illustrate) the time on the teaching clock.

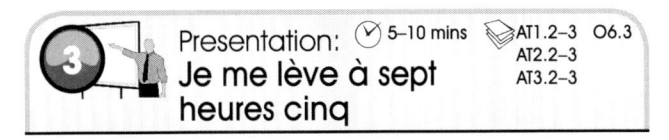

3. Presentation: 5–10 mins — *Je me lève à sept heures cinq*
AT1.2–3, AT2.2–3, AT3.2–3, O6.3

Materials
CD-ROM, whiteboard; teaching clock.

Description
Tap on each picture to hear the question and answer for what time Polly does each action. Use the additional features to practise word classes, or to record your own version of each word.

Delivery
- We hear the question *Tu [te lèves] à quelle heure?* followed by Polly's illustrated answer *Je [me lève] à…*
- Point out that *à* means 'at' when telling the time. You may also wish to highlight the different pronouns used in the question/answer (*ton/mon*).
- Pupils listen and repeat.
- Continue for all seven activities and repeat if further practice is required.

Refer to the Introduction for notes on the *Record* and *Word* features.

Extension
Run the presentation again with the sound turned off. Pupils can look at the picture and say what they think Polly would be saying.

Support
Ask pupils to illustrate each time on the teaching clock to reinforce the learning of the different time phrases.

Knowledge about language

Devising questions for authentic use
The presentation in this lesson uses questions as well as the answer phrases. It's important to stress that pupils need to be able to ask questions as well as answer them in order to have a proper conversation. Try to encourage pupils to do this by getting them to play the part of the teacher as well as working with a partner.

Worksheet 3 *Parlez!* provides further practice in asking questions.

4. Oracy activity: 10 mins — *Tu te lèves à quelle heure?*
O6.4, AT1.3, AT2.3

Materials
Unit 9 Flashcards (Routine activities), teaching clock.

Description
Whole-class speaking activity about the timings of their daily routine.

Delivery
- Display the flashcards on the board so that you can point to the relevant card as you ask each question.

- Select a pupil and ask them a question, e.g. *Tu [te lèves] à quelle heure?* The pupil answers the question and illustrates the time on the teaching clock.
- Repeat until all seven routine activities have been covered at least once.

Extension
Invite two pupils to the front of the class. One answers your question, the other must illustrate the time mentioned on the teaching clock. Build up to pupils asking the questions too.

Support
After each question, pupils could briefly work with a partner to practise further the questions and answers: pupils ask each other the same question you have just used, and give their own answers.

Worksheet 3 *Parlez!* may be used from this point onwards.

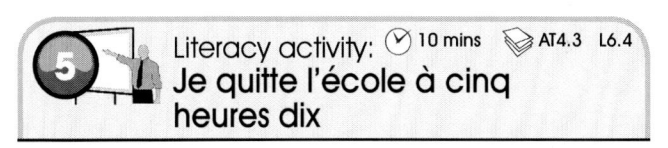

5. Literacy activity: Je quitte l'école à cinq heures dix
⏱ 10 mins   AT4.3   L6.4

Materials
CD-ROM, whiteboard.

Description
Tap on *Allez*. Look at what Polly and Bof do and what time they do it. Read the text at the bottom of the screen. Drag the text into the correct order.

Delivery
- Using the text tiles, pupils build a sentence which best describes the picture. This practises word order and patterns in sentences.
- When pupils are happy with their sentence they tap on *Fini*.
- Correct answers are rewarded with an appropriate animation, otherwise a 'life' is lost and pupils are invited to try again.
- Continue until all six sentences have been completed and repeat if further practice is required.

Support
If pupils are not confident about sentence-building, this activity can be done as a whole class activity: the class suggests what the sentence should be (and discusses their choices if necessary) before the pupil taps on *Fini*.

Worksheet 4 *Grammaire* may be used from this point onwards.

6. Plenary activity: Questions et réponses
⏱ 10 mins   AT1.3   O6.4   AT2.3

Materials
Unit 9 Flashcards (Routine activities), teaching clock, small bean bag.

Description
Pupils have further practice in making sentences about the timings of routine activities.

Delivery
- Divide the class into two teams. Place the flashcards face down.
- Throw the beanbag to a pupil in Team A, who selects a flashcard.
- Throw the beanbag to another child in the same team, who must set the teaching clock to a certain time.
- Team B must produce a sentence which corresponds to the clock and picture prompts, e.g. *Je prends mon petit déjeuner à huit heures cinq.*
- Team A can award up to two points for a fully correct answer. If Team A can produce the correct question for the given answer, they themselves win a point.
- Repeat until each team has had the chance to make at least four sentences.

Extension
More confident pupils could write out the questions and answers as well as say them.

Worksheet 3: Parlez!
⏱ 10–15 mins   AT1.3   O6.3   AT2.3–4   O6.4

Description
An information-gap activity to practise asking and answering questions about the times of routine activities. It may be used at any point after Activity 4.

Answers
A Je me lève à sept heures et quart. Je prends mon petit déjeuner à huit heures cinq. Je vais à l'école à neuf heures moins vingt. Je quitte l'école à trois heures vingt-cinq. Je prends mon dîner à six heures vingt. Je me couche à dix heures moins cinq.

B Je me lève à sept heures et quart. Je prends mon petit déjeuner à huit heures moins cinq. Je vais à l'école à huit heures vingt. Je quitte l'école à trois heures dix. Je prends mon dîner à sept heures moins vingt. Je me couche à dix heures cinq.

Worksheet 4: Grammaire
⏱ 10–15 mins   AT4.3   L6.4

Description
This provides practice in making affirmative sentences negative, and vice versa. It may be used at any point after Activity 5.

Answers
1 1 Je me lève à sept heures vingt-cinq.
   2 Je prends mon petit déjeuner à huit heures dix.
   3 Je vais à l'école à neuf heures moins vingt-cinq.
   4 Je prends mon déjeuner à midi et demi.
   5 Je quitte l'école à trois heures cinq.
   6 Je prends mon dîner à cinq heures et quart.
   7 Je me couche à neuf heures moins le quart.

2 1 Je me lève à sept heures et quart.
   2 Je prends mon petit déjeuner à huit heures moins vingt.
   3 Je vais à l'école à huit heures moins cinq.
   4 Je prends mon déjeuner à midi cinq.
   5 Je quitte l'école à quatre heures et demie.
   6 Je prends mon dîner à sept heures dix.
   7 Je me couche à dix heures moins le quart.

Unit 9 — Lesson 3

Lesson summary

Context
Asking and talking about breakfast

National criteria
KS2 Framework: **O6.1, O6.3, O6.4, L6.1, L6.2, L6.3, L6.4, IU6.1, IU6.2,**
Attainment Levels: **AT1.2–4, AT2.2–3; AT3.2–4, AT4.2–3**
Language Ladder Levels:
  Listening: **Grades 2–4**; Speaking: **Grades 2–3**;
  Reading: **Grades 2–4**; Writing: **Grades 2–3**

Cross-curricular links
Food technology

Key vocabulary
un chocolat chaud, un café, un jus de pomme, un croissant, un pain au chocolat, des céréales, une tartine

Language structures and outcomes
Qu'est-ce que tu prends au petit déjeuner? Je prends...

---

1. Starter activity: Le petit déjeuner — 5–10 mins — IU6.1 IU6.2

Materials
Unit 9 Flashcards (Breakfast items); magazine pictures of French breakfasts, if possible.

Description
A discussion/comparison of breakfast in Britain and in France.

Delivery
- Ask pupils to say what they have for breakfast, and decide whether there is a 'typical' breakfast that most British people have.
- Ask the class what they know about breakfast in France. Give them some basic information using the flashcards and/or magazine pictures: hot drinks may be drunk from a bowl at breakfast, and many children drink hot chocolate or warm milk; baguettes with butter/jam (*tartines*) are often 'dunked' in the hot drink by children and adults alike; people often have *croissants* and *pains au chocolat* at weekends; yoghurts and cereals are gaining in popularity now in France.

2. Animated story: La routine (2) — 10 mins — AT1.4 AT3.4 L6.1 L6.3 O6.1 O6.3 IU6.1 IU6.2

Materials
CD-ROM, whiteboard; Unit 9 Flashcards (Breakfast items).

Description
Watch and listen to this interactive story presenting the language for Lessons 3 and 4. You can pause and rewind the story at any point, or record your own version too.

Delivery
- Display the flashcards randomly on the board before pupils watch the animation.
- As they watch, pupils note which breakfast items are mentioned in the story.
- Play the story through and the class to identify the relevant flashcards. Ask pupils to summarise the story.
- Play the story through one more time to check/discuss answers.

Extension
Ask pupils to watch out for any breakfast items mentioned which are not on the flashcards (e.g. *du pain* and *de l'eau*).

Support
For less confident pupils you can pause the video after each breakfast item and collectively identify the relevant flashcard.

3. Presentation: Qu'est-ce que tu prends au petit déjeuner? — 5–10 mins — AT1.2 AT2.2 AT3.2 O6.3

Materials
CD-ROM, whiteboard; Unit 9 Flashcards (Breakfast items).

Description
Tap on the pictures to hear different breakfast foods and drinks being presented. Use the additional features to practise sound/spelling links, word classes and spelling, or to record your own version of each word.

Delivery
- Bof, Jake or Polly eats or drinks the tapped item and says what they have for breakfast using *Je prends...*
- Encourage pupils to repeat the answer each time.

Refer to the Introduction for notes on the *Record, Spell, Sound,* and *Word* features

Extension
- Revise *un/une/des* ('a', 'some') by asking pupils when each is used are used. Make sure they are clear about the meaning. Ask the class to name other food items and tell you what the definite article is e.g. **un** *sandwich,* **une** *pizza,* **des** *fraises*.

Support
Using the flashcards, repeat each part of the presentation.

4. Oracy activity: Je prends un café — 10 mins — AT1.3–4 O6.3

Materials
CD-ROM, whiteboard; Unit 9 Flashcards (Breakfast items).

Description
Tap on *Allez*. Listen to what each person wants for breakfast then put the right things in front of them.

Delivery
- The highlighted character requests two items for breakfast; pupils drag the requested items towards that character.
- Continue for all eight food and drink items and repeat if required.
- This is a good opportunity for pupils to gain practice in listening to short dialogues. Reassure them they do not have to understand every word in order to complete the activity.

Extension
Replay the audio and ask pupils to listen out for any opinion mentioned.

📄 Worksheet 5 *Grammaire* may be used from this point onwards.

5. Literacy activity: Je prends un chocolat chaud
⏱ 10 mins — AT3.3 L6.3 / AT4.3 L6.4

Materials
Pre-prepared word cards (see below).

Description
Pupils make sentences using word cards.

Delivery
- Prepare word cards on A4 card as follows:
  / qu'est-ce que / tu prends / au petit déjeuner / ? /
  / je prends / un jus de pomme / un café / un chocolat chaud / des céréales / un croissant
  / un pain au chocolat / une tartine / et /
- Stick the cards randomly on the board and divide the class into two teams. Invite a pupil from each team to the front.
- Pupil A must select the appropriate captions in order to ask Pupil B what they have for breakfast. Pupil B then selects appropriate captions to display a grammatically correct answer.
- Each team scores a point for a correct question/answer.

Extension
Make this activity more challenging by breaking down the captions even further, e.g. separating articles from nouns, separating pronouns from verbs. You could also revise food vocabulary from *Rigolo 1*, Unit 6 and add the question *Qu'est-ce que tu prends au déjeuner?*

Support
Invite two pupils from each team to come to the board each time so they can help each other form the sentences.

📄 Worksheet 6 *Lisez!* may be used from this point onwards.

6. Plenary activity: Je prends un café et des céréales
⏱ 5–10 mins — AT2.2–3 O6.4

Materials
Unit 9 Flashcards (Breakfast items); *Rigolo 1*, Unit 6 (Food items) for support and extension activities.

Description
Pupils practise making more sentences about what they have for breakfast.

Delivery
- Ask a pupil *Qu'est-ce que tu prends au petit déjeuner?*
- The pupil responds with one item, e.g. *Je prends un café*, before repeating the question to the next pupil.
- This pupil replies by repeating the first item and adding another e.g. *Je prends un café et des céréales*.
- Continue until all seven items have been mentioned.

Extension
Add the question *Qu'est-ce que tu prends au déjeuner?* plus additional food items from *Rigolo 1*.

Support
Give the relevant flashcard to each pupil after they have said a food item so that the following pupil(s) have visual prompts to help them if necessary.

Worksheet 5: Grammaire
⏱ 10 mins — AT4.2–3 L6.4

Description
This provides practice in using *prendre* to write about what food people eat at mealtimes. It may be used at any point after Activity 4.

Answers
1. 1. Je prends un café et un croissant.
   2. Il prend un jus de pomme et des céréales.
   3. Tu prends un café et une tartine.
   4. Je prends un chocolat chaud et un croissant.

2. 1. Au déjeuner il prend un sandwich au thon, un gâteau et un jus d'orange.
   2. Au déjeuner elle prend un sandwich au fromage, une pomme et un café.

Language learning strategies

Making predictions based on existing knowledge
In the last few units of *Rigolo 2*, pupils have the opportunity of reading more authentic-style texts in the worksheets. They will not necessarily have met all the language before but should be encouraged to use what they do know to work out or make educated guesses what new words/phrases might mean. For example, they have not met *s'entraîne* before but if you ask them to look in the middle of the word for an English word, they may be able to work it out. You can also encourage them to look at the rest of the sentence and ask them to use the context to work out unfamiliar words.

Worksheet 6: Lisez!
⏱ 10–15 mins — AT3.4 L6.1 / L6.2

Description
This provides practice in reading more authentic texts. It may be used at any point after Activity 5.

Answers
1. 1. la patinoire
   2. tous les jours de la semaine
   3. elle s'entraîne
   4. pendant une heure
   5. elle retourne
   6. des pâtes
   7. des fruits
   8. une compétition
   9. elle a gagné
   10. une coupe

2. 1. Monday–Friday
   2. 7:30 am
   3. 1 hour
   4. 5:00 pm
   5. (back) to the ice rink
   6. chicken, pasta and fruit
   7. Sunday
   8. a cup

Unit 9 (Lesson 4)

Lesson summary

Context
Talking about details of a typical day

National criteria
KS2 Framework: O6.1, O6.2, O6.3, O6.4, L6.1, L6.2, L6.3, L6.4, IU6.1, IU6.2, IU6.3
Attainment Levels: AT1.2–4, AT2.2–4; AT3.3–4, AT4.2–4
Language Ladder Levels:
  Listening: **Grades 2–4**; Speaking: **Grades 2–4**;
  Reading: **Grades 3–4**; Writing: **Grades 2–4**

Cross-curricular links
Art and Design, ICT (project work)

Key vocabulary
normalement, d'abord, ensuite, enfin, après l'école + language from Lesson 3

Language structures and outcomes
Je me lève, Je prends mon petit déjeuner, Je vais à l'école, Je prends mon déjeuner, Je quitte l'école, Je prends mon dîner, Je me couche, Je prends un chocolat chaud/un café/ un jus de pomme/un croissant/un pain au chocolat/des céréales/une tartine + other food items

---

1. Starter activity: 5–10 mins — AT1.2–3, AT2.2–3, O6.4
Je prends un jus de pomme

Materials
Unit 9 Flashcards (Routine activities and Breakfast items).

Description
Revision game using flashcards.

Delivery
- Hold up the flashcards from the unit to revise the phrases/breakfast items. Divide the class into two teams.
- Using the flashcards again as prompts, ask each team in turn full questions in order to elicit a full answer e.g. *Qu'est-ce que tu prends au petit déjeuner? – Je prends un chocolat chaud et une tartine.*
- Award a point for each correct answer.

2. Animated story: 5–10 mins — AT1.4, AT3.4, O6.1, O6.3, L6.1, L6.3, IU6.1, IU6.2
La routine (2)

Materials
CD-ROM, whiteboard.

Description
Watch and listen to this interactive story presenting the language for Lessons 3 and 4. You can pause and rewind the story at any point, or record your own version too.

Delivery
- Watch the animation again, this time to focus on the characters' accounts of their daily routines.
- Divide the class into four groups. Assign a character to each group (Jake, Polly, Nathalie, Olivier).
- Ask pupils to pay particular attention to 'their' character's routines as they watch the animation. After viewing ask each group to recount the routine, using question prompts if necessary, e.g. *Qu'est-ce que tu prends au petit déjeuner?*

Support
Write the characters' names on the board. Pause the story after each character speaks, then ask pupils to repeat what has been said.

3. Presentation: 10 mins — AT1.3–4, AT2.3–4, AT3.3–4, O6.1, O6.3, L6.1, IU6.1
Enfin, je me couche à neuf heures

Materials
CD-ROM, whiteboard.

Description
Tap on the pictures to hear Jake's daily routine. Use the additional features to record your own version of each sentence.

Delivery
- As Jake narrates each part of his daily routine, the text builds up line by line, giving pupils the opportunity to see a longer, continuous text.
- Pupils listen and repeat each line, using gestures to reinforce the language where appropriate. The accompanying text appears on screen as each scene is narrated.
- Continue for all six pictures and repeat if necessary.
- Point out and discuss the adverbs of time/sequence in the sentences (i.e. *normalement* ('usually'), *d'abord* ('first of all'), *ensuite* ('then'), *enfin* ('finally').

Refer to the Introduction for notes on the *Record* feature.

Support
Break down individual sentences into smaller parts for pupils to repeat. Practise each part separately, then try to put them together in a longer sentence.

Language learning strategies

Remember to take time out now and again to discuss with your pupils their language learning. Talk about how they're finding their French lessons. What do they find easy? What do they find most difficult? How do they remember words? How do they learn to put sentences together? How can they say what they want to say? What can they do when they don't understand? This lesson brings together language from the previous three lessons and allows them to put more language together to make longer sentences and paragraphs. Discuss how pupils cope with these longer passages and talk about how they might use language from previous units to incorporate into their work. Sharing ideas and experiences can give confidence to learners who may be finding language learning difficult.

Unit 9: Lesson 4

4. Oracy activity: Qu'est-ce que tu fais d'abord?
5–10 mins — AT1.3–4 O6.3, AT2.3–4 O6.4

Materials
Unit 9 Flashcards (Routine activities and Breakfast items); *Rigolo 1* Unit 6 Flashcards (Food items).

Description
A class activity practising talking about routines using sequencing adverbs.

Delivery
- Invite a confident pupil to the front of the class and ask them to go through a typical weekday routine. Prompt questions if necessary and suggest the use of *normalement, d'abord, ensuite, enfin* where appropriate.
- Ask pupils to work in pairs and to tell each other about their routines in the same way.

Extension
Some pupils may be able to write down their accounts after they have prepared them orally.

Worksheet 7 *Parlez!* may be used from this point onwards.

5. Literacy activity: Après l'école, je joue au football
10 mins — AT3.3–4 L6.1, L6.4

Materials
CD-ROM, whiteboard.

Description
Look at the pictures depicting Jake's day. Read the sentences at the bottom of the screen. Drag the sentences into the correct order.

Delivery
- Pupils re-order the sentences to match the sequence of pictures, and tap on *Fini*. There is a reward animation if the order is correct; otherwise, they are invited to try again.

Extension
Once the text is on the screen in the correct order, ask for volunteers to read the text aloud. Encourage pupils to try to sound as French as possible and to be expressive as possible. Play the text again to compare pronunciation.

Worksheet 8 *Écrivez!* may be used from this point onwards.

6. Plenary activity: Les différences
10–15 mins — AT4.3–4 IU6.1, L6.4 IU6.2, IU6.3

Materials
Possibly Unit 9 Flashcards and animations, to illustrate or check details.

Description
Pupils discuss what they have discovered about differences in the routines of French and British pupils.

Delivery
- Ask pupils to review what they have learned about differences in the routines of French and British pupils during this unit. Make notes on the board, or ask pupils to do so.
- You may wish to build up collectively some sentences on the board under the headings *En France* and *En Angleterre*, which pupils will be able to use in their forthcoming project.

Worksheet 7: Parlez!
10 mins — AT2.3–4 O6.2, O6.4

Description
This provides further speaking practice in asking and answering questions and giving a longer spoken presentation about daily routine. It may be used at any point after Activity 4.

Worksheet 8: Écrivez!
10 mins — AT3.4 L6.1, AT4.3–4 L6.2, L6.4

Description
This provides a longer account of a school day for further reading and writing practice. It may be used at any point after Activity 5.

Answers
1. **times mentioned:** sept heures dix; sept heures vingt-cinq, huit heures moins vingt, cinq heures moins le quart, sept heures, dix heures moins le quart
   drinks and food mentioned: un jus d'orange, du café et deux croissants, du poulet et des frites, une pizza, une pomme, une banane
2.
   1. 7:10 am
   2. orange juice, coffee and 2 croissants
   3. English and history
   4. It's not nice
   5. chicken and chips or pizza, an apple or a banana
   6. 9:45 pm

Project work: La routine en Grande-Bretagne et en France
1–2 hours — AT2.2–4 IU6.1, AT4.2–4 IU6.2, O6.2 IU6.3

Description
Pupils prepare a display about similarities and differences between their daily and school routine, and that of pupils in France.

Materials
Internet access and printer if possible; card and paper to display the pictures and text in the classroom or access to PowerPoint; emails or letters from French-speaking pupils if available.

Delivery
Encourage pupils to use all the language they have covered and to write as much as possible. Ideally, each group of pupils will make an oral presentation when their display is completed.

- If you have contact with a French school, pupils could email or send a questionnaire (based on some ideas from Worksheet 7) to the school.

If you do not have any French contacts, here are some points pupils may wish to include:

- French schools generally start earlier (8 am) and finish later (5 pm) in France. They often have a day off in the week (Wednesday or Thursday) but sometimes go in on Saturday morning. Sporting activities are usually offered mid-week when schools are closed.

- They often have 1½–2 hrs for lunch and usually have a three-course meal in the canteen with a starter, main course (with bread) and fruit or yoghurt.

- French children tend to go to bed earlier. Parents have to buy all their children's text books and stationery, and the children carry everything they need for the day in huge backpacks.

Rigolo 2 — Unit 10: Les transports

National criteria

KS2 Framework objectives

O6.1	Understand the main points and simple opinions in a spoken story, song or passage
O6.2	Perform to an audience
O6.3	Understand longer and more complex phrases or sentences
O6.4	Use spoken language confidently to initiate and sustain conversations and to tell stories
L6.1	Read and understand the main points and some detail from a short written passage
L6.2	Identify different text types and read short, authentic texts for enjoyment or information
L6.3	Match sound to sentences and paragraphs
L6.4	Write sentences on a range of topics using a model
IU6.1	Compare attitudes towards aspects of everyday life
IU6.2	Recognise and understand some of the differences between people
IU6.3	Present information about an aspect of culture

QCA Scheme of work

Unit 6	Ça pousse!
Unit 7	On y va
Unit 17	Le retour du printemps
Unit 21	Le passé et le présent
Unit 22	Ici et là

National Curriculum attainment levels

AT1.2–4, AT2.2–4, AT3.2–4, AT4.2–4

Language ladder levels

Listening: Breakthrough, Grades 2–4
Reading: Breakthrough, Grades 2–4
Speaking: Breakthrough, Grades 2–4
Writing: Breakthrough, Grades 2–4

5–14 guideline strands — Levels A–D

Listening
- Listening for information and instructions — A, B, C, D
- Listening and reacting to others — A, B, C, D

Speaking
- Speaking to convey information — A, B, C, D
- Speaking and interacting with others — A, B, C, D
- Speaking about experiences, feelings and opinions — A, B, C, D

Reading
- Reading for information and instructions — A, B, C, D
- Reading aloud — A, B, C, D

Writing
- Writing to exchange information and ideas — A, B, C, D
- Writing to establish and maintain personal contact — A, B, C, D
- Writing imaginatively to entertain — A, B, C, D

Unit objectives

- Talk about forms of transport
- Talk about where you're going and how you get there
- Talk about plans for a trip
- Buy tickets at the station

Key language

- *Où vas-tu? Je vais à l'école… en voiture, en bus, en train, en métro, à pied, à vélo, en avion, en bateau*
- *Où vas-tu? Comment vas-tu… ?*
  Je vais… à la boulangerie, au marché, à la piscine, au centre sportif, au château, au jardin public, au supermarché, à l'école… en voiture, etc.
- *Samedi, à 10 heures… D'abord, ensuite, enfin… Qu'est-ce qu'on va faire? On va… aller au parc d'attractions, prendre le train/l'avion, acheter des souvenirs, faire des manèges, regarder un film*
- *Bonjour [Monsieur]. Je voudrais des billets pour [Paris]. Combien de billets?*
  [Quatre] billets: [un] adulte et [trois] enfants. Aller-retour ou aller simple? [Aller-retour] s'il vous plaît. C'est combien? C'est [trente-cinq] euros. Le train part à quelle heure? [Dix heures et demie.]
  Merci [Monsieur]. Au revoir… Bon voyage!

Grammar and skills

- Use prepositions *en* and *à* with transports
- Listen for clues to meaning
- Use prepositions *au/à la/à l'* with places
- Using knowledge of word, text and structure to build texts
- Use *on va* + infinitives to talk about future plans
- Use time indicators
- Use context and previous knowledge to help reading
- Ask politely for things

Unit outcomes

Most children will be able to:
- Name some forms of transport
- Say how they get to various places
- Ask for tickets at a train station

Some children will also be able to:
- Use prepositions correctly with transports and places
- Start to write short texts
- Use *on va* + infinitive to talk about future plans
- Use strategies to deal with authentic reading texts

Unit 10 — Lesson 1

Lesson summary

Context
Talking about forms of transport

National criteria
KS2 Framework: O6.1, O6.3, O6.4, L6.1, L6.4, IU6.1, IU6.2
Attainment Levels: AT1.2–4, AT2.2, AT3.2–4, AT4.2–3
Language Ladder Levels:
    Listening: **Grades 2–4**; Speaking: **Grade 2**;
    Reading: **Grades 2–4**; Writing: **Grades 2–3**

Cross-curricular links
Geography, literacy, maths

Key vocabulary
en voiture, en bus, en train, en métro, à pied, à vélo, en avion, en bateau

Language structures and outcomes
Je vais à l'école en voiture, etc....

---

1 Starter activity: Les transports (5 mins — IU6.1 IU6.2)

Materials
Unit 10 Flashcards (Means of transport).

Description
An introduction to transport vocabulary.

Delivery
- Ask pupils questions in English about how they travel to various destinations, e.g. school, family visits, holidays.
- As pupils give answers, hold any relevant flashcards, say the word in French without too much emphasis, and stick the cards on the board.
- Continue with questions until all means of transport on the flashcards have been covered.
- Say the new words in French again and ask pupils if they can work out what each is in English. Ask them to explain how they guessed these things. What gave them clues? Did some sound like English words?

2 Video story: Je vais à la piscine (1) (10 mins — AT1.3–4, AT3.3–4, L6.1, O6.1, O6.3, IU6.1, IU6.2)

Materials
CD-ROM, whiteboard.

Description
Watch and listen to this video story presenting the language for Lessons 1 and 2. You can pause and rewind the story at any point.

Delivery
- Display the means of transport flashcards on the board. Ask pupils to note which means of transport are mentioned as they watch the video.
- Ask pupils to come to the board and circle the relevant flashcards. Say each means of transport in French, still without dwelling too much on the words.
- Play the whole video without stopping for pupils to enjoy and check whether they correctly identified all the means of transport in the video.
- Ask them to look for any cultural differences in the video.

Extension
Ask pupils to arrange the flashcards in the order in which they are mentioned in the video.

Support
Pause the video after each means of transport is mentioned. Ask pupils to come to the board and circle the relevant card.

Language learning strategies

Listening for clues to meaning
In the last few units of *Rigolo 2*, pupils will have the opportunity to hear longer texts and to hear familiar language in unfamiliar contexts. Both the video and the oracy activities now contain longer dialogues and pupils may not understand every word. Reassure them that this does not matter. Ask them to listen out for words they do know; this should be enough to understand the gist. If necessary, prepare them in advance by talking about the context and asking them to predict what they might hear. It can also be helpful to listen to the tone of voice used, as this will often help understanding.

3 Presentation: En avion (10 mins — AT1.2, AT2.2, AT3.2, O6.4)

Materials
CD-ROM; whiteboard.

Description
Tap on the pictures to hear the characters say how they get to the castle. Use the additional features to practise sound/spelling links, word classes and spelling, or to record your own version of each word.

Delivery
- The class hears how each character travels to *Château Rigolo* and repeats their answers, using gestures where possible.
- Continue for all eight pictures and repeat if further practice is required.

Refer to the Introduction for notes on the *Record*, *Spell*, *Sound* and *Word* features.

── Unit 10: Lesson 1 ──

4. Oracy activity: Je vais à l'école à pied
5–10 mins · AT1.3 · O6.1 O6.3

Materials
CD-ROM, whiteboard.

Description
Tap on *Allez*. Look at the photos. Listen to the conversation and choose the correct photo.

Delivery
- Before starting, check pupils that know the word *Angleterre*.
- The class will hear a conversation about where someone is going and how they get there; the pupil at the front must tap on the relevant picture. Remind pupils that they don't need to understand everything; just pick out familiar language.
- Tap on *Allez* to go on to the next dialogue.
- Continue for all six dialogues and repeat if further practice is needed.

Extension
Ask pupils to listen again and try to pick out any additional information.

Support
- Encourage less confident pupils to use the *Encore* button as much as necessary. Remind pupils that they don't need to understand everything that is said, just the key words.
- Look at the three pictures before listening and discuss what words they are likely to hear.

Worksheet 1 *Écrivez!* may be used from this point onwards

5. Literacy activity: Je vais à l'école en voiture
5–10 mins · AT4.2–3 · L6.4

Materials
Unit 10 Flashcards (Means of transport: pictures and captions).

Description
Team game in which pupils write about using different means of transport.

Delivery
- Display the picture and text flashcards on the board.
- Divide the class into teams.
- In turn, ask each team captain *Comment vas-tu à l'école?* and point to a card on the board. The team must either send someone to the board to write out their answer, or write the answer on a piece of paper to hand to you.
- Award one point for each correct answer.

Worksheet 2 *Lisez!* may be used from this point onwards.

6. Plenary activity: En bateau
10 mins · AT1.2 AT2.2 · O6.4

Materials
Unit 10 Flashcards (Means of transport: pictures only).

Description
Class survey of how pupils travel to school.

Delivery
- Display the relevant flashcards horizontally on the board. Draw vertical lines to make a chart.
- Ask each pupil *Comment vas-tu à l'école?* to elicit *Je vais à l'école [à pied]*. Keep a tally under each picture of how many pupils use that means of transport.
- Ask the class to count (in French) the results and discuss the survey findings.

Extension
Ask pupils to set up the chart and keep a record of the answers.

Worksheet 1: Écrivez!
10 mins · AT4.2 · L6.4

Description
This provides a crossword and a sentence-completion task about means of transport. It may be used any point after Activity 4.

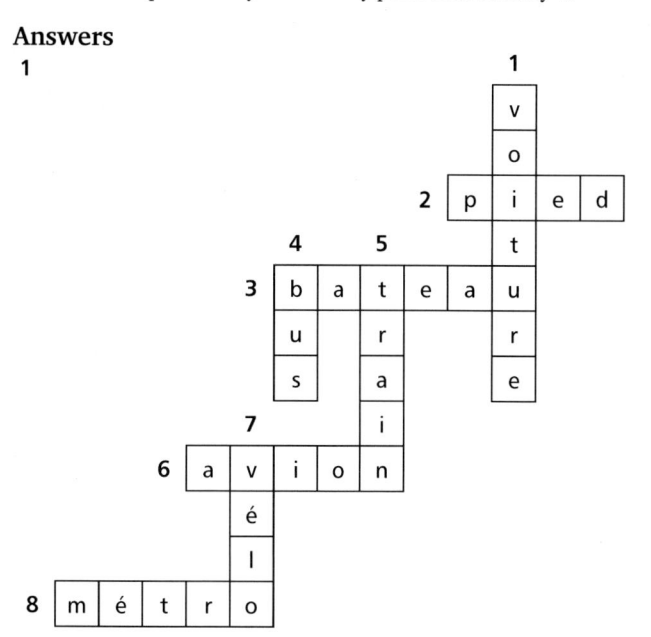

Answers

1

Crossword answers:
- 1 down: voiture (v/o/i/t/u/r/e)
- 2 across: pied
- 3 across: bateau
- 4 down: bus
- 5 down: train
- 6 across: avion
- 7 down: vélo
- 8 across: métro

2 1 à vélo 2 en voiture 3 en avion 4 en train

Worksheet 2: Lisez!
10 mins · AT3.2 AT4.2–3 · L6.4

Description
Thus provides further reading and writing practice about forms of transport. It may be used at any point after Activity 5.

Answers
1. D'abord, je vais à pied. Ensuite, je vais en bus. Enfin, je vais en métro.
2. D'abord, je vais en voiture. Ensuite, je vais en train. Enfin, je vais en avion.
3. D'abord, je vais à vélo. Ensuite, je vais en bateau. Enfin, je vais en bus.

Unit 10 — Lesson 2

Lesson summary

Context
Asking and talking about where you're going and how you get there

National criteria
KS2 Framework: **O6.1, O6.3, O6.4, L6.1, L6.4, IU6.1, IU6.2**
Attainment Levels: **AT1.2–4, AT2.2–3; AT3.2–4, AT4.2–4**
Language Ladder Levels:
  Listening: **Grades 2–4**; Speaking: **Grade 2–3**;
  Reading: **Grades 2–4**; Writing: **Grades 2–4**

Cross-curricular links
Geography, literacy

Language structures and outcomes
Où vas-tu? Comment vas-tu… ?
Je vais… à la boulangerie, au marché, à la piscine, au centre sportif, au château, au jardin public, au supermarché, à l'école
en voiture, en bus, en train, en métro, à pied, à vélo, en avion, en bateau

---

1. Starter activity: C'est la boulangerie (5 mins) — AT1.2, AT2.2, O6.4

Materials
CD-ROM, whiteboard; Unit 4 Flashcards (Places in the town).

Description
Quick revision of places around town.

Delivery
- Quickly re-play the presentation activity from Unit 4 Lesson 1 to refresh pupils' memories of places in the town.
- Finish with a quick team quiz using Unit 4 Flashcards.

2. Video story: Je vais à la piscine (1) (5–10 mins) — AT1.3–4, AT3.3–4, L6.1, O6.1, O6.3, IU6.1, IU6.2

Materials
CD-ROM, whiteboard; possibly Unit 4 Flashcards (Places in the town).

Description
Watch and listen again to this video story presenting the language for Lessons 1 and 2. You can pause and rewind the story at any point.

Delivery
- Tell pupils they will watch the video again and must listen out for any places around town. Ask them to put their hands up each time they recognise a place.
- Play the video and ask the class to tell you which places they heard. Also ask if they saw any other places in the film background which were not actually mentioned in the dialogue.

Extension
Ask pupil to listen also for any activities mentioned in the video.

Support
Pause the video after each place is mentioned and ask a pupil to point to the correct flashcard.

3. Presentation: Je vais au marché à vélo (5–10 mins) — O6.4, AT1.2–3, AT2.2–3, AT3.2–3

Materials
CD-ROM, whiteboard; Unit 4 Flashcards (Places in the town) and Unit 10 (Means of transport).

Description
Tap on the pictures to hear how Jake gets to each place. Use the additional features to practise sound/spelling links and word classes, or to record your own version of each question and answer exchange.

Delivery
- Pupils hear Gustave asking Jake how he gets to a particular place and Jake's reply.
- The class listens and repeats for each place and means of transport. Continue for all eight places and repeat if further practice is required.

Refer to the Introduction for notes on the *Record*, *Sound* and *Word* features.

Extension
- Focus on intonation when asking questions.
- Listen to the question and, if necessary, write it on the board. Explain that in French we sometimes change the order of words to ask questions. *Comment vas-tu…? Ou vas-tu?*

Support
- In order to check and reinforce comprehension, ask pupils to hold up the relevant flashcards after each conversation.
- Write the questions and answers on the board to help pupils see the same patterns repeated.

4. Oracy activity: Je vais à la piscine en bus (10 mins) — AT2.2–3, O6.4

Materials
Unit 4 Flashcards (Places in the town); map (for extension activity).

Description
Pupils practise saying how they get to various places around town.

Delivery
- Hold up the flashcards one by one and ask pupils *Comment vas-tu [à la piscine]?* Elicit full-sentence answers, e.g. *Je vais [à la piscine] [en bus]*.
- Continue until all places have been covered and as many means of transport as possible used.

Worksheet 3 *Parlez!* may be used from this point onwards.

---

102 — Rigolo 2 Teacher's Notes © Nelson Thornes Ltd 2008

Unit 10: Lesson 2

Extension
Use a map to ask additional questions, e.g. about how to get to places in France. Ask pupils if they've been to anywhere in France and how they got there.

5. Literacy activity: La journée de Nathalie
10 mins — AT3.3–4 L6.1

Materials
CD-ROM, whiteboard.

Description
Tap on *Allez*. Look at the pictures of where Nathalie is going. Drag the words into the correct order.

Delivery
- Before doing the activity, revise the expressions *d'abord, ensuite, enfin* and *après l'école*.
- Pupils look at the first picture and corresponding jumbled-up sentence describing it, then drag the text into the correct order.
- Tap on *Fini* to see if the sentence is correct.
- Continue until all six sentences have been covered, and repeat if necessary.
- This activity gives pupils the chance to see a longer text built up. At the end they can see the complete text on screen.

Extension
Divide the class into groups and ask each group to write out their suggested sentence before a pupil checks the answer on screen.

Support
This can be done as a whole-class activity: the class suggests what the sentence should be, and discusses their choices if necessary, before the pupil taps on *Fini*.

Worksheets 3 *Parlez!* and 4 *Grammaire* may be used from this point onwards.

Knowledge about language

Using knowledge of words, text and structure to build simple spoken and written passages.
Activities 5 and 6 give practice in building a short passage. Pupils have gradually been introduced to longer texts in listening and reading and, if they can cope, you can now start encouraging them to produce longer pieces of speaking and writing. Work together as a class to model such a text first, then allow pupils to adapt the text you've worked out together. This gives them the support they need to experiment more, once they are confident. At this stage, don't worry about mistakes they're making. It's more important for them to experiment a little and not to be frightened to produce language themselves.

6. Plenary activity: Je vais à Paris en train
10 mins — AT3.3–4 L6.1 / AT4.3–4 L6.4

Materials
Map of France, Unit 10 Flashcards (Means of transport).

Description
Brainstorm to build up a text about travel plans.

Delivery
- The aim is to build up a small text about travel, using time phrases.
- Using the map and a flashcard as illustrations, model a sentence along the lines of *D'abord, je vais à Paris en train*.
- Point to another place and flashcard and ask a pupil to continue the 'itinerary' as follows: *D'abord, je vais à Paris en train. Ensuite, je vais à [Nice] [en avion]*.
- Other pupils continue, using *ensuite* or *enfin* where relevant until a short text is built up.

Extension
As follow up, pupils adapt the text built up by the whole class to write about their own travel plans.

Support
This could be a group activity so that more confident pupils can help others build the sentences.

Worksheet 3: Parlez!
10 mins — O6.4 AT2.2–3

Description
This worksheet provides further speaking practice in places and means of transport. It may be used at any point after Activity 5.

Worksheet 4: Grammaire
10 mins — AT3.3 L6.1 / AT4.2 L6.4

Description
This worksheet provides further practice in using *au/à la/ à l'*. It may be used at any point after Activity 5.

Answers
1

à la	à l'	au
boulangerie (f)	école (f)	jardin public (m)
piscine (f)		marché (m)
montagne (f)		centre sportif (m)
campagne (f)		château (m)
		supermarché (m)
		bord de la mer (m)
		camping (m)

2
1. à la montagne, à la campagne, au jardin public, au bord de la mer
2. à la montagne
3. au supermarché, au marché
4. au bord de la mer
5. au centre sportif, au jardin public
6. à la boulangerie, au supermarché, au marché
7. à l'école

Unit 10 Lesson 3

Lesson summary

Context
Talking about plans for a trip

National criteria
KS2 Framework: **O6.1, O6.3, O6.4, L6.1, L6.2, L6.3, L6.4, IU6.1, IU6.2**
Attainment Levels: **AT1.3–4, AT2.3–4; AT3.2–4, AT4.3–4**
Language Ladder Levels:
  Listening: **Grades 3–4**; Speaking: **Grades 3–4**;
  Reading: **Grades 2–4**; Writing: **Grades 3–4**

Cross-curricular links
Literacy

Language structures and outcomes
samedi, à 10 heures, d'abord, ensuite, enfin
Qu'est-ce qu'on va faire? On va aller au parc d'attractions, on va prendre le train, on va prendre l'avion, on va acheter des souvenirs (au magasin), on va faire des manèges, on va regarder un film (au cinéma)

---

1 Starter activity: ⓥ 5 mins O6.3 AT1.3 / O6.4 AT2.3 / AT3.3
Qu'est-ce que tu vas faire?

Materials
CD-ROM, whiteboard; Unit 5 Flashcards (Holiday activities).

Description
Quick revision of using *je vais* + infinitive using the Presentation from Unit 5 Lesson 3.

Delivery
Write the basic structure on the board to remind pupils of the language pattern used before re-playing the Unit 5 Presentation.

Support
Use the flashcards to reinforce talking about future plans using *je vais* + infinitive.

---

2 Video story: ⓥ 10 mins AT1.4 O6.1 / AT3.4 O6.3 / L6.1 IU6.1 / IU6.2
Je vais à la piscine (2)

Materials
CD-ROM, whiteboard.

Description
Watch and listen to this video story presenting the language for Lessons 3 and 4. You can pause and rewind the story at any point.

Delivery
• Ask pupils to watch the first scene and tell you where the children are going, and how they are going to get there.

• Play the scene and go through the answers. Watch again if necessary.

Extension
Pupils can watch again and listen for any extra information.

Support
Pause the video during the first viewing and elicit answers as you go along.

---

3 Presentation: ⓥ 5–10 mins AT1.4 O6.1 / AT2.4 O6.3 / AT3.4 L6.1
On va aller au parc d'attractions

Materials
CD-ROM, whiteboard.

Description
Tap on the pictures to hear sentences about a planned day out. Use the additional features to record your own version of each sentence.

Delivery
• When pupils tap on the pictures, we hear Polly announcing their plans for the day out, building up sentence by sentence until the full text appears on screen.

• The whole class repeats each sentence as they hear it.

• Continue for all six pictures and repeat if further practice is required.

• Explain that *on* is used when speaking to mean 'we'. Point out that the structure *on va* + infinitive is used to say what we are planning to do.

Refer to the Introduction for notes on the *Record* feature.

Extension
• Ask pupils to look out for the different time expressions used in French, especially how we say 'at' + time, 'on' + day, etc.

• Ask pupils to tell you how to say 'take', 'watch', 'buy' in French.

Support
Go through each sentence slowly with the class, asking questions to ensure the pupils have understood what is being said.

---

4 Oracy activity: ⓥ 10 mins AT1.4 O6.1 / O6.3
On va prendre le train

Materials
CD-ROM, whiteboard.

Description
Tap on *Allez*. Listen to the characters' travel plans. Drag the pictures into the correct order according to what you hear.

Delivery
• This listening activity gives pupils the chance to hear longer dialogues.

• Pupils drag the pictures into the correct order according to the travel plans, then tap on *Fini* to see if their answer is correct.

• Repeat for all four conversations and repeat if required.

• By dividing the class into two groups you could make this into a team game, awarding a point for each correct answer.

---

104 — Rigolo 2 Teacher's Notes © Nelson Thornes Ltd 2008

Unit 10: Lesson 3

Extension
After each set of pictures, encourage pupils to try to come up with the sentences they've just heard. Play the audio again to check.

Support
To assist comprehension, focus pupils' attention on the pictures first and ask them to predict what they are going to hear.

5 Literacy activity: On va aller à Londres
10–15 mins   AT3.3–4 L6.1   AT4.3–4 L6.3 L6.4

Materials
If possible, pictures of Paris and London to illustrate your text.

Description
A class activity using *on va* + infinitive to build up a short text.

Delivery
- Ask pupils what they and their families are planning to do at the weekend, or during the holidays, to elicit a few sentences using *on va* + verb.
- Ask the class to help you plan an imaginary trip to Paris and write up your plans on the board, for example:

Mardi, on va aller à Paris.
D'abord, on va prendre le bus.
À 10 heures, on va prendre l'avion.
On va aller à la tour Eiffel.
On va aller à Disneyland Paris.
On va acheter des souvenirs au magasin.

- Divide the class into groups and ask them to plan a group trip to London. They then write up their plans using the Paris text as a model.
- If time allows, each group can read out their plans to the rest of the class.

Extension
Encourage pupils to use vocabulary they know from other units in their accounts.

Support
Go through possible plans for a London trip together orally before groups write out their plans.

Worksheets 5 *Grammaire* and 6 *Lisez!* may be used from this point onwards.

6 Plenary activity: On va prendre l'avion
10 mins   AT3.2–3 L6.4

Materials
Unit 10 Flashcards (Holiday activities); possibly *Rigolo 1* CD-ROM: Unit 5 Lesson 2, Karaoke song (*Chantez l'alphabet*) or the Lesson 2 Presentation (*L'alphabet*)

Description
Hangman game to practise the key language of this lesson.

Delivery
- If necessary, use the karaoke song or presentation to revise the alphabet. Alternatively, just go through the alphabet orally together.
- Revise the key language (see below) using the flashcard prompts.
- Play hangman with the following sentences:

On va aller au parc d'attractions.
On va prendre l'avion/le train.
On va acheter des souvenirs au magasin.
On va regarder un film au cinéma.
On va faire les manèges.

- Ask the pupil who guesses correctly to try and finish writing the sentence.

Extension
Introduce other activities and places already covered, but revise them before playing the game.

Worksheet 5: Grammaire
10 mins   AT3.3 L6.1   AT4.3 L6.4

Description
This gives further practice in using *aller* + infinitive to talk about future plans. It may be used at any point after activity 5.

Answers
1 1 vais 2 va 3 va 4 vais 5 va 6 vais 7 vas

2 1 c 2 a 3 d 4 g 5 b 6 e 7 f

3 2 On boit de la limonade.
3 On va manger du gâteau.
4 On écoute de la musique.
5 On va jouer au basket.
6 On va faire du sport.

Language learning strategies

Reading skills
Pupils are now being exposed to longer written texts in *Rigolo*. In the presentation for this lesson and in the video, they are hearing and seeing more language in unfamiliar contexts. Worksheet 6 gives them further practice in reading authentic texts. Remind them of strategies in coping with unfamiliar language:

- Read through and look for words they do understand.
- Look at pictures and the title, and see what the context is.
- Try to work out what some unknown words mean from the context, and also perhaps because they're similar to English words.
- As a last resort, they can look up some unknown words in a dictionary.

Worksheet 6: Lisez!
10 mins   AT3.3–4 L6.1   AT4.3–4 L6.2 L6.4

Description
This worksheet gives practice in reading an authentic text. It may be used at any point after activity 5.

Answers
1 1 theme park
2 15 euros
3 13 euros
4 12
5 20
6 France (Saint Jérôme)
7 00.33.3.55.92.02.09
8 picnic area (and a snack bar)
9 big wheel, toboggan, ghost train, dodgem boats, carousel, trampoline

Unit 10 — Lesson 4

Lesson summary

Context
Buying tickets at the station

National criteria
KS2 Framework: O6.1, O6.2, O6.3, O6.4, L6.1, L6.2, L6.3, L6.4, IU6.1, IU6.2, IU6.3
Attainment Levels: AT1.2–4, AT2.2–4; AT3.3–4, AT4.3–4
Language Ladder Levels:
- Listening: **Grades 2–4;** Speaking: **Grades 2–4;**
- Reading: **Grades 3–4;** Writing: **Grades 3–4**

Cross-curricular links
Numeracy, music, literacy

Language structures and outcomes
Bonjour [Mademoiselle].
Bonjour [Monsieur]. Je voudrais des billets pour [Paris].
Combien de billets?
[Quatre] billets: [un] adulte et [trois] enfants.
Aller-retour ou aller simple?
[Aller-retour] s'il vous plaît.
C'est combien?
C'est [trente-cinq] euros.
Le train part à quelle heure?
Le train part à [dix heures et demie].
Merci [Monsieur]. Au revoir.
Au revoir. Bon voyage!

---

1. Starter activity: Je voudrais... C'est combien?
5–10 mins — AT1.2, AT2.2, O6.4

Materials
Selection of flashcards depicting items which could be bought in a shop; pre-prepared cards each showing a variety of prices in euros; possibly *Rigolo 1* CD-ROM (Unit 11, Lesson 1 Presentation: *Je voudrais…*), whiteboard.

Description
Pupils revise numbers, asking politely for things and asking about the price of items.

Delivery
- If necessary, quickly revise numbers up to 60. You may also wish to use the *Rigolo 1* Unit 11 Presentation activity (see above) to revise asking for something in a shop.
- Invite two pupils to the front. Hand Pupil A a price card, and Pupil B a picture flashcard. Model a simple dialogue, along the lines of:
  – Bonjour [Mademoiselle]!
  – Bonjour [Monsieur].
  – Qu'est-ce que tu veux?
  – Je voudrais [un sandwich]. C'est combien?
  – Cinq euros, s'il vous plaît.
  – Voilà.
  – Merci. Au revoir [Mademoiselle]!
  – Au revoir [Monsieur].
- Repeat several times with other pupils and flashcards.

2. Video story: Je vais à la piscine (2)
10 mins — AT1.4, AT3.4, O6.1, O6.3, L6.1, IU6.1, IU6.2

Materials
CD-ROM, whiteboard.

Description
Watch and listen again to this video story presenting the language for Lessons 3 and 4. You can pause and rewind the story at any point.

Delivery
- Watch the second part of the video again, this time focusing on buying tickets at the station.
- Ask the class to note: how many tickets Chloé asks for, how much the tickets cost, the departure and arrival times of the train.
- Play the video through and elicit pupils' answers. Write them on the board.
- Play the scene through once more, pausing to check whether the answers on the board are correct.

Extension
Ask more confident pupils if they can also listen out for the ticket seller's questions.

Support
- During the first viewing, pause the film each time after Chloé speaks. Repeat chorally what she said.

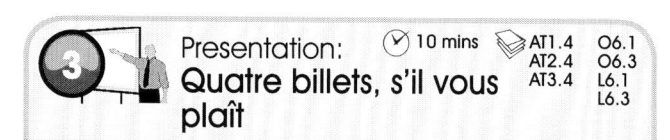

3. Presentation: Quatre billets, s'il vous plaît
10 mins — AT1.4, AT2.4, AT3.4, O6.1, O6.3, L6.1, L6.3

Materials
CD-ROM, whiteboard.

Description
Tap on the pictures to hear the dialogue and see the corresponding text. Use the additional features to record your own version of each part of the dialogue.

Delivery
- This presentation gradually builds up into a complete dialogue at the train station.
- Divide the class into two groups and invite a pupil to tap on the highlighted picture.
- Group A repeats the first speaker's sentence; Group B repeats the second speaker's sentence.
- Go through all the pictures, then repeat the activity. This time, Group A repeats after Speaker 2 and Group B repeats after Speaker 1. At the end, the whole dialogue is displayed.

Refer to the Introduction for notes on the *Record* feature.

Extension
Invite pairs of pupils to repeat and act out the dialogues after each scene.

Support
Chorally practise the dialogues after each scene until pupils are more familiar with the language and intonation.

4. Literacy activity: Je vais à Nice
10 mins — AT3.4, L6.1, L6.4

Materials
CD-ROM, whiteboard.

Description
Drag the words into the correct spaces to complete the sentences.

Delivery
- This is a gapped text to make pupils think about the structure of the sentences and to work out what might be missing. Ask them to predict what word might fit.
- Pupils select words to fill the gaps in the dialogue between Gustave and the ticket seller.

Extension
Ask pupils to suggest other words which could possibly fit into each gap. Invite pairs of pupils to re-enact the dialogue.

Support
Read through the completed dialogue together at the end of the activity. Half the class can read Gustave's lines; the other half can read the ticket-seller's part.

Worksheet 7 *Écrivez!* may be used from this point onwards.

5. Song: Je vais à Paris
10–15 mins — AT1.4, AT2.4, AT3.4, O6.1, O6.2, L6.1, L6.3, L6.4

Materials
CD-ROM, whiteboard.

Description
Watch and listen to the interactive karaoke song about travelling to different places. Choose either *Practice* or *Sing* mode: *Practice* to go through the song line by line; *Sing* to sing it all the way through. Switch the music and words on or off as you prefer, or try recording your own version.

Delivery
- Write the names of the three featured characters on the board (Nathalie, Olivier and Polly).
- Ask pupils to listen for the different means of transport featured in the song.
- Go through the song in *Practice* mode, checking general comprehension.
- Play the song through once more in *Sing* mode for pupils to sing along. If time allows, divide the class into groups and make this final stage into a karaoke competition. Pupils could perform the song at an assembly in front of fellow pupils/parents.

Extension
Copy the words of the song and cut it up into pieces of two lines. In groups, pupils reconstruct the song as you play it. Pupils could use the song as a model and write/sing their own additional verse.

Support
Cut up the song into individual verses. Pupils put them in the right order as they listen.

Worksheet 8 *Parlez!* may be used from this point onwards.

6. Plenary activity: Dialogues improvisés
10 mins — AT1.3–4, AT2.3–4, O6.2, O6.4

Materials
Unit 10 Flashcards (Means of transport and Holiday destinations); pictures of different possible destinations, e.g. chateau, theme park, places of interest.

Description
Pupils improvise short dialogues using flashcard prompts.

Delivery
- Place the flashcards in two piles: means of transport and destinations.
- Invite two pupils to the front of the class and hand one flashcard (from separate piles) to each pupil. For example, if pupils turn over *château* and *bateau*, model a dialogue between a 'ticket seller' and a 'tourist' along the lines of:
  – Bonjour!
  – Bonjour, je voudrais des billets de bateau.
  – Où vas-tu?
  – Je vais au château.
  – Combien de billets?
  – Deux billets. C'est combien?
  – C'est cinq euros.
Repeat with other pairs of pupils.

Extension
Encourage pupils to keep the dialogue going as long as possible, and to include language from previous units.

Support
Give pupils some cue cards with a suggested conversation, and ask them to change one or two elements.

Worksheet 7: Écrivez
10 mins — AT2.3, AT3.3, AT4.3, O6.2, O6.4, L6.1, L6.2

Description
This worksheet provides further writing and speaking practice to revise language from the unit. It may be used at any point after Activity 4.

Answers
Jake: **Le bus part à quelle heure?**
Mme Moulin: Le bus part à trois heures.
Mme Moulin: Qu'est-ce que tu veux?
Jake: **Je voudrais trois billets, s'il vous plait.**
Mme Moulin: On va aller où?
Jake: **On va aller au parc d'attractions.**
Jake: **C'est combien?**
Mme Moulin: C'est quatre-vingt huit euros.
Jake: Quatre-vingt huit euros!!!
Mme Moulin: Ahhh, tu veux trois billets aller-retour!
Jake: **Oui, trois billets aller-retour.**
Mme Moulin: Alors, c'est cent soixante euros.
Jake: Cent soixante euros! Non, merci, c'est trop cher…
Ça coûte 10 euros!

Worksheet 8: Parlez!
10 mins — AT2.3–4, O6.2, O6.4

Description
This worksheet provides further speaking practice in going on a trip and buying tickets. It may be used at any point after Activity 5. (You may wish to incorporate the work in this activity into the project work for this unit.)

Unit 10 Extra!

Project work: Un voyage en France
1 hours
AT2.3–4 O6.2
AT4.3–4 O6.4
L6.2 IU6.1
L6.4 IU6.2
     IU6.3

Description
Pupils plan a trip to a French-speaking country.

Materials
If possible, access to a PC (ideally with internet access for pupils to do research on their destination/download maps, etc.) and printer; maps and tourist brochures of French-speaking destinations; paper/card for displays.

Delivery

- Divide the class into pairs. Pupils decide where they want to go, how they will travel and what they are going to do there. They can write a paragraph about their plans using language from Lessons 1 to 3.

- Next, pupils can write a dialogue about buying the travel tickets (see Worksheet 8 *Parlez!* above).

- Each pair presents their travel plans to the class, and acts out their dialogue.

Sound/spelling activity: **Les sons 'o' et 'i'**
10–20 mins AT1.1 AT2.1

Description:
Practice mode:
Listen and practise pronouncing the 'o' sound and the 'i' sound on their own and then in words that have been covered in ***Rigolo*** so far.

Activity mode:
Listen to the words as they are read out. If they contain the 'o' sound, tap on the green button. If they don't contain the 'o' sound, tap on the red cross button. Repeat the process for 'i'. Listen carefully and choose your answer before the time runs out!

Delivery

- This sound/spelling activity focuses specifically on the 'o' and 'i' sounds.

- Select *Practice* and tap on *Next* to start this part. Then tap on *Allez*. The virtual teacher will say the 'o' sound and 'i' sound, first on their own and then with words that have been covered in ***Rigolo*** so far. Get the class to repeat the words chorally several times, checking the model each time using the *Encore* button. You can also use the *Record* feature here to compare a pupil's pronunciation more closely with the model.

- Once you have finished this part, tap on Activity to move on to test pupils' recognition of these sounds. Tap on *Allez* to start Activity 1. Pupils will hear one of 20 words read out in random order and must tap on the green button if they hear the 'o' sound or on the red cross if they don't. Pupils score a point when they correctly identify a word with 'o' within the time allowed. Tap on *Encore* to hear the word again and to re-start the time.

- Finally, in Activity 2, pupils repeat the above sequence, this time listening out for words with the 'i' sound.

- Repeat the activity if pupils need further practice.

Assessment for Units 9–10

Écoutez!

Play each audio 2–3 times, or more if necessary. Pause during each activity as required.

Total marks for listening: 20.

Activity 1 (AT1.2; O6.3)
Mark out of 10.

Answers
2 c, d 3 f, b 4 d, a 5 b, g 6 c, f

> 1 – Qu'est-ce que tu prends au petit déjeuner?
>   – Moi, je prends un chocolat chaud et une tartine.
> 2 – Qu'est-ce que tu prends au petit déjeuner?
>   – Moi, je prends un jus de pommes et un croissant.
> 3 – Qu'est-ce que tu prends au petit déjeuner?
>   – Euh… je prends des céréales et un café.
> 4 – Qu'est-ce que tu prends au petit déjeuner?
>   – Euh, je prends un croissant et un chocolat chaud.
> 5 – Qu'est-ce que tu prends au petit déjeuner?
>   – Moi, je prends un café et une tartine.
> 6 – Qu'est-ce que tu prends au petit déjeuner?
>   – Moi, je prends un jus de pommes et des céréales.

Activity 2 (AT1.3–4; O6.1, O6.3)
Mark out of 10.

Answers
1 1 theme park 2 baker's 3 train 4 bus 5 souvenirs
2 1 plane 2 castle 3 car 4 swimming pool 5 watching film

> 1 Samedi, on va aller au parc d'attractions.
>   D'abord, on va à la boulangerie.
>   À neuf heures, on va prendre le train.
>   Ensuite, on va prendre le bus.
>   Enfin, on va acheter des souvenirs au magasin.
> 2 Dimanche, on va prendre l'avion pour aller en Italie.
>   Lundi, on va aller au château.
>   On va aller au château en voiture.
>   Ensuite, on va aller à la piscine.
>   Enfin, on va regarder un film au cinéma.

Parlez!

Pupils can work in pairs for the speaking tasks. If it is not possible to assess each pair, then assess a few pairs for each assessment block and mark the rest of the class based on the spoken work they do in class.

Total marks for speaking: 20.

Activity 1 (AT2.2–3; O6.4)
10 marks (2 per sentence).

Answers

(*any 5 sentences*)
Je me lève (à + *any time*)
Je prends mon petit déjeuner (à + *any time*)
Je vais à l'école (à + *any time*)
Je prends mon déjeuner (à + *any time*)
Je quitte l'école (à + *any time*)
Je prends mon dîner (à + *any time*)
Je me couche (à + *any time*)

Activity 2 (AT2.3–4; O6.4)
10 marks.

Answers
Bonjour!
Bonjour (Monsieur). Je voudrais des billets pour (Marseille).
Combien de billets?
Un(e) adulte et deux enfants.
Aller-retour ou aller simple?
Aller simple s'il vous plaît. C'est combien?
C'est trente euros.
Le train part à quelle heure?
Le train part à dix heures et quart.
Merci, Monsieur, Au revoir!
Au revoir.

Lisez!

Total marks for reading: 20.

Activity 1 (AT3.2; L6.1)
Mark out of 10.

Answers
1 j, c; 2 g, d; 3 f, a; 4 h, b, 5 i, e

Activity 2 (AT3.4; L6.1)
Mark out of 10.

Answers
1 6:45 am
2 has breakfast
3 (apple juice and) bread with jam
4 7.45 am
5 on foot
6 has lunch
7 leaves school
8 cycling
9 goes to bed
10 asks Chloé what time she goes to bed

Écrivez!

Total marks for writing: 20.

Activity 1 (AT4.2; L6.4)
Mark out of 10 (2 per sentence).

Answers
1 Je vais au marché en bus.
2 Je vais à l'école à pied.
3 Je vais au jardin public à vélo.
4 Je vais au supermarché en voiture.
5 Je vais en centre sportif en train.

Activity 2 (AT4.3–4; L6.4)
Mark out of 10.

Rigolo 2 — Unit 11: Le sport

National criteria

KS2 Framework objectives

O6.1	Understand the main points and simple opinions in a spoken story, song or passage
O6.2	Perform to an audience
O6.3	Understand longer and more complex phrases or sentences
O6.4	Use spoken language confidently to initiate and sustain conversations and to tell stories
L6.1	Read and understand the main points and some detail from a short written passage
L6.2	Identify different text types and read short, authentic texts for enjoyment or information
L6.3	Match sound to sentences and paragraphs
L6.4	Write sentences on a range of topics using a model
IU6.1	Compare attitudes towards aspects of everyday life
IU6.2	Recognise and understand some of the differences between people
IU6.3	Present information about an aspect of culture

QCA Scheme of work

Unit 8	Argent de poche
Unit 14	Je suis le musicien
Unit 18	Les planètes
Unit 22	Ici et là

National Curriculum attainment levels

AT1.2–4, AT2.2–4, AT3.2–4, AT4.2–4

Language ladder levels

Listening:	Breakthrough, Grades 2–4
Reading:	Breakthrough, Grades 2–4
Speaking:	Breakthrough, Grades 2–4
Writing:	Breakthrough, Grades 2–4

5–14 guideline strands — Levels A–D

Listening
Listening for information and instructions	A, B, C, D
Listening and reacting to others	A, B, C, D

Speaking
Speaking to convey information	A, B, C, D
Speaking to convey information	A, B, C, D
Speaking about experiences, feelings and opinions	A, B, C, D

Reading
Reading for information and instructions	A, B, C, D
Reading aloud	A, B, C, D

Writing
Writing to exchange information and ideas	A, B, C, D
Writing to establish and maintain personal contact	A, B, C, D
Writing imaginatively to entertain	A, B, C, D

Unit objectives

- Talk about which sports you like
- Say what you think of different sports
- Give reasons for preferences
- Talk about a sporting event

Key language

- *Tu aimes quels sports? J'aime la natation, le vélo, la danse, le football, le tennis, l'équitation, la gymnastique, le roller*
- *Qu'est-ce que tu préfères? J'aime, Je n'aime pas, Je déteste, J'adore, Je préfère…* [+ names of sports]
  J'aime… mais/et je préfère…
- *J'aime [le football] parce que c'est amusant, facile, passionnant*
  Je n'aime pas [le football] parce que c'est ennuyeux, cher, difficile
- *Le samedi on va au match de foot.*
  On mange un sandwich et on boit un chocolat chaud.
  On regarde [Bordeaux] contre [Lyon].
  Le match commence à trois heures.
  X marque un but. C'est passionnant!
  Lyon gagne 2–0.

Grammar and skills

- Use the definite article with sports
- Spot patterns in French
- Use conjunctions *et* and *mais*
- Devise and ask questions
- Give reasons for opinions
- Use known language in new contexts
- Read and write longer texts
- Present information about sports

Unit outcomes

Most children will be able to:

- Talk about sports they like
- Express their preferences about different sports
- Ask questions about sports
- Say one or two sentences about a sporting event

Some children will also be able to:

- Give reasons for preferences
- Use conjunctions to make longer sentences
- Understand and write longer texts

Unit 11 — Lesson 1

Lesson summary

Context
Talking about which sports you like

National criteria
KS2 Framework: **O6.1, O6.3, O6.4, L6.1, L6.3, L6.4, IU6.1, IU6.2**
Attainment Levels: **AT1.2–4, AT2.2–3; AT3.2–4, AT4.2**
Language ladder levels:
   Listening: **Grades 2–4**; Speaking: **Grades 2–3**;
   Reading: **Grades 2–4**; Writing: **Grade 2**

Cross-curricular links
PE, literacy

Key vocabulary
le vélo, la danse, le football, le tennis, l'équitation, la gymnastique, le roller

Language structures and outcomes
Tu aimes quels sports? J'aime [la natation].

---

1. Starter activity: Les sports
5–10 mins — IU6.1 IU6.2

Materials
Unit 11 Flashcards (Sporting activities).

Description
A quick revision of sports and a brief introduction to some new ones.

Delivery
- Stick the picture flashcards on the board or hold them up, and ask pupils which ones they can say in French.
- Hold up the text flashcards and invite pupils to match the words to the pictures on the board. (Go over any unknown words very briefly at this stage as they will be covered later in the lesson.)

2. Animated story: Le grand match (1)
10 mins — AT1.3–4 O6.1, AT3.3–4 O6.3, L6.1 L6.3

Materials
CD-ROM, whiteboard; Unit 11 Flashcards (Sports activities).

Description
Watch and listen to this interactive story presenting the language for Lessons 1 and 2. You can pause and rewind the story at any point, or record your own version too.

Delivery
- Keep the flashcards displayed on the board and ask pupils to note whether all activities are mentioned in the animation.
- Play the story through, so that pupils can confirm which of the flashcard activities were mentioned.
- Summarise the story and key words together, then replay the story through one more time.

Extension
Ask pupils to place the sports flashcards in the order in which they appear in the story.

Support
Pause the story each time an activity is mentioned and point to the relevant flashcard during the first viewing.

3. Presentation: Tu aimes quels sports?
5–10 mins — AT1.2 O6.1, AT2.2, AT3.2

Materials
CD-ROM, whiteboard.

Description
Tap on the characters to hear them talk about which sports they like. Use the additional features to practise sound/spelling links, word classes and spelling, or to record your own version of each word.

Delivery
- The whole class listens to each sentence and repeats, miming each action to reinforce learning.
- Continue for all eight characters and repeat if further practice is required.
- You may wish to point out the importance of the definite article in French in these sentences, and encourage pupils to learn the article (*le/la/l'*) together with the sport.

Refer to the Introduction for notes on the *Record*, *Sound*, *Spell*, and *Word* features.

4. Oracy activity: J'aime le vélo
5–10 mins — AT2.2–3 O6.4

Materials
CD-ROM, whiteboard.

Description
Tap on *Allez*. Look at the symbols in the speech bubbles and say what you think each character is saying.

Delivery
- Gustave asks each character what sport(s) they like.
- Pupils use the clues to say the answer before tapping on the audio-check button to hear the model response. Where two sports are pictured, encourage pupils to use *et* e.g. *J'aime la danse et le football*.
- Pupils tap on the tick if their answer is correct. Otherwise, they tap on the cross and try again.
- Continue for all eight scenes and repeat if further practice is required.

Unit 11: Lesson 1

Support
Make this into a team activity so that less confident pupils can work together on the answer before saying it out loud.

Worksheet 1 *Écrivez!* may be used from this point onwards.

5. Literacy activity: J'aime le roller
5–10 mins AT3.2 L6.3

Materials
Unit 11 Flashcards (Sports activities: pictures and captions).

Description
Writing practice in the sports activities covered so far.

Delivery
- Display the caption flashcards randomly on the board.
- Invite a pupil to the front. Read out one of the captions and ask the pupil to point to the correct one.
- Ask pupils, in pairs, to look at the words on the board and to make three groups of words. Don't give any clues at this stage, but pupils will hopefully arrange the words according the article used (*le/la/l'*.) Invite a pair to the board to demonstrate their grouping and discuss together.
- Discuss how the French say 'I like **the** football' whereas in English we don't use an article.
- Allow the class two minutes to study the captions on the board, asking them to pay attention to the spelling and the articles. Remove the cards. Pupils write a list of as many of the words as possible, including the correct article. Go through the answers together, displaying the cards on the board as you do so.

Extension
Encourage accuracy with spelling when doing the writing part of the activity.

Support
Make the third part of the activity more like a dictation (with or without spelling out each word) for pupils who need more support.

Worksheet 2 *Grammaire* may be used from this point onwards.

Knowledge about language
Always encourage pupils to spot patterns in the foreign language. Use the categorising activity in Activity 5 to talk about gender again and reinforce what seeing *le* or *la* in front of a word tells you (i.e. that it is masculine or feminine).

6. Plenary activity: J'aime la gymnastique
5–10 mins AT2.2 O6.4 AT3.2 L6.3

Materials
Unit 11 Flashcards (Sports activities).

Description
Flashcard pairs game to further practise language from this lesson.

Delivery
- Divide the class into two teams. Stick the picture flashcards, face-down, on the board.
- Say one of the sports out loud, holding up the caption card at the same time. Invite the teams, in turn, to guess where the matching picture card is.
- Each time a team correctly identifies a card they score a point.

Worksheet 1: Écrivez!
5–10 mins AT4.2 L6.4

Description
A crossword and a sentence-building activity to practise writing about sports. This worksheet may be used at any point after Activity 4.

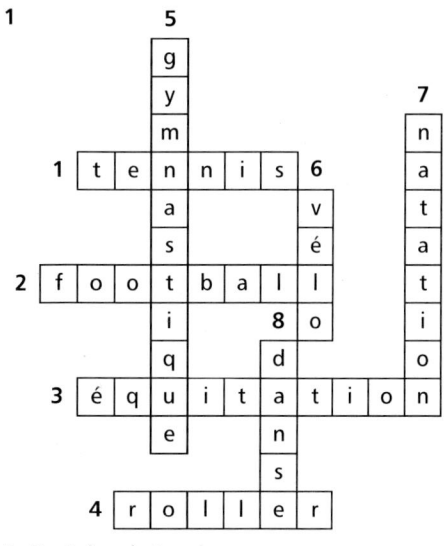

Answers
1

			5						
			g					7	
			y					n	
			m					a	
1	t	e	n	n	i	s	6	a	
			a				v	t	
			s				é	a	
2	f	o	o	t	b	a	l	l	
			i			8	o		t
			q			d			i
3	é	q	u	i	t	a	t	i	o	n
			e			n			
						s			
4	r	o	l	l	e	r			

2 2 J'aime le tennis.
   3 J'aime le roller et l'équitation.
   4 J'aime le vélo et la danse.
   5 J'aime le football, le roller et la gymnastique.
   6 J'aime le tennis, le vélo et la natation.

Worksheet 2: Grammaire
10 mins

Description
This worksheet provides further practice in gender of nouns. It may be used at any point after Activity 5.

Answers

masculine (**le**)	feminine (**la**)
le vélo	la danse
le tennis	l'équitation
le football	la gymnastique
le roller	la natation
le sport	la musique
le marché	la boulangerie
le balcon	la campagne
le jardin	la veste
le chapeau	l'informatique
le salon	la voiture

Unit 11 (Lesson 2)

Lesson summary

Context
Saying what you think of different sports

National criteria
KS2 Framework: O6.1, O6.3, O6.4, L6.1, L6.3, L6.4
Attainment levels: AT1.3–4, AT2.2–3; AT3.2–4, AT4.3
Language ladder levels:
 Listening: **Grades 3–4**; Speaking: **Grades 2–3**;
 Reading: **Grades 2–4**; Writing: **Grade 3**

Cross-curricular links
PE, literacy, numeracy

Language structures and outcomes
Qu'est-ce que tu préfères? J'aime, Je n'aime pas, Je déteste, J'adore, Je préfère... [+ names of sports]. [J'aime]...mais/et [je préfère]...

1. Starter activity: J'aime la natation (5 mins, AT2.2, AT3.2, O6.4)

Materials
Unit 11 Flashcards (Sports activities).

Description
A warm-up activity revising sports.

Delivery
- Divide the class into two teams.
- Invite a pupil from Team A to the front of the class and show them a flashcard, in secret. The pupil must mime the sport to their team. Award two points if they say the correct answer within 20 seconds; one point for up to 40 seconds.
- Continue with all the flashcards, alternating between the teams.

2. Animated story: Le grand match (1) (5–10 mins, AT1.3–4, AT3.3–4, L6.1, L6.3, O6.1, O6.3)

Materials
CD-ROM, Unit 11 Flashcards (Sports activities).

Description
Watch and listen again to this interactive story presenting the language for Lessons 1 and 2. You can pause and rewind the story at any point, or record your own version too.

Delivery
- Write the characters' names on the board (Jake, Polly, Nathalie and Olivier).
- Re-play the story, focusing this time on the characters' opinions of the activities.
- Play the story through and ask pupils to listen carefully for the sports mentioned by each character, and whether they have a positive or a negative opinion about each sport.
- After viewing, invite pupils to stick the flashcards under the relevant characters and to write a cross (✗) or a tick (✓) next to each card to indicate whether the character likes or dislikes the sport.
- Watch the story again to check their answers.

Support
During the first viewing, pause the story after each sport is mentioned to give pupils time to position the cards on the board.

3. Presentation: J'aime le football mais je préfère le roller (5–10 mins, AT1.3, AT2.3, AT3.3, O6.3)

Materials
CD-ROM, whiteboard; Unit 11 Flashcards (Preferences).

Description
Tap on each character to hear their likes, dislikes, and preferences in sport. Use the additional features to practise word classes, or to record your own version of each word.

Delivery
- Pupils listen and repeat what each character says about which sports they like/dislike/prefer.
- Continue for all eight characters and repeat if further practice is required.
- Draw pupils' attention to the use of *et* ('and') and *mais* ('but') and encourage them to use these conjunctions in their own speaking.

Refer to the Introduction for notes on the *Record* and *Word* features.

Extension
Use the activity with the sound off and get pupils to say sentences according to the symbols.

Support
Break down the sentence into two halves. Pupils repeat each half after you, then try to say the two halves together to make the longer sentence.

Knowledge about language

Activity 4 provides another opportunity for pupils to devise questions for authentic use. This makes sure that pupils can ask questions as well as answer them, which is an important skill when having a conversation in any language.

4. Oracy activity: Je n'aime pas le vélo et je déteste la natation (10 mins, AT2.3, O6.4)

Materials
Worksheet 3 *Parlez!*, Unit 11 Flashcards (Sports activities and Preferences).

Description
A class survey about pupils' opinions of various sports using Worksheet 3.

Delivery
- Write out *J'aime/Je n'aime pas/Je déteste/J'adore/Je préfère* and display the flashcards on the board to use as prompts.
- Ask a few confident pupils *Tu aimes quels sports?* and elicit answers using the phrases on the board.
- Display Worksheet 3 on the whiteboard and explain that the class is going to conduct its own survey about sports. Model how this works before allowing pupils a few minutes to survey a small group of classmates. Move around the groups to monitor the activity and help where required.
- Pool the results at the end of the activity and discuss your findings.

Extension
Encourage more confident pupils to make longer, more complex sentences using *et* and *mais* as much as possible.

Support
Accept more basic, shorter answers from less confident pupils.

---

5 — Literacy activity: Tu préfères quels sports? — 10 mins — AT3.3 AT4.3 — L6.4

Materials
CD-ROM, whiteboard.

Description
Tap on *Allez*. Look at what each person is saying about different sports. Read the text at the bottom of the screen. Drag the text into the correct order.

Delivery
- Pupils look at the symbols in Marine's or Gustave's thought bubble and the text options at the bottom of the screen.
- Using the text tiles, they build a sentence which best describes the picture. (These sentences give practice in forming longer sentences using *et* and *mais*.)
- When pupils are happy with their sentence they tap on *Fini*.
- Continue until all six sentences have been completed and repeat if further practice is required.

Support
This activity can be done as a whole-class activity: the class suggests what the sentence should be, and discusses their choices if necessary, before the pupil taps on *Fini*.

Worksheet 4 *Lisez!* may be used from this point onwards.

---

6 — Plenary activity: Le jeu du ballon — 10 mins — AT2.3 — O6.4

Materials
Small soft toy, ball or beanbag.

Description
Pupils have further practice in making sentences about sports.

Delivery
- Throw the ball/toy to a pupil, who makes a sentence, e.g. *J'adore la danse*, before throwing the ball/toy to another pupil.
- The next pupil must say *J'adore la danse et [la gymnastique]* before throwing the ball/toy to a third pupil.
- Continue until all the sports have been mentioned, then start again with a different verb, e.g. *Je déteste…*

Worksheet 3: Parlez! — 10 mins — AT2.3 — O6.4

Description
A class survey about pupils' opinions of various sports. It may be used at any point after Activity 3 (see Activity 4 notes above).

Worksheet 4: Lisez! — 10 mins — AT3.2 AT4.3 — L6.4

Description
This worksheet provides practice in reading and writing longer sentences about opinions of sports. It may be used at any point after Activity 5.

Answers
1. 1 c 2 a 3 e 4 d 5 b
2.
   1. Je déteste la gymnastique et la danse mais j'adore le football.
   2. Je n'aime pas le tennis mais j'adore le vélo.
   3. J'aime le tennis et j'adore le roller mais je n'aime pas le football.
   4. J'aime la gymnastique mais je préfère l'équitation et la natation.
   5. J'aime le vélo et j'adore le football et le roller.

Unit 11 (Lesson 3)

Lesson summary

Context
Giving reasons for preferences

National criteria
KS2 Framework: O6.1, O6.3, L6.1, L6.3, L6.4
Attainment levels: AT1.3–4, AT2.3, AT3.3–4, AT4.3
Language ladder levels:
  Listening: **Grades 3–4**; Speaking: **Grade 3**;
  Reading: **Grades 3–4**; Writing: **Grade 3**

Cross-curricular links
PE, Literacy

Language structures and outcomes
J'aime [le football] parce que c'est amusant, facile, passionnant
Je n'aime pas [le football] parce que c'est ennuyeux, cher, difficile

---

1. Starter activity: C'est amusant
5–10 mins — O6.3

Description
A game in which pupils deduce the meaning of new adjectives.

Delivery
- Write two columns of adjectives on the board: one in French, the other comprising the equivalents in English (in random order, as below):

amusant	difficult
facile	expensive
passionnant	funny/good fun
ennuyeux	easy
cher	boring
difficile	exciting

- Allow pupils two minutes to work in pairs and match up the French and English words by looking for similarities between the French and English words, making sensible guesses, etc.

- Go through the answers and discuss how pupils worked out the meanings. They can often use similar strategies when dealing with unknown vocabulary in reading texts.

Support
Reduce the number of adjectives and focus only on those pairs which do have similarities.

---

2. Animated story: Le grand match (2)
10 mins — AT1.3–4, AT3.3–4, O6.1, O6.3, L6.1, L6.3

Materials
CD-ROM, whiteboard.

Description
Watch and listen to this interactive story presenting the language for Lessons 3 and 4. You can pause and rewind the story at any point, or record your own version too.

Delivery
- Ask pupils to try to understand the gist of the story as they watch.
- Ask the class to summarise the story.

Extension
Ask pupils to raise their hands each time they recognise an adjective from the previous activity.

Support
Pause the story after every couple of lines to check comprehension.

---

3. Presentation: J'aime le football parce que c'est passionnant
5–10 mins — AT1.3, AT2.3, AT3.3, O6.3

Materials
CD-ROM, whiteboard; Unit 11 Flashcards (Sporting activities).

Description
Tap on the characters to hear them give reasons for their preferences in sport. Use the additional features to practise sound/spelling links, word classes and spelling, or to record your own version of each word.

Delivery
- We hear a short descriptive statement, e.g. *C'est passionnant*, followed by a longer sentence, e.g. *J'aime le football parce que c'est passionnant*.
- Encourage pupils to repeat both statements each time. Check understanding of the adjectives.
- Continue for all six characters and repeat if further practice is required.

Refer to the Introduction for notes on the *Record, Spell, Sound* and *Word* features.

Support
Concentrate on some pupils just repeating the *C'est* + adjective rather than the whole sentence. Use mimes and facial expression to give further oral practice. Decide as a class which expressions should be used for each adjective, then continue using them throughout subsequent activities.

---

4. Oracy activity: J'aime le tennis parce que c'est amusant
10 mins — AT1.3–4, O6.1, O6.3

Materials
CD-ROM, whiteboard.

Description
Tap on *Allez*. Listen to the audio. For each dialogue, tap on a symbol and a word to match the audio.

Delivery
- Pupils select a symbol and the matching word as they hear it in the dialogue.
- Continue for all eight scenarios and repeat if required.
- Reassure pupils that they do not have to understand every word in the dialogue order to complete the activity – it is a good activity to practise listening for key words.

Support
As the sentences here are quite long, encourage less confident pupils to tap *Encore* as many times as necessary before selecting their answer.

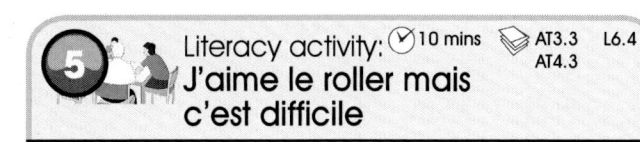

5. Literacy activity: J'aime le roller mais c'est difficile
10 mins — AT3.3, AT4.3 — L6.4

Materials
Pre-prepared word cards or captions written on the board (see below), Unit 11 Flashcards (Sports activities: pictures only).

Description
Pupils make sentences using word cards or captions on the board as prompts.

Delivery
- Prepare word cards on A4 card, or write these captions on the board as follows:
J'aime… (+ sports flashcards)
Je n'aime pas… (+ sports flashcards)
parce que c'est
amusant
facile
passionnant
ennuyeux
cher
difficile

- As a whole-class activity, practise making sentences together using these prompts.
- Divide the class into small groups and hold a competition to see how many different sentences each group can produce in five minutes.

Extension
Make the activity more challenging by breaking down the captions even further, e.g. *parce que c'est* becomes three separate captions. You could also adapt the sentences to include other vocabulary, e.g. school subjects (*Je n'aime pas les maths parce que c'est difficile*).

Worksheets 5 *Écrivez!* and 6 *Grammaire* may be used from this point onwards.

Language learning strategies
Always encourage your pupils to re-use language learned in one topic or context in a different one. It is important that pupils do not 'compartmentalise' language into specific chunks that can only be used for one purpose. Activities 5 and 6 give the opportunity to recycle language from previous units in a new context. Have a brainstorming session, recalling language which they could use here.

6. Plenary activity: C'est qui?
5–10 mins — AT1.3, AT4.3 — O6.3, L6.4

Description
Pupils guess the identity of someone in their class from a description of their likes and dislikes.

Delivery
- Make one or two sentences about a pupil in the class, e.g. *J'adore le football parce que c'est facile mais je n'aime pas les maths parce que c'est ennuyeux.*
- The other pupils must guess who you are talking about.
- Repeat and try to incorporate as many key words as possible.

Extension
Pupils could work in pairs or small groups to make up their own 'Guess who?' statement which they read/say out loud to the rest of the class. Encourage pupils to include vocabulary from previous units too.

Worksheet 5: Écrivez!
10 mins — AT4.3 — O6.3, L6.4

Description
This worksheet provides practice in writing longer sentences about why pupils like/dislike certain activities. It may be used at any point after Activity 5. (As an extension activity, pupils can write about other things they like/dislike, e.g. TV programmes and school subjects.)

Answers
1.
   1. J'aime le tennis mais c'est cher.
   2. J'adore l'équitation parce que c'est amusant et passionnant.
   3. Je préfère la danse parce que c'est facile et amusant.
   4. Je n'aime pas la natation parce que c'est ennuyeux et difficile.
   5. Je déteste le football parce que c'est ennuyeux. J'adore le tennis parce que c'est passionnant.
   6. J'aime le vélo parce que c'est amusant mais je préfère la gymnastique parce que c'est passionnant.

Worksheet 6: Grammaire
10 mins — AT4.3 — O6.3, L6.4

Description
This worksheet provides practice in writing longer sentences using conjunctions pupils have met so far. It may be used at any point after Activity 5.

Answers
1.
   1. J'aime le tennis et le football.
   2. J'adore l'équitation mais je n'aime pas la natation.
   3. Je préfère le roller parce que c'est amusant.
   4. Je n'aime pas la gymnastique parce que c'est ennuyeux.
   5. Je déteste la danse et je n'aime pas le tennis.
   6. J'aime le vélo et j'adore le football.

2.
   1. J'adore la danse et la gymnastique.
   2. J'aime l'équitation parce que c'est amusant.
   3. Je n'aime pas le roller mais j'aime le football.
   4. J'adore la gymnastique mais c'est cher.
   5. J'aime le football mais je préfère le tennis.
   6. J'aime la natation et/mais j'adore la gymnastique

Unit 11 (Lesson 4)

Lesson summary

Context
Talking about a sporting event

National criteria
KS2 Framework: O6.1, O6.2, O6.3, O6.4, L6.1, L6.2, L6.3, L6.4, IU6.1, IU6.2, IU6.3
Attainment levels: AT1.2–4, AT2.2–4; AT3.3–4, AT4.2–4
Language ladder levels:
- Listening: **Grades 2–4**; Speaking: **Grades 2–4**;
- Reading: **Grades 3–4**; Writing: **Grades 2–4**

Cross-curricular links
ICT (project work), Food technology, Art and design, PE, Literacy

Language structures and outcomes
Le samedi on va au match de foot.
On mange un sandwich et on boit un chocolat chaud.
On regarde [Bordeaux] contre [Lyon].
Le match commence à trois heures.
X marque un but. C'est passionnant!
Lyon gagne 2–0.

---

1. Starter activity: Qu'est-ce qu'on mange?
5–10 mins · AT1.2, AT2.2 · O6.4

Materials
All food and drink flashcards (*Rigolo 1* Units 6 & 11; *Rigolo 2* Units 3 & 9).

Description
Revision game using flashcards.

Delivery
- Hold up the flashcards and ask *Qu'est-ce que c'est?* for each to elicit words for food and drink.
- Make two columns on the board and write two headings: *Qu'est-ce qu'on mange?* and *Qu'est-ce qu'on boit?*
- Ask pupils to come to the board and place the flashcards in the correct column.

2. Animated story: Le grand match (2)
5–10 mins · AT1.3–4, AT3.3–4 · O6.1, O6.3, L6.1, L6.3

Materials
CD-ROM, whiteboard.

Description
Watch and listen again to this interactive story presenting the language for Lessons 3 and 4. You can pause and rewind the story at any point, or record your own version too.

Delivery
- Re-play the story, this time focusing on the opinions about sports and reasoning expressed by the characters.
- Play the story and ask pupils to repeat the opinions/reasoning sentences (and the numbers they heard, in context if possible).
- Encourage pupils to give you as much information as possible in French, then watch the story a second time.

Extension
Pupils try to listen out for extra information.

Support
Pause the story after each relevant line during the first viewing, and elicit the answers (numbers or opinions) to the comprehension task.

3. Presentation: Le match de football
10 mins · AT1.4, AT2.4, AT3.4 · O6.1, O6.3, L6.1, L6.2

Materials
CD-ROM, whiteboard.

Description
Tap on the pictures to hear an account of a trip to a football match. Use the additional features to record your own version of each phrase.

Delivery
- This is one of the longer presentations. It gives pupils the opportunity to see a longer text built up line by line.
- Pupils listen and repeat each sentence in sequence as they hear it, using gestures to reinforce the language where appropriate.
- The accompanying text appears on screen as each scene is narrated.
- Check that pupils understand each sentence before moving on to the next one.

Refer to the Introduction for notes on the *Record* feature.

Extension
Encourage pupils to break down the sentences so they can be adapted with other words, e.g. **On regarde** [*un film*], **on mange** [*une banane*], etc.

Support
Check comprehension of each line as it is played.

4. Oracy activity: Samedi, on va au match de football
5–10 mins · AT2.4, AT4.4 · O6.2, O6.4

Materials
Pre-prepared text on board.

Description
Reading aloud a longer text.

Delivery
- Focus on the complete text shown at the end of the Activity 3 Presentation (see above). Read it out to the class, adding gestures and varying your voice pitch as much as possible to 'animate' the story.

- Ask pupils to practise reading out the text in pairs, concentrating on pronunciation rather than speed of delivery. They can try to learn it by heart, if possible.

- Invite pupils to perform their version at the front of the class.

Extension
Go through the whole text and discuss what parts could be replaced with other words to change the story. Encourage more confident pupils to adapt the text before performing it to the class, e.g.
*Samedi, on va au match de **football** [tennis].On mange **un sandwich** [une pizza] et on boit **un chocolat** [un jus de pomme]. On regarde **Rigoloville** [favourite team] contre **Tigreville** [another favourite team]. Le match commence à trois [onze] heures.
Bof [favourite player] marque un but. C'est **passionnant** [facile]! **Rigoloville** [favourite team] gagne **20–3** [50–1]!*

5. Literacy activity: France–Italie
10 mins — AT3.4 — L6.1 L6.2

Materials
CD-ROM, whiteboard.

Description
Drag the text into the correct order to complete the account of the trip to a football match.

Delivery
- This is a gap-fill activity. Ask pupils why they selected a particular word to drag into the gap, i.e. it needed to be a noun, etc.

- When the text is complete it is read out by the Virtual Teacher.

Extension
Ask pupils to give other possible words that would fit in each gap, to get them thinking about adapting language for their own use.

Support
- Make this a whole-class activity. Encourage pupils to guess what sort of word is missing and think about predicting what comes next.

Worksheet 7 *Lisez!* may be used from this point onwards.

6. Plenary activity: En scène
10–15 mins — AT1.4 O6.2 — AT2.4 O6.4

Materials
Worksheet 8 *Parlez!*

Description
Using Worksheet 8, pupils practise reading aloud and adapting accounts of sporting events.

Delivery
- Allow pupils a few minutes to complete Activity 1 of the worksheet.

- In Activity 2, pupils could take turns to say a line, whilst their partner acts out what they are saying.

- Ask the rest of the class, who are listening, to pick out two or three main points from each dialogue.

Worksheet 7: Lisez!
10 mins — AT3.4 — L6.1 L6.2

Description
This worksheet provides authentic reading practice on the subject of sporting events. It may be used at any point after Activity 5.

Answers
1 2 P 3 N 4 G 5 Équipe 6 J
3 1e 2a 3c 4d 5b

Worksheet 8: Parlez!
10–15 mins — AT2.3–4 O6.2 / AT3.3–4 O6.4 / AT4.3–4 L6.4

Description
This worksheet gives practice in reading aloud and adapting accounts of sporting events. It may be used at any point after Activity 5.

Answers
1 1 *Samedi, on va au match de football.*
   2 On mange un sandwich et on boit un chocolat chaud.
   3 On regarde Rigoloville contre Tigreville.
   4 Le match commence à trois heures.
   5 Bof marque un but. C'est passionnant!
   6 Rigoloville gagne 20–3.

Knowledge about language

Intercultural understanding
Use the project at the end of each unit to encourage pupils to present information about an aspect of French culture. In this project, encourage them to present or include some information about sport in France, in the form of an electronic or an oral presentation. Encourage them to use good presentation techniques if speaking, i.e. speaking in a clear voice, trying to sound as French as possible if they're doing a small amount in French, sounding enthusiastic about their chosen subject. Ask others to evaluate their classmates' work, being as constructive and as positive as possible!

Project work: Les sports
1–2 hours — AT2.2–4 O6.2 / AT3.3–4 O6.3 / AT4.2–4 O6.4 / L6.1 IU6.1 / L6.2 IU6.2 / L6.4 IU6.3

Description
Pupils prepare a display about sporting activities.

Materials
Internet access and printer if possible; card and paper to display the pictures and text in the classroom, or access to PowerPoint; pictures of school sporting events or of French sports personalities.

Delivery
- Divide the class into groups and ask each group to cover a different event or sport, e.g. a school sports day; sports activities depicted in the websites of French primary schools; a school football match; an international sports event such as the Roland Garros tennis championships or Wimbledon; or something more personal such as horse-riding lessons. Each group must gather as many pictures as possible and write captions for each one.

- Encourage pupils to use all the language they have covered and to write as much as possible. Ideally, each group of pupils will make an oral presentation when their display is completed.

Rigolo 2 — Unit 12: On va faire la fête!

National criteria

KS2 Framework objectives

O6.1	Understand the main points and simple opinions in a spoken story, song or passage
O6.2	Perform to an audience
O6.3	Understand longer and more complex phrases or sentences
O6.4	Use spoken language confidently to initiate and sustain conversations and to tell stories
L6.1	Read and understand the main points and some detail from a short written passage
L6.2	Identify different text types and read short, authentic texts for enjoyment or information
L6.3	Match sound to sentences and paragraphs
L6.4	Write sentences on a range of topics using a model
IU6.1	Compare attitudes towards aspects of everyday life
IU6.2	Recognise and understand some of the differences between people
IU6.3	Present information about an aspect of culture

QCA Scheme of work

Unit 4	Portraits
Unit 6	Ça pousse!
Unit 7	On y va
Unit 21	Le passé et le présent
Unit 23	Monter un café
Unit 24	Quoi de neuf?

National Curriculum attainment levels

AT1.2–4, AT2.2–4, AT3.2–4, AT4.3–4

Language ladder levels

Listening: Breakthrough, Grades 2–4
Reading: Breakthrough, Grades 2–4
Speaking: Breakthrough, Grades 2–4
Writing: Breakthrough, Grades 3–4

5–14 guideline strands — Levels A–D

Listening
Listening for information and instructions — A, B, C, D
Listening and reacting to others — A, B, C, D

Speaking
Speaking to convey information — A, B, C, D
Speaking and interacting with others — A, B, C, D
Speaking about experiences, feelings and opinions — A, B, C, D

Reading
Reading for information and instructions — A, B, C, D
Reading aloud — A, B, C, D

Writing
Writing to exchange information and ideas — A, B, C, D
Writing to establish and maintain personal contact — A, B, C, D
Writing imaginatively to entertain — A, B, C, D

Unit objectives

- Revise forms of transport, places and future plans
- Revise descriptions of people and clothes
- Revise opinions of food and clothes
- Order food in a cafe

Revision of key language

- *Où vas-tu? Je vais au marché, au supermarché, au château, au jardin public, au centre sportif, à l'école, à la boulangerie, à la piscine, à la montagne, à la campagne*
  Comment vas-tu? Je vais en bus, en voiture, en avion, en train, en métro, en bateau, à pied, à vélo
  Qu'est-ce que tu vas faire samedi? Je vais/On va… regarder un film, visiter un parc d'attractions, nager, faire la fête, faire les manèges, prendre le train, prendre l'avion, acheter des souvenirs, faire du ski, faire du bateau, faire du sport, faire du vélo, voir mes grands-parents

- *Il/Elle est [+nationality]. Il/Elle est (n'est pas) grand(e), petit(e), sympa, drôle, sportif/sportive, timide, beau/belle, sévère, intelligent(e). Il/Elle a les cheveux longs/courts et les yeux bleus/marron/verts. Il/Elle a… ans. Il/Elle porte un pantalon, un t-shirt, un chapeau, une veste, une jupe, une chemise, des chaussures [+ colour]*

- *J'aime, Je n'aime pas, J'adore, Je déteste… le chocolat chaud, le café, le jus de pomme, les croissants, les pains au chocolat, les céréales, les tartines, les frites, les gâteaux, les bonbons, les pommes, les carottes, les haricots, les sandwichs au poulet/au thon/au fromage/à la tomate, les glaces au chocolat/à l'orange/à la fraise/à la vanille.*
  C'est bien, cool, chouette, nul, fantastique, délicieux, beau/belle, moche, trop grand, trop petit, trop cher, bon, mauvais… pour la santé

- *Qu'est-ce que tu veux/vous voulez manger/boire? Je voudrais un… s'il te plaît, s'il vous plaît. Merci. C'est combien? C'est… euros. Voilà… Merci, au revoir*

Revision grammar and skills

- Prepositions: *au/à la/à l'* + places; *en/à* + means of transport
- Use *je vais* + infinitive to talk about future plans
- Revisit known language in a different context
- Use 3rd person verbs including *avoir* and *être*
- Use agreement of adjectives
- Use negatives
- Re-combine known language in different ways
- Express opinions in different ways
- Use plurals of food words
- Use reading strategies to cope with authentic texts
- Ask for things politely
- Present information on an aspect of French culture using song and sketches

Unit outcomes

Most children will be able to:
- Revise and re-use language met in previous units
- Describe someone in one or two sentences
- Express opinions
- Ask for food and drink in a café

Some children will also be able to:
- Re-combine known language in different ways
- Form sentences in the present and future tenses
- Use and apply grammar rules more confidently including negatives, prepositions and agreement of adjectives

Unit 12 — Lesson 1

Lesson summary

Context
Revising forms of transport, places, and immediate future plans

National criteria
KS2 Framework: O6.1, O6.2, O6.3, O6.4, L6.1, L6.2, L6.3, L6.4, IU6.1, IU6.2, IU6.3
Attainment levels: AT1.2–4, AT2.2–4, AT3.4, AT4.3–4
Language ladder levels:
 Listening: **Grades 2–4**; Speaking: **Grades 2–4**;
 Reading: **Grade 4**; Writing: **Grades 3–4**

Cross-curricular links
Geography, music, drama

Language structures and outcomes
Talking about forms of transport and immediate future (all revision)
Où vas-tu? Je vais au marché, au château, au supermarché, au jardin public, au centre sportif, à l'école, à la boulangerie, à la piscine, à la montagne, à la campagne
Comment vas-tu? Je vais en bus, en voiture, en avion, en train, en métro, en bateau, à pied, à vélo
Qu'est-ce que tu vas faire samedi? Je vais/On va… regarder un film, visiter un parc d'attractions, nager, faire la fête, faire les manèges, prendre le train, prendre l'avion, acheter des souvenirs, faire du ski, faire du bateau, faire du sport, faire du vélo, voir mes grands-parents

---

General note for Unit 12
The aim of the unit is to revise language met so far in *Rigolo* and to see known language in new contexts, in different combinations and in longer texts. Throughout this unit, the outcome should be that pupils prepare for a final party, performance (of song) or event (see Project work in Lesson 4) or a combination of all of the above in a French day at school. Lesson 1 revises going to places, immediate future plans and forms of transport.

1 Starter activity: 5–10 mins — Je vais au marché à vélo
AT1.2–4 O6.3
AT2.2–4 O6.4

Materials
CD-ROM, whiteboard; Units 4 and Unit 10 Flashcards (Places in the town and Means of transport).

Description
A quick revision of transport and places using the Unit 10 Lesson 2 Presentation.

Delivery
- Invite pupils to the front to tap on the highlighted places on screen.
- Pupils hear Gustave asking Jake where he is going and how he gets there.
- The class listens and repeats for each place/means of transport.

Extension
Use all relevant flashcards to extend the revision to all the vocabulary for means of transport and places.

2 Video story: 10 mins — Au café (1)
AT1.4 O6.1
AT3.4 O6.3
L6.1 IU6.1
L6.3 IU6.2

Materials
CD-ROM, whiteboard.

Description
Watch and listen to this video story presenting the language for Lessons 1 and 2. You can pause and rewind the story at any point.

Delivery
- Play the video through without stopping and ask pupils to listen out for:
 a the different places around town
 b the different forms of transport
 c any cultural differences they can spot in the film.
- After viewing, go through the answers together. Ask pupils more detailed questions about the content of the film to check full comprehension.
- Replay the whole video without stopping for pupils to enjoy and check the points you have discussed together.

Extension
Focus on the language related to future plans. Ask pupils to see how many sentences about future plans they can remember.

Support
Work through the dialogue line by line after the initial viewing, asking questions to check comprehension.

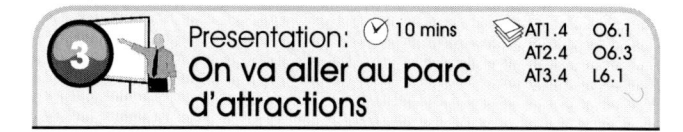

3 Presentation: 10 mins — On va aller au parc d'attractions
AT1.4 O6.1
AT2.4 O6.3
AT3.4 L6.1

Materials
CD-ROM, whiteboard; Units 5 and 10 Flashcards (Holiday destinations and Means of transport).

Description
Revision of future plans using the Unit 10 Lesson 3 Presentation.

Delivery
- Re-play the Unit 10 Presentation, to revise future plans using *on va* + infinitive.
- We hear Polly announcing plans for the day out and the whole class repeats each sentence.
- Continue for all six pictures and repeat if further practice is required. A longer text is gradually built up on screen.
- Remind the class that *on* is used when speaking to mean 'we', and *je* means 'I'. Remind pupils also that the structure *on va/je vais* + another verb is used to say what we are planning to do.
- Hand out flashcards to pairs of pupils and individuals to elicit further sentences using *on va* or *je vais*.

— Unit 12: Lesson 1 —

Extension
Use flashcards from previous units to extend and practise the language covered there, e.g. Unit 5 Flashcards (Holiday activities). Prepare some short dialogues with the class using *je vais* + infinitive. More able pupils could then look at each line and suggest adapting one element to produce a new sentence, e.g. On va aller [au cinéma].

4. Oracy activity: Je vais au marché
5–10 mins · AT1.4 · O6.1 O6.3

Materials
CD-ROM, whiteboard.

Description
Tap on *Allez*. Look at the pairs of pictures showing three different situations. Listen to the conversation and choose the correct pair of pictures.

Delivery
- The class will hear a conversation between Jake and Madame Chanson about Jake's plans (where he's going, how he's getting there and what he's going to do there). Pupils tap on the relevant pair of pictures.

Extension
Ask pupils to try to pick out any extra information they hear in the dialogues.

Support
Encourage less confident pupils to use the *Encore* button as much as necessary. Remind them that they don't need to understand everything that is said, just the key words. Look at the three pairs of pictures before listening and discuss what words they are likely to hear.

Worksheet 1 *Parlez!* may be used from this point onwards

5. Song: On va faire la fête
10–15 mins · AT1.4 O6.1 / AT2.4 O6.2 / AT3.4 O6.3 / AT4.3–4 L6.1 L6.3 / IU6.3 L6.2 L6.4

Materials
CD-ROM, whiteboard; *Rigolo 1* Unit 11 and *Rigolo 2* Unit 10 Flashcards (Party activities and Holiday activities).

Description
Watch and listen to the interactive karaoke song practising revision of intentions with *on*. Choose either *Practice* or *Sing* mode: *Practice* to go through the song line by line; *Sing* to sing it all the way through. Switch the music and words on or off as you prefer, or try recording your own version.

Delivery
- Write the names Polly, Jake, Nathalie and Didier on the board.
- Ask pupils to listen to the song all the way through in *Sing* mode and note which activities each character will be doing at the party.
- Elicit answers from the class and note suggestions on the board under the relevant names (remember that *manger, chanter, boire* and *danser* will appear for all four characters).
- Ask pupils to make sentences about who is going to do what, using the different formats (which you can also write on the board): Je vais… On va… [Nathalie/Elle/Didier/Il] va…
- Play the song through in *Practice* mode, checking the answers on the board after pupils have sung each line.

- You can either play the song again, in *Sing* mode, for pupils to join in with the singing and actions, or organise a karaoke competition in teams.

Extension
Print out and cut up the lyrics. Ask pupils to recreate the song after listening to it all the way through. Pupils could also perform the song, changing the names to those of pupils in their class to personalise it, as part of the special French event or day (see Lesson 4 Project work).

Support
Use the activity flashcards to revise the language as necessary: hand out the flashcards and ask pupils to hold them up as they hear the activities in the song. Encourage pupils to memorise the song in groups and see who can remember it best.

Worksheet 2 *Grammaire* provides further exploitation of the song with a gapped text and may be used from this point onwards.

6. Plenary activity: Des sketchs
10 mins · AT1.4 O6.1 / AT2.3–4 O6.2 / IU6.3 O6.4

Materials
Units 4, 5 and 10 Flashcards (Places in the town, Holiday activities and Means of transport).

Description
Pupils recreate dialogues based on a model in the video.

Delivery
- Play the following video extract again, and write the dialogue on the board:
  - Ou vas-tu?
  - Je vais <u>au centre sportif</u>. Je vais <u>faire de la danse</u>.
  - <u>Je n'aime pas la danse</u>. C'est <u>difficile.</u>
  - Non, c'est <u>très facile.</u>
  - Comment vas-tu <u>au centre sportif</u>?
  - D'abord, je vais <u>en bus.</u> Ensuite, je vais <u>à pied.</u>
- Brainstorm other places they can go, things they can do and how to get there. Replace the underlined expressions in the dialogue, using the flashcards as prompts if needed.
- In pairs, ask pupils to do quick improvisations based loosely on this pattern.

Extension
Pupils try to include language they've learned previously.

Worksheet 1: Parlez!
10 mins · AT1.4 O6.4 / AT2.4 L6.4 / AT4.3

Description
This worksheet provides further speaking practice in places and future plans. It may be used at any point after Activity 4.

Worksheet 2: Grammaire
10 mins · AT1.4 L6.1 / AT3.4 L6.3 / O6.1 IU6.1

Description
This provides further exploitation of the karaoke song with a gapped text and more creative writing. It may be used at any point after Activity 5.

Answers
1 1 va 2 on 3 va 4 faire 5 vais 6 écouter 7 regarder 8 faire

Unit 12 (Lesson 2)

Lesson summary

Context
Revising descriptions of people and clothes

National criteria
KS2 Framework: **O6.1, O6.3, O6.4, L6.1, L6.2, L6.3, L6.4, IU6.1, IU6.2**
Attainment Levels: **AT1.2–4, AT2.2–4, AT3.2–4, AT4.3–4**
Language ladder levels:
   Listening: **Grades 2–4**; Speaking: **Grades 2–4**;
   Reading: **Grades 2–4**; Writing: **Grades 3–4**

Cross-curricular links
Literacy, Food technology

Language structures and outcomes
Il/Elle est [+nationality]. Il/Elle est (n'est pas) grand(e), petit(e), sympa, drôle, sportif/sportive, timide, beau/belle, sévère, intelligent(e). Il/Elle a les cheveux longs/courts et les yeux bleus/marron/verts. Il/Elle a… ans. Il/Elle porte un pantalon, un t-shirt, un chapeau, une veste, une jupe, une chemise, des chaussures [+ colour]

General note
This lesson revises descriptions of people and clothes and use of the 3rd person. As with Lesson 1, concentrate on re-activating and consolidating previously learnt language and combining it in new ways. Build on pupils' increasing confidence by encouraging them to experiment with the language.

1. Starter activity: Elle est belle (5 mins) — AT1.2–3 O6.1, AT2.2–3 O6.3, AT3.2–3

Materials
Rigolo 1 Units 3 and 7, *Rigolo 2* Unit 1 Flashcards (Descriptions); magazine pictures of celebrities.

Description
A warm-up game to revise descriptions of people.

Delivery
Using the magazine pictures or pupils in the class as models, elicit as many descriptions as possible using the target language outlined above.

Extension
More confident pupils could work in pairs/small groups to write down as many sentences as possible about the 'model'. Focus their attention on the agreement of adjectives.

Support
If necessary, you could use any of the following presentations for further revision practice: *Rigolo 1* Unit 7 (Lessons 1, 3 or 4); *Rigolo 2* Unit 1 (Lesson 4) or Unit 8 (Lesson 3).

2. Video story: Au café (1) (5 mins) — AT1.4 O6.1, AT3.4 O6.3, L6.1 IU6.1, L6.3 IU6.2

Materials
CD-ROM, whiteboard.

Description
Watch and listen again to this video story presenting the language for Lessons 1 and 2. You can pause and rewind the story at any point.

Delivery
● Tell pupils they will watch the video again and must listen out this time for the description of Romain.

● Elicit a full description and replay that extract again if necessary for pupils to check their answers.

Extension
Ask more confident pupils to describe Léa from the shots in the film.

3. Presentation: Il est sportif (5–10 mins) — AT1.4 O6.1, AT2.4 O6.3, AT3.4 L6.1

Materials
CD-ROM, whiteboard; *Rigolo 1* Units 3 and 7, *Rigolo 2* Unit 1 Flashcards (Descriptions) for extension and support.

Description
Tap on the pictures to hear the descriptions. Use the additional features to record your own version of each phrase.

Delivery
● This presentation revises age, nationality, details of eyes, hair, personality and clothes.

● Pupils first hear a sentence describing Polly and Olivier. When the next highlighted picture is tapped, the descriptive sentence is added to the previous text. Pause after each new line is added to the text and check understanding.

● Continue for all six pictures and repeat if further practice is required.

Refer to the Introduction for notes on the *Record* feature.

Extension
More confident pupils could talk about other *Rigolo* characters using flashcards or pictures on screen.

Support
Use flashcards to do further revision of descriptions if necessary, concentrating on age, nationality, and personality adjectives.

4. Oracy activity: Les descriptions (10 mins) — AT2.3–4 O6.4

Materials
Rigolo 1 character flashcards.

Description
Pupils practise describing *Rigolo* characters in as much detail as possible.

Delivery
● Divide the class into two teams.

Rigolo 2 Teacher's Notes © Nelson Thornes Ltd 2008 — 125

- Stick three of the character flashcards on the board. Ask: *C'est qui?* and begin to describe the characters sentence by sentence. Talk about age (*il/elle a... ans*), nationality (*il/elle est francais(e)*, etc.), appearance/personality (*il/elle est drole*, etc.), clothes (*il/elle porte une chemise bleue*, etc.). By selecting characters of the same sex you can make the game more or less challenging!

- The first team to identify correctly the character described wins a point.

- Repeat with another three cards, and so on.

Extension
- To make the game more challenging, stick up four or five flashcards at a time. More confident pupils could call out the descriptions and the other team must guess the identity of the character.

- You could also describe teachers/other staff in your school, and pupils must identify them from your description.

Support
Reduce the number of characters to just two, to enable less confident pupils to participate.

5 Literacy activity: Monsieur Chanson est comment?
10 mins — AT3.4 L6.1 L6.4

Materials
CD-ROM, whiteboard.

Description
Drag the words at the bottom into the correct spaces.

Delivery
- Look at the gapped text with the class. Ask pupils if they can tell you what sort of words are missing from each space (verb? adjective? noun? pronoun?). Can they suggest some words that might fit?

- Pupils then drag the word tiles into the most appropriate place in the text. The resulting sentences describe Monsieur Chanson, Madame Chanson, and Nathalie.

Extension
- Divide the class into groups. Before doing the whiteboard activity, ask each group to write out their version of the three descriptions and check their answers as you go through the activity.

- After doing the drag and drop, more able pupils could write their own version, fitting other possible words into the gaps.

Support
- This can be done as a whole-class activity: the class suggests what the sentence should be (and discusses their choices if necessary).

- Give pupils just two possible alternatives for each space.

Worksheets 3 *Lisez!* and 4 *Grammaire* may be used from this point onwards.

6 Plenary activity: On cherche Madame Moulin
5–10 mins — AT2.3–4 O6.4 AT4.3–4 L6.4

Materials
Card, picture of Madame Moulin.

Description
An additional class activity to practise describing someone in detail.

Delivery
- Prepare a ('Wanted') poster of Madame Moulin, perhaps using a cut-out from her flashcard in *Rigolo 1*, Unit 1.

- Tell pupils Madame Moulin is wanted by the police for acts of sabotage against the Mills family. Brainstorm a detailed description of her with the whole class, and write the description (or ask a pupil to write it) on the board.

Extension
Pupils could make their own *Recherché* posters for other *Rigolo* characters.

Worksheet 3: Lisez!
10 mins — AT3.4 L6.1 L6.2

Description
This worksheet provides practice in reading and understanding authentic texts. It may be used at any point after Activity 5.

Answers
2 1 les chaussures de tennis
   2 le pantalon bleu
   3 la belle jupe rose
   4 la veste noire
   5 la chemise rouge
   6 le t-shirt jaune

Worksheet 4: Grammaire
10 mins — L6.4 AT4.3–4

Description
This provides further practice in 3rd person forms of *avoir* and *être* and agreement of adjectives. It may be used at any point after Activity 5.

Answers
1 1 a 2 est 3 grand 4 sportif 5 vert 6 a 7 est
   8 petite 9 intelligente 10 belle

Unit 12 Lesson 3

Lesson summary

Context
Revising opinions of food and clothes

National criteria
KS2 Framework: O6.1, O6.3, O6.4, L6.1, L6.2, L6.3, IU6.1, IU6.2
Attainment levels: AT1.2–4, AT2. 2–4; AT3.2–4
Language ladder levels:
  Listening: **Grades 2–4**; Speaking: **Grades 2–4**;
  Reading: **Grades 2–4**

Cross-curricular links
Food technology

Key vocabulary
Revision: *J'aime, Je n'aime pas, J'adore, Je déteste… le chocolat chaud, le café, le jus de pomme, les croissants, les pains au chocolat, les céréales, les tartines, les frites, les gâteaux, les bonbons, les pommes, les carottes, les haricots, les sandwichs au poulet/au thon/au fromage/à la tomate, les glaces au chocolat/à l'orange/à la fraise/à la vanille. C'est bien, cool, chouette, nul, fantastique, délicieux, beau/belle, moche, trop grand, trop petit, trop cher, bon, mauvais… pour la santé*

General note on Lesson 3
Lesson 3 revises different ways of expression opinions about food and clothes using either *j'aime, je n'ame pas, j'adore, je déteste* or *c'est* + adjectives. As with previous lesson, one of the main aims is to revise language and to combine known language in different context and in different combinations. We would like pupils to be adventurous in their use of known language and not just to use it in set phrases and in the context in which they originally learned it. Don't worry if pupils make some mistakes with their language. It's more important that they experiment and enjoy their language learning rather than achieving 100% accuracy.

① Starter activity: Je n'aime pas les haricots
⏱ 5 mins · AT1.3 AT2.3 · O6.3 O6.4

Materials
Units 3 and 9 Flashcards (Food items).

Description
Quick revision of giving opinions about food.

Delivery
● Brainstorm and write on the board the various ways in which you can express likes/dislikes, i.e. *j'aime, je n'aime pas, j'adore, je déteste.*

● Brainstorm all ways in which pupils have learnt to express their opinions, and write them in positive/negative columns on the board:
Positive: *C'est… bien, cool, chouette, fantastique, délicieux, beau, belle, bon, bon pour la santé*
Negative: *C'est… nul, moche, trop grand, trop petit, trop cher, mauvais, mauvais pour la santé*

● Hold up one of the food flashcards and ask: *Qu'est-ce que c'est? C'est…* Ask: *Tu aimes les…?* Pupils give their individual opinions.

● Then continue with the clothes. Pupils reply using *C'est* + an adjective (see the list of key language above)

② Video story: Au café (2)
⏱ 10 mins · AT1.4 AT3.4 L6.1 L6.3 · O6.1 O6.3 IU6.1 IU6.2

Materials
CD-ROM, whiteboard.

Description
Watch and listen to this video story presenting the language for Lessons 3 and 4. You can pause and rewind the story at any point.

Delivery
● Ask pupils to summarise what happened in the first part of this video. Tell the class that Lucas and Thomas are going in to the café owned by Chloé's family, and that she is helping out there today.

● Write the names Lucas and Thomas in two columns. Ask pupils to note what food each boy eats, and any opinions they express about food.

● Play the video through then complete the table on the board together.

Support
Pause the video during the first viewing and elicit answers as you go along.

③ Presentation: C'est beau mais c'est trop grand
⏱ 10 mins · AT1.2–3 AT2.2–3 AT3.2–3 · O6.3 O6.4

Materials
CD-ROM, whiteboard.

Description
Revision of opinions about clothes using the Unit 8 Lesson 2 Presentation.

Delivery
● Invite pupils to tap first on Olivier, then on Didier, who is trying on t-shirts. He appears from behind the curtain and describes the t-shirt, in response to Olivier's question.

● Pupils listen to and repeat the question, then do the same for the answer.

Extension
Bring in a selection of catalogues/magazines featuring clothes for men and women, and older children/teenagers if possible. Ask pupils to work in groups and to comment on several items of clothing using the target structures and vocabulary.

― Unit 12: Lesson 3 ―

4. Oracy activity: C'est super mais c'est trop cher
10 mins — AT1.4 — O6.1, O6.3

Materials
CD-ROM, whiteboard.

Description
Tap on *Allez*. Look at the three pictures and listen to the conversation between Jake and Polly. Select the picture that best matches their conversation.

Delivery
- This provides practice in listening to longer exchanges and asking pupils to pick out key words and phrases. Pupils select the picture which best matches the conversation.
- By dividing the class into two groups you could make this into a team game, awarding a point for each correct answer.

Extension
Ask pupils to listen for any extra details they can understand.

Support
Focus pupils' attention first on the pictures and ask them to predict what they are going to hear.

5. Literacy activity: La carte
15 mins — AT3.4, IU6.2 — L6.1, L6.2

Materials
Worksheet 5 *Lisez!*; French–English dictionaries.

Description
Pupils extract information from an authentic menu.

Delivery
- This worksheet provides further practice in reading authentic texts and helps pupils to develop reading strategies.
- Focus pupils' attention on the menu: ask them to identify the three sections and ask how much a few individual items cost.
- Allow pupils a few minutes to complete the answers to each activity, in pairs or individually. If available, allow pupils to check unknown words in a dictionary.
- At the end of Activity 2, take a few minutes to go through the menu in detail. Ask pupils to imagine they are on holiday in France with someone who doesn't understand any French and they must translate the menu for them.

Extension
In groups, pupils could devise their own menu.

Language learning strategies

Reading strategies
When dealing with authentic texts, discuss various strategies with your pupils and apply them to the menu:
- Skim though and say what type of reading text this is: is it a newspaper article, a diary, a story, a menu?
- Scan the text and see if they understand anything at all. From what they do understand, what can they tell you about the text?
- Deduce any more words because they look like English words, or from the context in which an unknown word is used.
- Use the French–English part of a dictionary to look up words they feel are important but can't guess. Allow them to look up a maximum of 10 words; they must choose which words to look up.
- Go back and read the text again. How much more do they understand?

6. Plenary activity: C'est bon?
10–20 mins — AT1.3, AT2.3 — O6.3, O6.4, IU6.2

Materials
Real food and drink items if possible (see food list in the lesson summary above); otherwise food and drink flashcards or plastic play food; possibly blindfold.

Description
Pupils taste and/or describe food items.

Delivery
- Bring in as many items of food and drink that we have covered in *Rigolo* for pupils to taste and comment on.
- Place the items on a table and ask pupils to gather round. Go through the items one by one, asking *Qu'est-ce que c'est?* to elicit the words.
- Ask for a volunteer to taste an item and give their opinion. If possible, you could blindfold the pupil so that they must first identify the food or drink item, then give their opinion.
- Repeat with as many items and pupils as feasible.
- If real food/drink isn't available, you could use plastic play food (blindfolded pupils feel and guess what the food is and say what they think of it) or flashcards (one pupil describes an item, another must identify the correct card and give their opinion).

Worksheet 5: Lisez!
10 mins — AT3.4, IU6.1, IU6.2 — L6.1, L6.2

Description
This worksheet provides further practice in reading authentic texts and discussing reading strategies (see Activity 5 notes above).

Answers
1
1. fromage
2. thon
3. frites
4. poulet
5. gâteau au chocolat
6. glace à la vanille
7. glace à la fraise
8. jus d'orange
9. jus de pomme
10. chocolat chaud

2
1. le sandwich poulet
2. la pizza maison
3. le gâteau du jour
4. la coupe Marcel
5. le sandwich Marcel

Worksheet 6: Parlez!
10 mins — AT2.4 — O6.4

Description
This provides further practice in asking and answering questions about school, clothes, food and sports. It may be used at any point after Activity 5.

Unit 12 — Lesson 4

Lesson summary

Context
Ordering food in a café

National criteria
KS2 Framework: O6.1, O6.2, O6.3, O6.4, L6.1, L6.2, L6.3, L6.4, IU6.1, IU6.2, IU6.3
Attainment levels: AT1.3–4, AT2.3–4; AT3.4, AT4.4
Language ladder levels:
  Listening: **Grades 3–4**; Speaking: **Grades 3–4**;
  Reading: **Grade 4**; Writing: **Grade 4**

Cross-curricular links
Geography, FT, Drama, ICT, Art and design

Language structures and outcomes
Qu'est-ce que tu veux/vous voulez manger/boire?
Je voudrais un... s'il te plaît, s'il vous plaît. Merci.
C'est combien? C'est... euros. Voilà... Merci, au revoir

General notes on Lesson 4
This lesson focuses on ordering food in a café so that pupils can set up their own café for their end-of-term event and serve other pupils/teachers/parents. Encourage them to learn the part of the customer and the waiter.

1. Starter activity: Quatre billets, s'il vous plaît (5 mins)
AT1.4, AT2.4, AT3.4 — O6.1, O6.3, L6.1, L6.3

Materials
CD-ROM, whiteboard.

Description
Revision of asking politely for things using the Unit 10 Lesson 4 Presentation.

Delivery
- Invite pupils to tap on the highlighted pictures. The whole class listens to and repeats both question and answer as a quick revision activity.
- After re-playing the presentation, ask pupils what the French is for 'please', 'thank you', 'I would like', 'how much is it?', 'hello' and 'goodbye'.

Extension
Invite pairs of pupils to the front so they can repeat and act out the dialogues after each scene.

Support
- First revise numbers if necessary.
- Practise the dialogues chorally after each scene until pupils are more familiar with the language and intonation.

2. Video story: Au café (2) (5–10 mins)
AT1.4, AT3.4 — O6.1, O6.3, L6.1, L6.3, IU6.1, IU6.2

Materials
CD-ROM, whiteboard.

Description
Watch and listen again to this video story presenting the language for Lessons 3 and 4. You can pause and rewind the story at any point.

Delivery
- Ask pupils this time to listen out in particular for the language used to order and pay for food. Write the key expressions on the board as pupils suggest them.
- Go through the language used by Chloé to ask what the customers want to order, and to give the price at the end. Again, write pupils' suggestions on the board.
- Ask pupils to tell you if they can see any cultural differences between British and French cafés.
- If time allows, play the video through one more time for pupils to double-check their answers/observations.

Support
During the first viewing pause the video after each line and repeat chorally what is said.

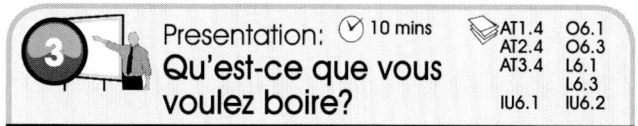

3. Presentation: Qu'est-ce que vous voulez boire? (10 mins)
AT1.4, AT2.4, AT3.4 — O6.1, O6.3, L6.1, L6.3, IU6.1, IU6.2

Materials
CD-ROM, whiteboard.

Description
Tap on the pictures to hear the dialogue. Use the additional features to record your own version of each exchange.

Delivery
- Divide the class into two groups. Group A repeats Gustave's sentence; Group B repeats Madame Moulin's sentence.
- Go through all the pictures, then repeat the activity. This time, Group A repeats after Madame Moulin and Group B repeats after Gustave.
- After the last speaker, the whole conversation appears on screen. Use it to practise the complete series of dialogues.

Refer to the Introduction for notes on the *Record* feature.

Extension
Invite pairs of pupils to the front so they can repeat and act out the dialogues after each scene. Ask for volunteers to perform the whole conversation at the end.

Support
Practise the dialogues chorally after each scene until pupils are more familiar with the language and intonation.

4. Literacy activity: Voilà une limonade (5–10 mins)
AT3.4 — L6.1, L6.3

Materials
CD-ROM, whiteboard

Description
Tap on *Allez*. Drag the words into the correct order.

Unit 12: Lesson 4

Delivery
- Pupils look at the pictures and drag the word tiles into the correct order.
- When they are satisfied with their sentence, pupils tap on *Fini*. There is a reward animation for a correct answer; otherwise the Virtual Teacher invites them to try again.

Support
Read through the completed dialogue together at the end of the activity. Half the class reads Polly's lines and the other half read Bof's.

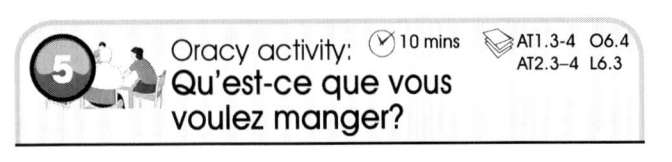

5 Oracy activity: Qu'est-ce que vous voulez manger?
10 mins — AT1.3-4 O6.4 / AT2.3-4 L6.3

Materials
Food and drink flashcards (see above) or plastic/play food; pre-prepared euro money cards.

Description
Pupils re-enact the dialogue from Activity 4 (see above).

Delivery
- Display the final dialogue from Activity 4 and invite two pupils to the front to act out the scenes using props.
- Ask the class to make suggestions as to how the dialogue could be changed, e.g. different food and drink items, prices. Experiment with some of the suggestions, inviting more pupils to act out the amended dialogues at the front.

Extension
Allow pupils to work in small groups and make up their own dialogues.

Worksheets 7 *Écrivez!* and 8 *Lisez!* may be used from this point onwards.

5 Plenary activity: Des conversations au café
10–15 mins — AT1.3-4 O6.2 / AT2.3-4 O6.4 / IU6.3

Materials
Worksheet 7 *Écrivez!*; food and drink flashcards or plastic/play food; pre-prepared euro money cards.

Description
Pupils perform short dialogues based on those they have adapted in Worksheet 7 *Écrivez!*

Delivery
- Read through the dialogue on the worksheet together.
- Adapt the first couple of lines as a whole-class activity if necessary, then allow up to five minutes for pupils to complete the adaptation in pairs.
- Move around the class to monitor and help the children act out the conversation. Encourage them to learn their lines by heart.
- Invite pairs to the front to perform the role play using props to the rest of the class.

Extension
Encourage more able pupils to use language from other units too.

Support
With your help, pupils could adapt the dialogues in groups rather than pairs.

Worksheet 7: Écrivez!
10–16 mins — AT2.4 O6.2 / AT4.4 O6.4 / L6.4 IU6.3

Description
Pupils adapt and perform dialogues about ordering food and drink in a café (see Activity 6 above).

Worksheet 8: Lisez!
10 mins — AT3.4 O6.2 / IU6.3 L6.1 / L6.2

Description
This worksheet provides further practice in reading longer texts and acting out scenes. It may be used at any point after Activity 5.

Answers
2 **circled in black** un sandwich au thon, une pizza, des carottes
  circled in red je n'aime pas (la pizza), je déteste ça, c'est trop cher
  circled in blue soixante-dix

Intercultural understanding
Use the project work suggestion below to give pupils opportunities to present information about any aspect of French culture. It may be that they can set up a café just for their own class, or perform a song for another class, or on a larger scale set up a more adventurous café for parents and teachers. By setting up a French café, they can show others what sort of things they would see on a menu, what currency would be used, what drinks/food they could order and how French people would ask for things in a café. They can perform songs and sketches and also possibly use ICT to prepare menus for the tables.

Unit 12 Extra!

Project work: 1–3 hours AT2.4 IU6.1 / AT3.4 IU6.2 / AT4.4 IU6.3 / L6.4 O6.2 / O6.4
La fête

Description
A task or performance (or both!) to combine as much language as possible from the whole of the *Rigolo* curriculum.

Materials
Depending on project work chosen, access to a PC and printer, paper and card for displays, real food and drink items, euros.

Delivery
The project is the culmination of the whole of *Rigolo*. You can choose a selection of the following, or combine them in a day devoted to French activities. You could perhaps invite parents to pupils' own café in the afternoon to see some of their performances.

- The class prepares a French café for another class, parents or teachers.
- They plan the menu, prepare the café, and act as waiters and waitresses.
- Pupils plan and present a sketch which takes place in a French café.
- Pupils perform a song that they've adapted from the original one in Lesson 1 of this unit.
- Pupils prepare a display of descriptions of people. This could be, for example, a selection of *Recherché* posters for staff at the school!

Sound/spelling activity: 10 mins AT1.1 / AT2.1
Le son 'ez'

Description:
Practice mode:
Listen and practise pronouncing the 'ez' sound on its own and then in words that have been covered in *Rigolo* so far.

Activity mode:
Listen to the words and phrases and count how many times you hear the 'ez' sound in each, then tap on the correct number on the screen.

Delivery
- This sound/spelling activity focuses specifically on the 'ez' sound, sometimes spelled 'et', 'ez', 'ai' 'é' and 'er'.

- Select *Practice* and tap on *Next* to start this part. Then tap on *Allez*. The Virtual Teacher will say the 'ez' sound as part of words that have been met in *Rigolo*. For each of these, get the class to repeat the words chorally several times, checking the model each time using the *Encore* button. You can also use the *Record* feature here to compare a pupil's pronunciation more closely with the model.

- Once you have finished this part, choose *Activity* to move on to test pupils' recognition of these sounds. Tap on *Allez* to start. Pupils will hear 12 phrases read out. For each phrase, they must work out how many 'ez' sounds they hear. They tap on the correct number button on screen, between 0 (if they don't hear it at all) and 4. To show pupils how the activity works, tap on the *Example* button. You can tap on *Encore* to hear the phrase again. Ask the whole class to vote on how many times they hear the sound and ask individual pupils to come forward to select the right number.

- When they have selected the right number, the phrase will appear on screen and the 'ez' sound will be highlighted at the appropriate point in the audio. Click on the *Encore* button if you want to hear the phrase again and review their answer.

- Repeat the activity if pupils need further practice.

Assessment for Units 11–12

Écoutez!

Play each audio 2–3 times, or more if necessary. Pause during each activity as required.

Total marks for listening: 20.

Activity 1 (AT1.2–3; O6.3)
Mark out of 10.

Answers

	swim	bike	riding	tennis	gym	♥	♥♥	♥✗	♥♥✗
e.g.			(✓)				(✓)		
1				✓				✓	
2	✓								✓
3					✓		✓		
4		✓					✓		
5			✓					✓	

> Example:
> – Tu aimes quels sports?
> – Moi, j'adore l'équitation, oui j'adore ça!
> 1 – Quels sports est-ce que tu n'aimes pas?
> – Moi, je n'aime pas le tennis. Non je n'aime pas ça.
> 2 – Et toi, Luc, quels sports est-ce que tu n'aimes pas?
> – Moi, je déteste la natation. Oui, je déteste la natation.
> 3 – Et toi, Sophie, quels sports est-ce que tu aimes?
> – Moi, j'adore la gymnastique. C'est super!
> 4 – Et toi, Thomas, quels sports est-ce que tu aimes?
> – Moi, j'aime le vélo. Oui, j'aime ça.
> 5 – Et toi, Delphine, quels sports est-ce que tu n'aimes pas?
> – Moi, je n'aime pas l'équitation. C'est difficile.

Activity 2 (AT1.4; O6.3)
Mark out of 10.

Answers

	Où?	Transport?	Activité?
e.g.	marché	bus	jouer au football
1	café	pied	la gymnastique
2	cinéma	voiture	un film
3	centre sportif	vélo	1 la natation 2 jouer au tennis

Example:
- *Où vas-tu ce week-end?*
- *Samedi, je vais au marché.*
- *Comment vas-tu au marché?*
- *J'y vais en bus.*
- *Et qu'est-ce que tu vas faire dimanche?*
- *Dimanche, je vais jouer au football.*
- *Mm, super!*

1 - *Où vas-tu ce week-end?*
   - *Samedi, je vais au café.*
   - *Comment vas-tu au café?*
   - *J'y vais à pied.*
   - *Et qu'est-ce que tu vas faire dimanche?*
   - *Dimanche, je vais faire de la gymnastique. J'adore la gymnastique!*

2 - *Où vas-tu ce week-end?*
   - *Samedi, soir je vais au cinéma.*
   - *Comment vas-tu au cinéma?*
   - *J'y vais en voiture.*
   - *Qu'est-ce que tu vas regarder?*
   - *Je vais regarder un film comique.*
   - *Super!*

3 - *Où vas-tu ce week-end?*
   - *Samedi, je vais au centre sportif.*
   - *Comment vas-tu au centre sportif?*
   - *J'y vais à vélo.*
   - *Et qu'est-ce que tu vas faire au centre sportif?*
   - *D'abord, je vais faire de la natation, ensuite je vais jouer au tennis.*
   - *J'adore le sport!*

Parlez!

Pupils can work in pairs for the speaking tasks. If it is not possible to assess each pair, then assess a few pairs for each assessment block and mark the rest of the class based on the spoken work they do in class.

Total marks for speaking: 20

Activity 1 (AT2.2–3; O6.4)
10 marks (2 per mini-dialogue).

Answers
1 - Je voudrais une pizza, s'il vous plaît.
   - Voilà.
   - C'est combien?
   - C'est sept euros.
2 - Je voudrais une glace s'il vous plaît.
   - Voilà.
   - C'est combien?
   - C'est deux euros.
3 - Je voudrais un sandwich au fromage s'il vous plaît.
   - Voilà.
   - C'est combien?
   - C'est cinq euros.
4 - Je voudrais un gâteau s'il vous plaît.
   - Voilà.
   - C'est combien?
   - C'est quatre euros.
5 - Je voudrais un croissant s'il vous plaît.
   - Voilà.
   - C'est combien?
   - C'est trois euros.

Activity 2 (AT2.3–4; O6.4)
10 marks.

Lisez!

Total marks for reading: 20.

Activity 1 (AT3.2; L6.1)
Mark out of 10.

Answers
1 **1** g, i **2** j, f **3** a, d **4** c, h **5** b, e

Activity 2 (AT3.4; L6.1)
Mark out of 10.

Answers
2 **1** Sarah **2** Luc **3** Luc **4** Sarah **5** Luc **6** 3.30 **7** 20 **8** France **9** by car **10** 8.00

Écrivez!

Total marks for writing: 20.

Activity 1 (AT4.2–3; L6.4)
Mark out of 10 (2 per sentence).

Answers
(*any 5 sentences – reasons not necessary but denote slightly higher level*)

1 1 J'adore le football.
   2 Je n'aime pas le tennis.
   3 J'aime l'équitation.
   4 Je déteste la natation.
   5 J'adore le vélo.
   6 J'adore les frites.
   7 J'aime les pizzas.
   8 J'aime les gâteaux.
   9 Je déteste les glaces.
   10 J'aime les pommes.

Activity 2 (AT4.3–4; L6.4)
Mark out of 10.

Rigolo 2

Appendix 1

Scheme of work

Unit 1: Salut, Gustave!

Lesson	Objective	Context/Key language	Grammar/skills	National criteria
1	Greet people and give and personal information	Greetings and personal information: *Bonjour/Salut! Comment t'appelles-tu? Je m'appelle… Ça va ? Oui, ça va bien/Non, ça ne va pas/Comme ci comme ça Tu es français(e)/britannique ? Oui/Non je suis… Quel âge as-tu ? J'ai… ans*	• Ask and answer questions	Framework: O5.1, O5.3, L5.1, L5.2, L5.3, IU5.1 NC Attainment levels: AT1.2–3, AT2.1–3, AT3.2–3, AT4.2–3 Language ladder: Listening: Grades 1–3; Speaking: Grades 1–3; Reading: Grades 2–3; Writing: Grades 2–3
2	Ask and talk about sisters and brothers	*Tu as des frères ou des sœurs? J'ai un(e) /deux/trois frères/sœurs Je n'ai pas de frères ou de sœurs*	• Recognise and use plural forms • Use a negative	Framework: O5.1, O5.3, L5.1, L5.2, L5.3, IU5.1 NC Attainment levels: AT1.2–3, AT2.1–2, AT3.2–3, AT4.2 Language ladder: Listening: Grades 2–3; Speaking: Grades 1–2; Reading: Grades 2–3; Writing: Grade 2
3	Say what people have and have not using 3rd person *avoir*	*Il a/Elle a… Il/Elle n'a pas de… +* Revised nouns: *une sœur, un frère, un vélo, une guitare*	• Use 3rd person *avoir* in positive and negative statements • Manipulate language by changing an element in a sentence	Framework: O5.1, O5.3, O5.4, L5.1, L5.2, L5.3, IU5.1 NC Attainment levels: AT1.1–3, AT2.2–3, AT3.2–3, AT4.2–3 Language ladder: Listening: Grades 2–3; Speaking: Grades 2–3; Reading: Grades 2–3; Writing: Grades 2–3
4	Say what people are like using 3rd person *être* including negatives.	*Il/Elle est…, Il/Elle n'est pas… drôle, sportif(ve), sympa, timide , beau/ belle, sévère, grand(e), petit(e), intelligent(e), français(e), britannique* (all revised apart from *beau/belle*)	• Use 3rd person *être* in positive and negative sentences • Understand and use agreements of adjectives (singular) • Recognise patterns in simple sentences	Framework: O5.1, O5.3, O5.4, L5.1, L5.2, L5.3, IU5.1 NC Attainment levels: AT1.2–3, AT2.2, AT3.2–3, AT4.2–3 Language ladder: Listening: Grades 2–3; Speaking: Grade 2; Reading: Grades 2–3; Writing: Grades 2–3
Extra!	Project work: descriptions of people or celebrities	Summary of above language	• Prepare a short presentation	Framework: L5.1, L5.2, L5.3, O5.4 NC Attainment levels: AT3.2–3, AT4.2–3 Language ladder: Speaking: Grades 2–3; Writing: Grades 2–3

Rigolo 2 Teacher's Notes © Nelson Thornes Ltd 2008

Unit 2: À l'école

Lesson	Objective	Context/Key language	Grammar/skills	National criteria
1	Name school subjects	C'est… l'anglais, le français, le sport, l'histoire-géo, les sciences, les maths, la musique	• Understand and use the definite article correctly: le/la/l'/les	Framework: O5.1, O5.2, O5.3, L5.1, L5.3, IU5.1, IU 5.2 NC Attainment levels: AT1.1–3, AT2.1, AT3.1–3, AT4.1–2 Language ladder: Listening: Grades 1–3; Speaking: Grade 1; Reading: Grades 1–3; Writing: Grades 1–2
2	Talk about likes and dislikes at school	J'aime /Je n'aime pas + subjects C'est bien/cool/nul	• Express opinions • Use correct intonation when asking a question	Framework: O5.1, O5.2 O5.3, L5.1, L5.2, L5.3, IU5.1, IU5.2 NC Attainment levels: AT1.1–3, AT2.1–2, AT3.2–3, AT4.2 Language ladder: Listening: Grades 1–3; Speaking: Grades 1–2; Reading: Grades 1–3; Writing: Grade 2
3	Ask and say the time	Quelle heure est-il? Il est une heure et quart. Il est trois heures moins le quart. Il est trois heures et demie. Il est midi/minuit	• Understand that there is not always a direct equivalent to each English word in French	Framework: O5.1, O5.2, O5.3, L5.1, L5.2, L5.3, IU5.1, IU5.2 NC Attainment levels: AT1.2–3, AT2.2, AT3.2–3, AT4.2 Language ladder: Listening: Grades 2–3; Speaking: Grade 2; Reading: Grades 2–3; Writing: Grade 2
4	Talk about timings of the school day	La recré, le déjeuner, l'école commence à… heure(s) et finit à…	• Use song to help memorise language • Form longer sentences	Framework: O5.1, O5.2, O5.3, O5.4, L5.1, L5.2, L5.3, IU5.1, IU5.2, IU5.3 NC Attainment levels: AT1.2–3, AT2.2–3, AT3.2–3, AT4.2 Language ladder: Listening: Grades 2–3; Speaking: Grades 2–3; Reading: Grades 2–3; Writing: Grades 2–3
Extra!	Project work: School in France Sound/spelling activity for Units 1–2 Assessment for Units 1–2	Summary of above language, and Unit 1	Use the internet to find information	Framework: O5.1, O5.3, L5.1, L5.3, IU5.1, IU5.2, IU5.3 NC Attainment levels: AT1.1–3, AT2.1–3, AT3.1–3, AT4.1–2 Language ladder: Listening: Grades 1–3; Speaking: Grades 1–3; Reading: Grades 1–3; Writing: Grades 1–3

Unit 3: La nourriture

Lesson	Objective	Context/Key language	Grammar/skills	National criteria
1	Ask politely for food items	*Je voudrais… s'il vous plaît un sandwich au poulet, un sandwich au thon, un sandwich au fromage, un sandwich à la tomate, une glace au chocolat, une glace à l'orange, une glace à la fraise, une glace à la vanille*	• Understand and use au/à la/à l' when referring to flavours of foods • Learn gender when learning new words	Framework: O5.1, O5.3, L5.1, L5.2, L5.3, IU5.1 NC Attainment levels: AT1.2–3, AT2.2, AT3.1–3, AT4.2 Language ladder: Listening: Grades 2–3; Speaking: Grade 2; Reading: Grades 1–3; Writing: Grade 2
2	Describe how to make a sandwich	*les tomates, le thon, le fromage, une baguette, le beurre* *Mangez, Coupez, Prenez, Mettez*	• Give instructions in the vous form • Prepare a short presentation	Framework: O5.1, O5.3, O5.4, L5.1, L5.2, L5.3, IU5.1 NC Attainment levels: AT1.2–3, AT2.2–3, AT3.2–3, AT4.2–3 Language ladder: Listening: Grades 2–3; Speaking: Grades 2–3; Reading: Grades 2–3; Writing: Grade 2
3	Express opinions about food	*J'aime /Je n'aime pas … les gâteaux, les frites, les bonbons, les pommes, les carottes, les haricots*	• Understand and use negatives • Use the plural form of some food vocabulary • Integrate new vocabulary into previously learned language	Framework: O5.1, O5.2, O5.3, L5.1, L5.2, L5.3, IU5.1 NC Attainment levels: AT1.2–3, AT2.2, AT3.2–3, AT4.2–3 Language ladder: Listening: Grades 2–3; Speaking: Grade 2; Reading: Grades 2–3; Writing: Grades 2–3
4	Talk about healthy and unhealthy food	*[Les carottes], C'est bon pour la santé* *Ce n'est pas bon pour la santé*	• Use known language in a new context	Framework: O5.1, O5.2, O5.3, O5.4, L5.1, L5.2, L5.3, IU5.1 NC Attainment levels: AT1.2–3, AT2.2–3, AT3.2–3, AT4.2–3 Language ladder: Listening: Grades 2–3; Speaking: Grades 2–3; Reading: Grades 2–3; Writing: Grades 2–3
Extra!	Project work: finding out about French lunches and writing instructions for favourite sandwich	Summary of above language	• Use the internet to find information • Use a dictionary for unknown words	Framework: O5.4, L5.1, L5.3, IU5.1 NC Attainment levels: AT1.2–3, AT2.2–3, AT3.2–3, AT4.2–3 Language ladder: Listening: Grades 2–3; Speaking: Grades 2–3; Reading: Grades 1–3; Writing: Grades 2–3

Unit 4: En ville

Lesson	Objective	Context/Key language	Grammar/skills	National criteria
1	• Name places in the town	Qu'est-ce que c'est? C'est… la boulangerie, le centre sportif, le château, l'école, le jardin public, le marché, la piscine, le supermarché	• Use le/la/l' correctly with places	Framework: O5.1, O5.3, L5.1, L5.3, IU5.2, IU5.3 NC Attainment levels: AT1.1–3, AT2.1–2, AT3.1–3, AT4.1–2 Language ladder: Listening: Grades 1–3; Speaking: Grades 1–3; Reading: Grades 1–3; Writing: Grades 1–2
2	• Ask the way and give directions	[La piscine] s'il vous plaît? Tournez à droite/à gauche. Allez tout droit. D'abord… ensuite… enfin… + directions	• Use sequencers d'abord, ensuite, enfin to say longer sentences. • Give instruction using the vous form	Framework: O5.1, O5.3, O5.4, L5.1, L5.2, L5.3, IU5.1, IU5.2, IU5.3 NC Attainment levels: AT1.2–3, AT2.2–3, AT3.2–3, AT4.3 Language ladder: Listening: Grades 2–3; Speaking: Grades 2–3; Reading: Grade 3; Writing: Grade 3
3	• Say where you are going	Où vas-tu? Je vais au château/centre sportif/jardin public/marché/supermarché Je vais à la boulangerie/piscine Je vais à l'école	• Use prepositions au/à la /à l' with places • Recognise language patterns and deduce rules	Framework: O5.1, O5.3, L5.1, L5.2, L5.3, IU5.1, IU5.2, IU5.3 NC Attainment levels: AT1.2–3, AT2.2–3, AT3.2–3, AT4.2–3 Language ladder: Listening: Grades 2–3; Speaking: Grades 2–3; Reading: Grades 2–3; Writing: Grades 2–3
4	• Give the time and say where you are going	Il est [deux] heures. Je vais au/à la/à l' + places	• Incorporate known language into new structures	Framework: O5.1, O5.3, O5.4, L5.1, L5.2, L5.3, IU5.1, IU5.2, IU5.3 NC Attainment levels: AT1.2–3, AT2.2–3, AT3.2–3, AT4.3 Language ladder: Listening: Grades 2–3; Speaking: Grades 2–3; Reading: Grades 2–3; Writing: Grades 2–3
Extra!	Project work: Researching a town in France Sound/spelling activity for Units 3–4 Assessment for Units 3–4	Summary of above language, and Unit 3	• Use the internet to find information	Framework: O5.1, O5.2, O5.3, O5.4, L5.1, L5.2, L5.3, IU5.1, IU5.2, IU5.3 NC Attainment levels: AT1.1–3, AT2.2–3, AT3.2–3, AT4.1–3 Language ladder: Listening: Grades 1–3; Speaking: Grades 2–3; Reading: Grades 2–3; Writing: Grades 1–3

Unit 5: En vacances

Lesson	Objective	Context/Key language	Grammar/skills	National criteria
1	Ask and say where you're going on holiday	*Où vas-tu en vacances?* *Je vais à la campagne.* *Je vais à la montagne.* *Je vais au bord de la mer.* *Je vais au camping.* *Je vais au parc d'attractions.*	• Use *au/à la /à* correctly with places • Recognise patterns and apply knowledge of rules	Framework: O5.1, O5.2 O5.3, L5.1, L5.2, L5.3, IU5.2 NC Attainment levels: AT1.2–3, AT2.2, AT3.2–3, AT4.2–3 Language ladder: Listening: Grades 2–3; Speaking: Grade 2; Reading: Grades 2–3; Writing: Grades 2–3
2	Express opinions about holidays	*J'aime ça. Je n'aime pas ça* *J'adore ça. Je déteste ça.*	• Express opinions	Framework: O5.1, O5.2, O5.3, L5.1, L5.2, L5.3, IU5.2 NC Attainment levels: AT1.2–3, AT2.2–3, AT3.2–3, AT4.2–3 Language ladder: Listening: Grades 2–3; Speaking: Grades 2–3; Reading: Grades 2–3; Writing: Grades 2–3
3	Talk about what you're going to do on holiday	*Qu'est-ce que tu vas faire en vacances?* *Je vais faire du bateau.* *Je vais faire du ski.* *Je vais nager.* *Je vais faire du sport.* *Je vais faire du vélo.* *Je vais voir mes grands-parents.* *Je vais faire les manèges.*	• Use *je vais* + infinitive to talk about future plans • Apply grammatical knowledge to make sentences	Framework: O5.1, O5.2, O5.3, L5.1, L5.2, L5.3, IU5.2 NC Attainment levels: AT1.2–3, AT2.2–3, AT3.2–3, AT4.2–3 Language ladder: Listening: Grades 2–3; Speaking: Grades 2–3, Reading: Grades 2–3; Writing: Grades 2–3
4	Talk about holiday plans	Consolidation of all the above	• Make longer sentences	Framework: O5.1, O5.2, O5.3, O5.4, L5.1, L5.2, L5.3, IU5.1, IU5.2 NC Attainment levels: AT1.2–3, AT2.2–3, AT3.2–3, AT4.2–3 Language ladder: Listening: Grades 2–3; Speaking: Grades 2–3; Reading: Grades 2–3; Writing: Grades 2–3
Extra!	Project work: finding out about French theme parks and presenting information to rest of class	Summary of above language	• Use the internet to find information • Read authentic texts	Framework: O5.2, O5.4, L5.1, L5.2, L5.3, IU5.1, IU5.2 NC Attainment levels: AT2.2–3, AT3.2–3, AT4.2–3 Language ladder: Speaking: Grades 2–3; Reading: Grades 2–3; Writing: Grades 2–3

Unit 6: Chez moi

Lesson	Objective	Context/Key language	Grammar/skills	National criteria
1	Name rooms in the house	*Chez moi, il y a une salle de bains/ une cuisine/une salle à manger/des WC/un salon/un balcon/un jardin/deux chambres*	• Use *il y a* + indefinite article • Prepare a short presentation	Framework: O5.1, O5.2, O5.3, L5.1, L5.3, IU5.2, IU5.3 NC Attainment levels: AT1.1–3, AT2.1–2, AT3.1–3, AT4.1–2 Language ladder: Listening: Grades1–3; Speaking: Grades 1–2; Reading: Grades 1–3; Writing: Grades 1–2
2	Describe rooms in the house	*C'est … grand/petit/vert/blanc/bleu/ jaune/rose/rouge* *C'est grand et rouge*	• Use *c'est* + adjectives • Join sentences with *et* • Practise new language with a friend	Framework: O5.1, O5.2, O5.3, O5.4, L5.1, L5.2, L5.3, IU5.2, IU5.3 NC Attainment levels: AT1.1–3, AT2.1–3, AT3.2–3, AT4.2–3 Language ladder: Listening: Grades 1–3; Speaking: Grades 1–3; Reading: Grades 2–3; Writing: Grades 2–3
3	Say what people do at home	*Qu'est-ce qu'il/elle fait? Il/Elle mange [un sandwich]/regarde la télé/écoute de la musique/lit [un livre] /joue avec l'ordinateur/joue au tennis*	• Use 3rd person verbs • Manipulate language by changing an element in a sentence	Framework: O5.1, O5.3, O5.4, L5.1, L5.2, L5.3, IU5.2, IU5.3 NC Attainment levels: AT1.2–3, AT2.2–3, AT3.2–3, AT4.2–3 Language ladder: Listening: Grades 2–3; Speaking: Grades 2–3; Reading: Grades 2–3; Writing: Grades 2–3
4	Say what people do and where	Activities in the home + *dans le salon/ les WC*, etc.	• Use and understand both the indefinite and definite articles • Make longer sentences	Framework: O5.1, O5.2, O5.3, L5.1, L5.2, L5.3, IU5.2, IU5.3 NC Attainment levels: AT1.2–3, AT2.2–3, AT3.2–3, AT4.2–3 Language ladder: Listening: Grades 2–3; Speaking: Grades 2–3; Reading: Grades 2–3; Writing: Grades 2–3
Extra!	Project work: researching and making a display / presentation of homes in France and GB Sound/spelling activity for Units 5–6 Assessment for Units 5–6	Summary of above language, and Unit 5	• Use the internet to find information • Prepare a presentation	Framework: O5.1, O5.2, O5.3, O5.4, L5.1, L5.2, L5.3, IU5.2, IU5.3 NC Attainment levels: AT1.1–3, AT2.1–3, AT3.1–3, AT4.2–3 Language ladder: Listening: Grades 1–3; Speaking: Grades 2–3; Reading: Grades 2–3; Writing: Grades 2–3

Unit 7: Le week-end

Lesson	Objective	Context/Key language	Grammar/skills	National criteria
1	Ask and talk about regular activities	Qu'est-ce que tu fais [le mercredi/le samedi]? Le lundi… j'écoute de la musique, je joue (au basket), je mange [du gâteau], je regarde [la télé], je bois [du chocolat chaud], je fais du vélo, je fais du roller Tu fais…? joues…? regardes…?	• Use several verbs in 1st person • Recognise patterns in French • Build longer sentences • Adapt sentences to say different things	Framework: O6.1, O6.3, O6.4, L6.1, L6.4, IU6.1, IU6.2 NC Attainment levels: AT1.2–4, AT2.2–4, AT3.2–4, AT4.3 Language ladder: Listening: Grades 2–4; Speaking: Grades 2–4; Reading: Grades 2–4; Writing: Grade 3
2	Say what you don't do	Je n'écoute pas… Je ne regarde pas… Je ne joue pas… Je ne bois pas de… Je ne mange pas de… Je ne fais pas de… (+ activities from Lesson 1 + negatives)	• Use negatives	Framework: O6.1, O6.2, O6.3, O6.4, L6.1, L6.2, L6.3, L6.4, IU6.1 NC Attainment levels: AT1.2–4, AT2.2–4, AT3.2–4, AT4.2–3 Language ladder: Listening: Grades 2–4; Speaking: Grades 2–4; Reading: Grades 2–4; Writing: Grades 2–3
3	Ask and say what other people do	Qu'est-ce qu'il/elle fait le week-end? … le lundi matin/après-midi/soir? Le lundi matin, il/elle… fait [du sport/du vélo], écoute [la radio/des CD], mange [un sandwich], boit [du jus d'orange], regarde(la télé), joue [au tennis/au foot]	• Use verbs in 3rd person • Listen for clues	Framework: O6.1, O6.3, O6.4, L6.1, L6.2, L6.3, L6.4, IU6.1 NC Attainment levels: AT1.2–4, AT2.2–4, AT3.2–4, AT4.3–4 Language ladder: Listening: Grades 2–4; Speaking: Grades 2–4; Reading: Grades 2–4; Writing: Grades 3–4
4	Talk about what you like/dislike doing	Est-ce que tu aimes faire/écouter/jouer/regarder…? J'aime, Je n'aime pas, J'adore, Je déteste… faire du vélo, écouter des CD/la radio, regarder la télé, jouer au football/tennis, faire du sport	• Use j'aime/je n'aime pas, etc. with an infinitive	Framework: O6.1, O6.2, O6.3, O6.4, L6.1, L6.3, L6.4, IU6.1 NC Attainment levels: AT1.2–4, AT2.2–4, AT3.2–4, AT4.3–4 Language ladder: Listening: Grades 2–4; Speaking: Grades 2–4; Reading: Grades 2–4; Writing: Grades 3–4
Extra!	Project work: weekly profile of an English and a French young person.		• Prepare a PowerPoint presentation. • Plan and prepare a task and evaluate others	Framework: O6.2, O6.4, L6.4, IU6.1, IU6.2 NC Attainment levels: AT2.3–4, AT4.3–4 Language ladder: Speaking: Grades 3–4; Writing: Grades 3–4

Unit 8: Les vêtements

Lesson	Objective	Context/Key language	Grammar/skills	National criteria
1	Ask and say what clothes you'd like	*Qu'est-ce que tu veux? Tu veux... ? Je voudrais un t-shirt, un pantalon, un chapeau, une veste, une jupe, une chemise, des chaussures, des lunettes de soleil + et*	• Using *des* with plural words	Framework: O6.1, O6.2, O6.3, O6.4, L6.1, L6.4, IU6.1, IU6.2 NC Attainment levels: AT1.1–4, AT2.1–3, AT3.1–4, AT4.2–3 Language ladder: Listening: Grades 1–4; Speaking: Grades 1–3; Reading: Grades 1–4; Writing: Grades 2–3
2	Give opinions about clothes	*C'est comment? C'est moche, beau, trop grand, trop petit, trop cher... et/mais...*	• Giving opinions using *c'est...* • Using *et* and *mais* to make longer sentences	Framework: O6.1, O6.2, O6.3, O6.4, L6.1, L6.4, IU6.1, IU6.2 NC Attainment levels: AT1.2–4, AT2.2–4, AT3.2–4, AT4.2–4 Language ladder: Listening: Grades 2–4; Speaking: Grades 2–4; Reading: Grades 2–4; Writing: Grades 2–4
3	Say what clothes you wear	*Je porte... un pantalon, un chapeau, un t-shirt, une veste, une chemise, une jupe, des chaussures, des lunettes de soleil...* *rose, orange, marron, rouge(s), jaune(s), vert(e)(s), bleu(e)(s), noir(e)(s), blanc(s), blanche(s)*	• Agreement of adjectives • Practising new language with a friend	Framework: O6.1, O6.2, O6.3, O6.4, L6.1, L6.2, L6.3, L6.4 IU6.1, IU6.2 NC Attainment levels: AT1.2–4, AT2.2–3, AT3.2–4, AT4.3–4 Language ladder: Listening: Grades 2–4; Speaking: Grades 2–3; Reading: Grades 2–4; Writing: Grades 3–4
4	Ask and talk about prices (including 60–80)	*C'est combien? Ça coûte [soixante-douze] euros* Numbers 60 to 80	• Techniques for memorising language	Framework: O6.1, O6.2, O6.3, O6.4, L6.1, L6.2, L6.3, IU6.1, IU6.2 NC Attainment levels: AT1.1–4, AT2.1–4, AT3.1–4, AT4.2–4 Language ladder: Listening: Grades 1–4; Speaking: Grades 1–4; Reading: Grades 1–4; Writing: Grades 2–4
Extra!	• Project work: presenting a PowerPoint presentation or display of uniform and contrasting with what a French young person would wear for school • Sound/spelling activity for Units 7–8 • Assessment for Units 7–8	Summary of above language, and Unit 7	Using PowerPoint	Framework: O6.3, O6.4, L6.1, L6.2, L6.4, IU6.1, IU6.2, IU6.3 NC Attainment levels: AT1.1–4, AT2.1–3, AT3.2–4, AT4.2–4 Language ladder: Listening: Grades 2–4; Speaking: Grades 3–4; Reading: Grades 2–4; Writing: Grades 3–4

Unit 9: Ma journée

Lesson	Objective	Context/Key language	Grammar/skills	National criteria
1	Ask and talk about daily routine	*Je me lève, Je prends mon petit déjeuner, Je vais à l'école, Je prends mon déjeuner, Je quitte l'école, Je prends mon dîner, Je me couche*	• Use 1st person present tense including some reflexives	Framework: O6.1, O6.3, O6.4, L6.1, L6.3, L6.4, IU6.1, IU6.2 NC Attainment levels: AT1.2–4, AT2.2, AT3.2–4, AT4.2–3 Language ladder: Listening: Grades 2–4; Speaking: Grade 2; Reading: Grades 2–4; Writing: Grades 2–3
2	Talk about times of daily routine	Daily routine phrases (Lesson 1) + à… une heure, deux heures (moins) cinq, dix, vingt, vingt-cinq	• Make longer sentences with times • Formulate questions	Framework: O6.1, O6.3, O6.4, L6.1, L6.3, L6.4, IU6.1, IU6.2 NC Attainment levels: AT1.2–4, AT2.2–4, AT3.2–4, AT4.3 Language ladder: Listening: Grades 2–4; Speaking: Grades 2–4; Reading: Grades 2–4; Writing: Grade 3
3	Ask and talk about breakfast	*Qu'est-ce que tu prends au petit déjeuner? Je prends… un chocolat chaud, un café, un jus de pomme, un croissant, un pain au chocolat, des céréales, une tartine*	• Use et to join sentences, together • Cope with longer reading texts	Framework: O6.1, O6.3, O6.4, L6.1, L6.2, L6.3, L6.4, IU6.1, IU6.2 NC Attainment levels: AT1.2–4, AT2.2–3, AT3.2–4, AT4.2–3 Language ladder: Listening: Grades 2–4; Speaking: Grades 2–3; Reading: Grades 2–4; Writing: Grades 2–3
4	Talk about details of a typical day	*normalement, d'abord, ensuite, enfin, après l'école* + language from Lesson 3	• Use adverbs and time expressions to make longer paragraphs • Reflect and share ideas about language learning	Framework: O6.1, O6.2, O6.3, O6.4, L6.1, L6.2, L6.3, L6.4, IU6.1, IU6.2, IU6.3 NC Attainment levels: AT1.2–4, AT2.2–4, AT3.3–4, AT4.2–4 Language ladder: Listening: Grades 2–4; Speaking: Grades 2–4; Reading: Grades 3–4; Writing: Grades 2–4
Extra!	Project work: similarities and differences in daily routine in France and GB		• Prepare a display/presentation.	Framework: O6.2, IU6.1, IU6.2, IU6.3 NC Attainment levels: AT2.2–4, AT4.2–4 Language ladder: Speaking: Grades 2–4; Writing: Grades 2–4

Unit 10: Les transports

Lesson	Objective	Context/Key language	Grammar/skills	National criteria
1	Talk about forms of transport	*Où vas-tu? Je vais à l'école… en voiture, en bus, en train, en métro, à pied, à vélo, en avion, en bateau*	• Use prepositions *en* and *à* with transports • Listen for clues to meaning	Framework: O6.1, O6.3, O6.4, L6.1, L6.4, IU6.1, IU6.2 NC Attainment levels: AT1.2–4, AT2.2, AT3.2–4, AT4.2–3 Language ladder: Listening: Grades 2–4; Speaking: Grade 2; Reading: Grades 2–4; Writing: Grades 2–3
2	Ask and talk about where you're going and how you get there	*Où vas-tu? Comment vas-tu … ? Je vais… à la boulangerie, au marché, à la piscine, au centre sportif, au château, au jardin public, au supermarché, à l'école en voiture, en bus, en train, en métro, à pied, à vélo, en avion, en bateau*	• Use propositions *au/à la /à l'* with places • Using knowledge of word, text and structure to build texts	Framework: O6.1, O6.3, O6.4, L6.1, L6.4, IU6.1, IU6.2 NC Attainment levels: AT1.2–4, AT2.2–3, AT3.2–4, AT4.2–4 Language ladder: Listening: Grades 2–4; Speaking: Grades 2–3; Reading: Grades 2–4; Writing: Grades 2–4
3	Talk about plans for a trip	Time/order indicators: *Samedi, à 10 heures… D'abord, ensuite, enfin… On va + infinitive* (future plans): *Qu'est-ce qu'on va faire? On va aller au parc d'attractions, on va prendre le train, on va prendre l'avion, on va acheter des souvenirs (au magasin), on va faire des manèges, on va regarder un film [au cinéma]*	• Use *on va* + infinitives to talk about future plans • Use time indicators • Use context and previous knowledge to help reading skills	Framework: O6.1, O6.3, O6.4, L6.1, L6.2, L6.3, L6.4, IU6.1, IU6.2 NC Attainment levels: AT1.3–4, AT2.3–4, AT3.2–4, AT4.3–4 Language ladder: Listening: Grades 3–4; Speaking: Grades 3–4; Reading: Grades 2–4; Writing: Grades 3–4
4	Buy tickets at the station	*Bonjour [Mademoiselle]. Bonjour [Monsieur]. Je voudrais des billets pour [Paris]. Combien de billets? [Quatre] billets: [un] adulte et [trois] enfants. Aller-retour ou aller simple? [Aller-retour] s'il vous plaît. C'est combien? C'est [trente-cinq] euros. Le train part à quelle heure? Le train part à [dix heures et demie]. Merci [Monsieur]. Au revoir. Au revoir. Bon voyage!*	Ask politely for things	Framework: O6.1, O6.2, O6.3, O6.4, L6.1, L6.2, L6.3, L6.4, IU6.1, IU6.2 NC Attainment levels: AT1.2–4, AT2.2–4, AT3.3–4, AT4.3 Language ladder: Listening: Grades 2–4; Speaking: Grades 2–4; Reading: Grades 3–4; Writing: Grade 3
Extra!	• Project work: plan a trip to a French-speaking country • Sound/spelling activity for Units 9–10 • Assessment for Units 9–10	Summary of above language, and Unit 9	Give a short presentation	Framework: O6.1, O6.2, O6.3, O6.4, L6.1, L6.2, L6.4, IU6.1, IU6.2, IU6.3 NC Attainment levels: AT1.1–4, AT2.1–4, AT3.2–4, AT4.2–4 Language ladder: Listening: Grades 2–4; Speaking: Grades 2–4; Reading: Grades 2–4; Writing: Grades 2–4

Unit 11: Le sport

Lesson	Objective	Context/Key language	Grammar/skills	National criteria
1	Talk about which sports you like	*Tu aimes quels sports? J'aime la natation, le vélo, la danse, le football, le tennis, l'équitation, la gymnastique, le roller*	• Use the definite article with sports • Spot patterns in French	Framework: O6.1, O6.3, O6.4, L6.1, L6.3, L6.4, IU6.1, IU6.2 NC Attainment levels: AT1.2–4, AT2.2–3, AT3.2–4, AT4.2 Language ladder: Listening: Grades 2–4; Speaking: Grades 2–3; Reading: Grades 2–4; Writing: Grade 2
2	Say what you think of different sports	*Qu'est-ce que tu préfères? J'aime, Je n'aime pas, Je déteste, J'adore, Je préfère…* [+ names of sports] *J'aime… mais/et je préfère…*	• Use conjunctions *et* and *mais* • Devise and ask questions	Framework: O6.1, O6.3, O6.4, L6.1, L6.3, L6.4 NC Attainment levels: AT1.3–4, AT2.2–3, AT3.2–4, AT4.3 Language ladder: Listening: Grades 3–4; Speaking: Grades 2–3; Reading: Grades 2–4; Writing: Grade 3
3	Give reasons for preferences	*J'aime [le football] parce que c'est amusant, facile, passionnant Je n'aime pas [le football] parce que c'est ennuyeux, cher, difficile*	• Give reasons for opinions • Use known language in new contexts	Framework: O6.1, O6.3, L6.1, L6.3, L6.4 NC Attainment levels: AT1.3–4, AT2.3, AT3.3–4, AT4.3 Language ladder: Listening: Grades 3–4; Speaking: Grade 3; Reading: Grades 3–4; Writing: Grade 3
4	Talk about a sporting event	*Le samedi on va au match de foot. On mange un sandwich et on boit un chocolat chaud. On regarde [Bordeaux] contre [Lyon]. Le match commence à trois heures. X marque un but. C'est passionnant! Lyon gagne 2–0.*	• Read and write longer texts • Present information about sports	Framework: O6.1, O6.2, O6.3, O6.4, L6.1, L6.2, L6.3, L6.4 NC Attainment levels: AT1.2–4, AT2.2–4, AT3.3–4, AT4.3–4 Language ladder: Listening: Grades 2–4; Speaking: Grades 2–4; Reading: Grades 3–4; Writing: Grades 3–4
Extra!	Project work: making a PowerPoint presentation or display on an aspect of sport	Summary of above language	• Use the internet to find information • Present information about sports	Framework: O6.2, O6.3, O6.4, L6.1, L6.2, L6.4, IU6.1, IU6.2, IU6.3 NC Attainment levels: AT2.2–4, AT3.3–4, AT4.2–4 Language ladder: Speaking: Grades 2–4; Reading: Grades 3–4; Writing: Grades 2–4

Unit 12: On va faire la fête!

Lesson	Objective	Context/Key language	Grammar/skills	National criteria
1	Revise forms of transport, places and immediate future plans	Revision: *Où vas-tu? Je vais au marché, au château, au supermarché, au jardin public, au centre sportif, à l'école, à la boulangerie, à la piscine, à la montagne, à la campagne* *Comment vas-tu? Je vais en bus, en voiture, en avion, en train, en métro, en bateau, à pied, à vélo* *Qu'est-ce que tu vas faire samedi? Je vais/On va… regarder un film, visiter un parc d'attractions, nager, faire la fête, faire les manèges, prendre le train, prendre l'avion, acheter des souvenirs, faire du ski, faire du bateau, faire du sport, faire du vélo, voir mes grands-parents*	• Prepositions: *au/à la/à l'* + places; *en/à* + transports • Use *je vais* + infinitive to talk about future plans • Revisit known language in a different context	Framework: O6.1, O6.2, O6.3, O6.4, L6.1, L6.2, L6.3, L6.4, IU6.1, IU6.2, IU6.3 NC Attainment levels: AT1.2–4, AT2.2–4, AT3.4, AT4.3–4 Language ladder: Listening: Grades 2–4; Speaking: Grades 2–4; Reading: Grade 4; Writing: Grades 3–4
2	Revise descriptions of people and clothes	Revision: *Il/Elle est [+ nationality]. Il/Elle est (n'est pas) grand(e), petit(e), sympa, drôle, sportif/sportive, timide, beau/belle, sévère, intelligent(e). Il/Elle a les cheveux longs/courts et les yeux bleus/marron/verts. Il/Elle a… ans. Il/Elle porte un pantalon, un t-shirt, un chapeau, une veste, une jupe, une chemise, des chaussures* [+ colour]	• Use 3rd person verbs including *avoir* and *être* • Use agreement of adjectives • Use negatives • Re-combine known language in different ways	Framework: O6.1, O6.3, O6.4, L6.1, L6.2, L6.3, L6.4, IU6.1, IU6.2 NC Attainment levels: AT1.2–4, AT2.2–4, AT3.2–4, AT4.3–4 Language ladder: Listening: Grades 2–4; Speaking: Grades 2–4; Reading: Grades 2–4; Writing: Grades 3–4
3	Revise opinions of food and clothes	Revision: *J'aime, Je n'aime pas, J'adore, Je déteste… le chocolat chaud, le café, le jus de pomme, les croissants, les pains au chocolat, les céréales, les tartines, les frites, les gâteaux, les bonbons, les pommes, les carottes, les haricots, les sandwichs au poulet/au thon/au fromage/à la tomate, les glaces au chocolat/à l'orange/à la fraise/à la vanille.* *C'est bien, cool, chouette, nul, fantastique, délicieux, beau/belle, moche, trop grand, trop petit, trop cher, bon, mauvais… pour la santé*	• Express opinions in different ways • Use plurals of food words • Use reading strategies to cope with authentic texts	Framework: O6.1, O6.3, O6.4, L6.1, L6.2, L6.3, IU6.1, IU6.2 NC Attainment levels: AT1.2–4, AT2.2–4, AT3.2–4 Language ladder: Listening: Grades 2–4; Speaking: Grades 2–4; Reading: Grades 2–4

Unit 12: On va faire la fête!

Lesson	Objective	Context/Key language	Grammar/skills	National criteria
4	Order food in a cafe.	Qu'est-ce que tu veux/vous voulez manger/boire? Je voudrais un… s'il te plaît, s'il vous plaît. Merci. C'est combien? C'est… euros. Voilà… Merci, au revoir	• Ask for things politely	Framework: O6.1, O6.2, O6.3, O6.4, L6.1, L6.2, L6.3, L6.4, IU6.1, IU6.2, IU6.3 NC Attainment levels: AT1.3–4, AT2.3–4, AT3.4, AT4.4 Language ladder: Listening: Grades 3–4; Speaking: Grades 3–4; Reading: Grade 4
Extra!	• Project work: preparing for a French day or event; setting up a café and performing songs and sketches • Sound/spelling activity for Units 11–12 • Assessment for Units 11–12	Summary of above language, and Unit 11	• Present information on an aspect of French culture using song and sketches	Framework: O6.2, O6.3, O6.4, L6.1, L6.4, IU6.1, IU6.2, IU6.3 NC Attainment levels: AT1.1–4, AT2.1–4, AT3.2–4, AT4.2–4 Language ladder: Listening: Grades 2–4; Speaking: Grades 2–4; Reading: Grades 2–4; Writing: Grades 2–4

Appendix 2
KS2 Framework mapping grid

Rigolo 2

Year 5 objectives	1	2	3	4	5	6
O5.1 Prepare and practise a simple conversation, re-using familiar vocabulary and structures in new contexts	✓	✓	✓	✓	✓	✓
O5.2 Understand and express simple opinions		✓	✓	✓	✓	✓
O5.3 Listen attentively and understand more complex phrases and sentences	✓	✓	✓	✓	✓	✓
O5.4 Prepare a short presentation on a familiar topic	✓					
L5.1 Re-read frequently a variety of short texts	✓	✓	✓	✓	✓	✓
L5.2 Make simple sentences and short texts	✓	✓	✓	✓	✓	✓
L5.3 Write words, phrases and short sentences, using a reference source	✓	✓	✓	✓	✓	✓
IU5.1 Look at further aspects of their everyday life from the perspective of someone from another country	✓	✓	✓	✓	✓	✓
IU5.2 Recognise similarities and differences between places				✓		✓
IU5.3 Compare symbols, objects or products which represent their own culture with those of another country		✓				✓

Year 6 objectives	7	8	9	10	11	12
O6.1 Understand the main points and simple opinions in a spoken story, song or passage		✓	✓	✓	✓	✓
O6.2 Perform to an audience		✓		✓	✓	✓
O6.3 Understand longer and more complex phrases or sentences		✓	✓	✓	✓	✓
O6.4 Use spoken language confidently to initiate and sustain conversations and to tell stories		✓	✓	✓	✓	✓
L6.1 Read and understand the main points and some detail from a short written passage		✓	✓	✓	✓	✓
L6.2 Identify different text types and read short, authentic texts for enjoyment or information		✓	✓	✓	✓	✓
L6.3 Match sound to sentences and paragraphs		✓	✓	✓	✓	✓
L6.4 Write sentences on a range of topics using a model	✓	✓	✓	✓	✓	✓
IU6.1 Compare attitudes towards aspects of everyday life		✓	✓	✓	✓	✓
IU6.2 Recognise and understand some of the differences between people		✓	✓	✓	✓	✓
IU6.3 Present information about an aspect of culture		✓	✓	✓	✓	✓

✓ = Objective is covered in this unit on the CD-ROM

Rigolo 2
Appendix 3
5–14 National Guidelines mapping grid

Strands and attainment targets	1	2	3	4	5	6	7	8	9	10	11	12
Listening												
Listening for information and instructions	A, B, C	A, B, C	A, B, C	A, B, C	A, B, C	A, B, C	A, B, C, D	A, B, C, D	A, B, C, D	A, B, C, D	A, B, C, D	A, B, C, D
Listening and reacting to others	A, B, C	A, B, C	A, B, C	A, B, C	A, B, C	A, B, C	A, B, C, D	A, B, C, D	A, B, C, D	A, B, C, D	A, B, C, D	A, B, C, D
Speaking												
Speaking to convey information	A, B, C	A, B, C	A, B, C	A, B, C	A, B, C	A, B, C, D	A, B, C, D	A, B, C, D	A, B, C, D	A, B, C, D	A, B, C, D	A, B, C, D
Speaking and interacting with others	A, B, C	A, B, C	A, B, C	A, B, C	A, B, C	A, B, C, D	A, B, C, D	A, B, C, D	A, B, C, D	A, B, C, D	A, B, C, D	A, B, C, D
Speaking about experiences, feelings and opinions	A, B, C	A, B, C	A, B, C	A, B	A, B, C	A, B, C	A, B, C	A, B, C, D	A, B, C, D	A, B, C, D	A, B, C, D	A, B, C, D
Reading												
Reading for information and instructions	A, B, C	A, B, C	A, B, C	A, B, C	A, B, C	A, B, C	A, B, C, D	A, B, C, D	A, B, C, D	A, B, C, D	A, B, C, D	A, B, C, D
Reading aloud	A, B, C	A, B, C	A, B, C	A, B, C	A, B, C	A, B, C	A, B, C, D	A, B, C, D	A, B, C, D	A, B, C, D	A, B, C, D	A, B, C, D
Writing												
Writing to exchange information and ideas	A, B, C	A, B, C	A, B, C	A, B, C	A, B, C	A, B, C, D	A, B, C, D	A, B, C, D	A, B, C, D	A, B, C, D	A, B, C, D	A, B, C, D
Writing to establish and maintain personal contact	A, B	A, B	A, B	A, B	A, B, C	A, B	A, B, C, D	A, B, C, D	A, B, C, D	A, B, C, D	A, B, C, D	A, B, C, D
Writing imaginatively to entertain	A, B, C	A, B, C	A, B, C	A, B, C	A, B, C	A, B, C	A, B, C	A, B, C, D	A, B, C, D	A, B, C, D	A, B, C, D	A, B, C, D

Rigolo 2 units

Rigolo 2

Appendix 4
Flashcards

Unit 1
New character
1. Gustave

Sisters / brothers
2. J'ai un frère.
3. J'ai une sœur.
4. J'ai deux frères.
5. J'ai deux sœurs.
6. Je n'ai pas de frères ou de sœurs.

New adjectives and negatives
7. Il est beau.
8. Il n'est pas beau.
9. Elle est belle.
10. Elle n'est pas belle.

Unit 2
School subjects
1. l'anglais
2. le français
3. le sport
4. l'histoire-géo
5. la musique
6. les sciences
7. les maths

Likes / dislikes
8. J'aime…
9. Je n'aime pas…

School day
10. l'école
11. la récré
12. le déjeuner

Unit 3
Sandwiches and ice-creams
1. un sandwich au poulet
2. un sandwich au thon
3. un sandwich au fromage
4. un sandwich à la tomate
5. une glace au chocolat
6. une glace à la vanille
7. une glace à la fraise
8. une glace à l'orange

Healthy / unhealthy food items
9. les frites
10. les gâteaux
11. les bonbons
12. les pommes
13. les carottes
14. les haricots

Unit 4
Places in the town
1. la boulangerie
2. le centre sportif
3. le château
4. l'école
5. le jardin public
6. le marché
7. la piscine
8. le supermarché

Unit 5
Holiday destinations
1. à la montagne
2. à la campagne
3. au camping
4. au bord de la mer
5. au parc d'attractions

Likes / dislikes
6. J'adore…
7. Je déteste…

Holiday activities
8. faire du ski
9. faire du sport
10. faire du vélo
11. faire du bateau
12. nager
13. voir mes grands-parents
14. faire les manèges

Unit 6
Rooms / places in the home
1. un salon
2. une cuisine
3. une salle à manger
4. une salle de bains
5. des WC
6. une chambre
7. un balcon
8. un jardin

Activities in the home
9. Il lit un livre.
10. Elle mange un sandwich.
11. Elle joue avec l'ordinateur.
12. Il écoute de la musique.
13. Il regarde la télé.

Unit 7
Activities with *je*
1. Je regarde la télé.
2. J'écoute de la musique.
3. Je fais du vélo.
4. Je fais du roller.
5. Je joue au basket.
6. Je mange du gâteau.
7. Je bois du chocolat chaud.

Activities with *il / elle*
8. Il fait du sport.
9. Il écoute la radio.
10. Elle joue au foot.
11. Il fait du vélo.
12. Il regarde la télé.
13. Elle regarde un film.

Unit 8
Clothes
1. un pantalon
2. une veste
3. une chemise
4. un t-shirt
5. un chapeau
6. une jupe
7. des chaussures
8. des lunettes de soleil

Opinions about clothes
9. C'est trop petit.
10. C'est trop grand.
11. C'est trop cher.
12. C'est beau.
13. C'est moche.

Unit 9
Daily routine
1. Je me lève.
2. Je prends mon petit déjeuner.
3. Je vais à l'école.
4. Je prends mon déjeuner.
5. Je quitte l'école.
6. Je prends mon dîner.
7. Je me couche.

Breakfast items
8. un jus de pomme
9. un café
10. un chocolat chaud
11. des céréales
12. un croissant
13. un pain au chocolat
14. une tartine

Unit 10
Forms of transport
1. en bus
2. en voiture
3. en train
4. en bateau
5. à vélo
6. à pied
7. en métro
8. en avion

Plans for a trip
9. On va aller au parc d'attractions.
10. On va prendre le train.
11. On va prendre le bus.
12. On va acheter des souvenirs au magasin.
13. On va faire les manèges.
14. On va regarder un film au cinéma.

Unit 11
Sports
1. le football
2. la danse
3. le roller
4. la gymnastique
5. la natation
6. le tennis
7. le vélo
8. l'équitation

Preferences
9. Je préfère…
10. J'aime…
11. Je n'aime pas…
12. Je déteste…
13. J'adore…